ASE Guide to Secondary Science Education

Edited by
Valerie Wood-Robinson

The **Association** *for* **Science Education**

Published by the Association for Science Education
College Lane, Hatfield, Herts AL10 9AA

ISBN 0 86357 406 8 (2007: 978 0 86357 406 1)

Executive Editor: Helen Johnson
Design and page layout: Colin Barker
Cover photos: (top to bottom) Courtesy of: Comberton Village College (AST Richard Waller and pupil Tom Adams); Wellcome Photo Library ('Plague Nation by Stan's Café'); Wales Science Year; Science Learning Centre East Midlands (2).
Printed by Piggott Black Bear Ltd, Cambridge, England

Contents

Section 3

About the authors

Philip Adey taught chemistry in Barbados before embarking on curriculum development, teacher education and research into cognitive barriers to learning. He is now Emeritus Professor of Cognition, Science, and Education at King's College London and an independent consultant trading as 'Developing Intelligence'.

Hilary Asoko is a senior lecturer at the University of Leeds, where she is involved in teacher education programmes and research in science education. Her particular interests are in children's conceptual development in science and how this can be supported in the classroom.

Derek Bell is Chief Executive of the Association for Science Education. He has extensive insight into teaching and learning in science through his own teaching, research and experience in teacher education. He maintains contact with a wide range of organisations.

Paul Black, OBE, is Emeritus Professor at King's College London, where he directed the education department from 1976 to 1989. He retired in 1995. In the 1980s he helped direct national surveys of school science performance for the Assessment of Performance Unit (APU). In 1987–1988 he was chair of the Task Group on Assessment and Testing, which set out the basis for national testing in England and Wales.

Peter Borrows is Director of CLEAPSS. Before that he was a science adviser, having previously spent over 20 years as a teacher and head of department in London schools. He has been a member of the ASE Safeguards Committee since the late 1960s and was its chair for 21 years.

Phil Bunyan is a senior regional adviser for the Secondary National Strategy, which grew out of the Key Stage 3 Strategy. He has been part of the science team from its outset in 2001. Previously he was the science inspector in Nottinghamshire and before that worked in Northamptonshire and South London.

Andrew Clegg is a science education consultant working from the UK and Namibia. He was formerly a science teacher in Yorkshire and Somerset and one-time head of the Department of Mathematics and Science Education at the University of Botswana.

Sandra Duggan is an experienced researcher, currently working in the School of Applied Social Science, University of Durham.

Mick Dunne is Programme Manager for all postgraduate initial teacher education courses and Science Education Leader at Bradford College. He is a member of the Editorial Board of *Primary Science Review* and has a particular interest in environmental education.

Rosemary Feasey is a freelance science education consultant and author. She was the first person from a primary background to become national Chair of the Association for Science Education.

Richard Gott is Professor of Education in the School of Education, University of Durham.

Paul Hamer, **Jasmin Chapman** and **Barbara Allmark** are all directors of The Learners' Co-operative Ltd. In addition to their work for the co-operative, Paul is currently Secondary Strategy Science Consultant for Plymouth LEA, Jasmin is teaching part-time at Lipson Community College, Plymouth and Barbara trains teachers at the College of St Mark & St John, Plymouth.

Wynne Harlen, OBE, was Professor of Science Education at the University of Liverpool from 1985 to 1990, before becoming Director of the Scottish Council for Research in Education. She is now visiting professor in education at the University of Bristol. She was editor of *Primary Science Review* from 1999 to 2004.

Chris Harrison is a lecturer at King's College London, where she leads the Assessment for Learning Research Group whose publications include the Black Box series. She is a popular speaker at national and international conferences.

Martin Hollins is a freelance consultant who was leader of the science and technology team at the Qualifications and Curriculum Authority (QCA) until recently. After science teaching in Malawi, Surrey and London, he has worked in curriculum development and teacher education. Posts have included director of the University of Bath 5–16 project and director of the North London Science Centre.

Edgar Jenkins taught chemistry and biology in secondary schools before joining the University of Leeds where he served as Head of the School of Education and Director of the Centre for Studies in Science and Mathematics Education. He is the author of many books and articles and is now Emeritus Research Professor at Leeds.

Brenda Keogh and **Stuart Naylor** currently work independently as writers, researchers, publishers, consultants and professional development providers for teachers, as Millgate House Publishing and Consultancy. They both have extensive experience in teacher education as well as working as teachers and advisory teachers.

John Leach is Professor of Science Education and Head of the School of Education at the University of Leeds. He has a longstanding research interest in teaching and learning science in classrooms. His recent work addresses the design and dissemination of research-informed

science teaching materials. John previously taught chemistry and science in English secondary schools.

Robin Millar is Professor of Science Education at the University of York. His work involves initial teacher education and CPD for science teachers. He has also played a leading role in several major research and development projects, including *Twenty First Century Science*.

Roger Mitchell is Acting Head Teacher at Ripple Junior School in Barking. He has served on a variety of advisory panels including those for the DfES, QCA and the DTI and is currently Chair of ASE Primary Science Committee. He has particular interests in promoting the effective use of ICT and in developing quality dialogue in science lessons.

Philip Morris was a science teacher and senior manager for over 21 years, and is now an independent education consultant, specialising in the use of ICT, and part-time lecturer on the initial teacher training course at Sheffield Hallam University.

Labrini Nikolaou is an experienced science teacher. She has carried out research and curriculum development at King's College London in the areas of teaching physics concepts, scientific enquiry and classroom dialogue.

Jonathan Osborne is Chair of Science Education at King's College London and President-Elect of the North American National Association for Research on Science Teaching. He taught in London Schools for nine years before becoming an advisory teacher and then joining King's as a lecturer.

Alan Peacock edits *Primary Science Review* and formerly ran the Primary Science PGCE Programme at the University of Exeter. He has worked extensively in Africa, and has published research, textbooks and teachers' guides. He is now a consultant in environmental education.

Chris Peel is the advisory technician at CLEAPSS where his role includes developing and delivering courses for technicians, advising technicians and writing and updating CLEAPSS publications. Previously Chris had been a science technician in schools and colleges for over 30 years.

Mary Ratcliffe is Professor of Science Education at the University of Southampton and Director of the Science Learning Centre South East. She taught in comprehensive schools in East Anglia and has been Chair of ASE (1996/97). Her research and development interests are in pupils' and teachers' reactions to socio-scientific issues and the development of effective learning and assessment practice.

Michael Reiss is Professor of Science Education at the Institute of Education, University of London, Chief Executive of Science Learning Centre London, and holds various visiting professorships. He is director of the Salters-Nuffield Advanced Biology Project, a member of the Farm Animal Welfare Council and editor of the journal *Sex Education*.

Ian Richardson, HMI, became the specialist adviser for science in 2003. He has taught science in a wide range of social contexts and worked in Cheshire LEA Advisory Team. As Professional Officer for science at the National Curriculum Council he participated in two revisions of the science Orders for England. As an independent consultant he wrote textbooks, worked on the development of KS2 and KS3 national tests and teacher professional development in science and management.

Kay Sample has taught in both secondary and middle schools, has been an Advisory Teacher for Science and is now a Leading Consultant and manager of the Science team in Northumberland.

Phil Scott is Professor of Science Education at the University of Leeds. He taught physics and science in high schools for 15 years, becoming a head of science, before starting his university career with the Children's Learning in Science Research Group.

Lynne Symonds works actively with science teachers from many parts of the world to encourage the sharing of ideas. She is currently Chair of the ASE International Committee and of The Commonwealth Association for Science, Technology and Maths Educators.

Jenny Versey is Chair of the ASE's 11–19 Committee. She has 25 years' experience of teaching science and in curriculum development, and eight years' experience as Science Strategy Manager for the London Borough of Enfield. Her current work includes induction tutoring for graduate and overseas-trained teachers.

John Wardle is Director of the Science Learning Centre Yorkshire and the Humber. Both in teaching and teacher training roles John has specialised in the field of ICT in science, developing projects such as Schools Online and the Science Consortium.

Rod Watson is a senior lecturer in science education at King's College London. He has directed several national projects aimed at improving scientific enquiry in schools, including the AKSIS project and the SKEES project.

Valerie Wood-Robinson taught for over 30 years in secondary schools, with intervals as a teacher-trainer and an LEA adviser and inspector. She has worked on curriculum research and development projects at both Leeds University and Kings' College London and elsewhere. Valerie is a member of ASE Publications Committee and has edited several books published by ASE.

Lynne Wright is an experienced primary teacher, Ofsted inspector of primary and nursery schools and teacher educator, with expertise in many aspects of science education. She is a member of the ASE Publications Committee.

Introduction

The previous edition of the *ASE Guide to Secondary Science Education* was published in 1998. It has been a popular and highly regarded resource and inspiration for all concerned with secondary science education. Considerable changes have taken place, which are continuing as science education develops into the 21st century, and these are represented in this new edition. This is a completely new book, not a revised version of the previous *Guide*, although several familiar topics are revisited, and several well-known authors are contributing again.

The purpose of the *Guide* is to provide both an account of current thinking about the fundamental aims and philosophy underpinning science education and, furthermore, informed views on how these ideas and values can be translated into practice. Starting from a consideration of *why* we teach science, teachers are in the best position to use ideas of *how* to teach that can be found in curriculum materials and in other ASE publications. However, in some chapters, there are strong hints towards the 'how-to-do', especially in non-negotiable matters such as safety. The *Guide* is key reading for all teachers and trainees and particularly for newly qualified teachers.

The book attempts to cover a wide range of topics and the chapters are necessarily short. However, there are many references to published sources and to websites as guidance to readers requiring further details. The book is not intended to be read from cover to cover, although the order of chapters provides a sequential narrative for those who wish to do that. The intention is to provide a source of information and inspiration on those topics of interest to the reader at any one time. The authors include professors and lecturers of science education, inspectors, advisers and consultants, head teachers and class teachers, educational consultants and the Chief Executive of ASE. In editing, I have attempted to collate the work of this wide cross-section of science educationists into a coherent book, while maintaining the authors' individual styles to illustrate their respective points of view.

Some perennial matters that are revisited include the purposes of science education, the importance of attitudes and values, the identification of quality in science education, the nature of children's learning, the engagement of all pupils, the importance of learning to investigate, the use of information and communication technology, and health and safety matters. The chapters relating to these topics reflect fresh thinking as well as consolidation of well-established ideas. At the same time there is now more to say about looking forward to the 21st century with the benefit of historical hindsight, and about professional development, particularly with the instigation of the national and regional science learning centres and with the increasing role of support staff. Attention is given to transfer from primary to secondary school, to school self-evaluation, to formative use of assessment including pupils' self-assessment, to talk and dialogue in the classroom and to developing children's thinking skills and creativity. Chapters on these subjects reflect some of the exciting developments taking place in the last few years.

Some changes of policy, in England particularly, have taken place since the publication of the 1998 *Guide*. Initiatives, including the Key Stage 3 Strategy (now the Secondary National Strategy), the QCA Scheme of Work, and currently changes to post-14 provision and assessment, have had a considerable effect on what and how teachers teach and are reflected in the pages of the *Guide*. While it is inevitable that some issues specific to England are discussed, reference is made to policies and practice in Scotland, Wales and Northern Ireland where these differ from those in England. Indeed, one early chapter takes a global view of how science education is practised across the UK and beyond. We intend the *Guide* to be of interest and use to those engaged in secondary science teaching worldwide. Specific terminology, for example that of year groups, is explained to enable readers to relate examples to their familiar educational systems. We acknowledge that different terminology is used in different systems and different institutions. Common terms such as 'school', 'head of department', 'scheme of work', and so on are used to encompass entities that may have alternative titles in certain contexts. Pseudonyms have been used in examples about named pupils and teachers.

Organisation of the *Guide*

The chapters fall into three groups having different levels of focus. The early chapters deal with issues at a national level, where matters of overall goals and policies are discussed. Following these are chapters relating to policy matters and their application in practice at the school departmental level, including decisions about how provision for learning science can extend beyond the classroom and across the primary–secondary transition. The final chapters are more relevant to planning and implementation at the classroom level, illustrating current thinking on these matters rather than providing details of how and what to teach. Several themes pervade the *Guide*, appearing even in chapters not explicitly focused on them. Teaching for understanding, which entails the active involvement of learners, is a recurrent theme, as is the recognition of 'quality' science learning, by pupils, teachers and observers alike. Self-evaluation at all levels, from individual pupils' reflection on their own learning to whole departments' examination of their quality, appears as another theme. Concern for opportunities for a wider and more relevant science education for the 21st century also runs through the chapters. Cross-references between chapters, and a comprehensive but not exhaustive index, enable readers to pursue these and other themes throughout the book.

About half the chapters contain material that is common with chapters on the same topic in the companion *ASE Guide to Primary Science Education*, edited by Wynne Harlen. We believe this common approach is helpful in emphasising the continuity in children's science education. In some cases the linked chapters are very similar; in others there are different examples and references to practice that suit one or other context; and in others again more substantial differences in treatment of a topic were seen as appropriate. The *Secondary Guide* contains little detail about the management of school science at school and departmental level, to avoid duplication of material in other ASE publications (e.g. *ASE/SEP CD for Heads of Science and Principal Teachers*; *The beginning science teacher's induction handbook*; and *Safeguards in the school laboratory*, 11th edition) whereas the *Primary Guide* includes chapters on subject management of importance to primary science subject leaders.

Contributors

The contributors are all members of the ASE who are committed to, and experienced in, developing science education. Notes about the authors can be found on pages v to vii. In general the expertise of the authors ranges across the whole gamut of issues related to secondary science but for this *Guide* they have been asked to address just one part of it. Adopting such a focus is quite difficult and some overlap, despite editorial intervention, is inevitable. The *Guide* cannot encompass every aspect of secondary science education and no doubt some gaps will be identified, for which I take full responsibility. I was privileged to be asked to be the editor of this book and to work with the authors, to whom I am extremely grateful. They willingly agreed to write and to meet a tight schedule at periods when there were heavy demands on their time. I am particularly appreciative of the experienced support of Wynne Harlen, without whose generous guidance during the parallel editing of our complementary guides, my task would have been far more daunting. I also thank Helen Johnson for her patient technical editing and Colin Barker for converting the texts into attractive and well-designed publications.

Valerie Wood-Robinson

November 2005

Section 1 National level: Setting the scene

Chapter 1

Science education for the 21st century

There are several different arguments for including science as a core subject in the curriculum. The different demands made on

Robin Millar and
Jonathan Osborne

the science curriculum, however, create a tension between the needs of teaching science for understanding in everyday life and of teaching science for future specialist jobs. The *Beyond 2000* seminars explored ways of resolving this tension. This led to the development of a possible solution in the form of the *Twenty First Century Science* curriculum (for key stage 4 in England). This is an exciting opportunity, unique in the world, to test a solution to the curriculum dilemma of scientific literacy versus science for specialists.

Perspectives on purpose and change

It often seems that the science curriculum is constantly changing – sometimes in relatively small ways, sometimes more significantly. Are these changes making it steadily better? Your answer is likely to depend on what you think the *purpose* of science education is. This in turn will depend on what you think education is for; for example, whether you think of it primarily in terms of developing every individual's knowledge and skills, or of satisfying the needs of society for people with a range of capabilities and expertise, or of handing on valued knowledge to new generations. Sometimes we emphasise the *intrinsic* value of learning: some things are worth learning simply because they are interesting and hence life-enhancing. At other times we may emphasise *instrumental* reasons for learning: some things are worth learning because of what this then enables us to do.

These different perspectives cannot be regarded as right or wrong, better or worse. Rather they indicate the complexity of the role we expect science education to fulfil. People's views reflect their values and so differ from person to person, group to group. There are many 'stakeholders' with an interest in the science curriculum; their values and priorities may differ. Our expectations of the science curriculum also change with time. Curriculum change may be more about improving its 'fit' to a changing external context than about improvement in absolute terms. We might then ask: how well suited is the science curriculum to the needs of young people growing up in the early years of the 21st century? And what kinds of changes do we believe are needed to enable it to satisfy those needs better?

Arguments for teaching science

Our expectations of the school science curriculum are reflected in the range and variety of the arguments put forward to justify the place of science as a core subject. Four common arguments are given below.

The 'reliable and useful knowledge' argument

This starts from the view that science offers us the best available explanations of the material world. Science explains, for instance, why we have night and day, how the body functions, what is happening when new substances are made, and so on. Some knowledge of these explanations is essential to function effectively in contemporary society, where so much of our everyday world is a product of, or is influenced by, scientific knowledge and its technological applications. As well as being practically useful, enabling the individual to understand scientific explanations in the media or engage in a conversation with their doctor about their health, the study of science develops 'scientific habits of mind', a rational way of tackling questions and problems, based on empirical evidence and an agreed (though revisable) framework of ideas, that enhance the individual's ability to cope with everyday life.

The economic argument

This springs from the recognition that developed industrial economies are increasingly dependent on their scientific and technological base. Increasingly, what we sell is a product of the 'added value' that such knowledge is able to generate. This in turn is highly dependent on a supply of scientists and technologists at all levels. Figure 1.1, for instance, shows the proportion of the civilian population in the USA employed in science and engineering in 1983, 1993 and 2002. In the UK, and Europe more generally, the picture is similar (High Level Group for Human Resources and Technology, 2004). Several key professions (such as medicine) also require a sound basic knowledge of science.

From this perspective, school science is seen as providing a pre-professional training, and acts essentially as a sieve for selecting those who will enter academic science and the professions that have a scientific base, or follow courses of scientific vocational training. Any 'wastage' is justified by the claim that all students learn something useful, and that everyone ultimately benefits from the material gains that science makes possible.

The cultural argument

This is the argument that science is one of the great achievements of our culture – the shared heritage that forms the backdrop to the language and discourse

Figure 1.1
Proportion of the civilian population in the USA employed in science and engineering (National Science Board, 2004).

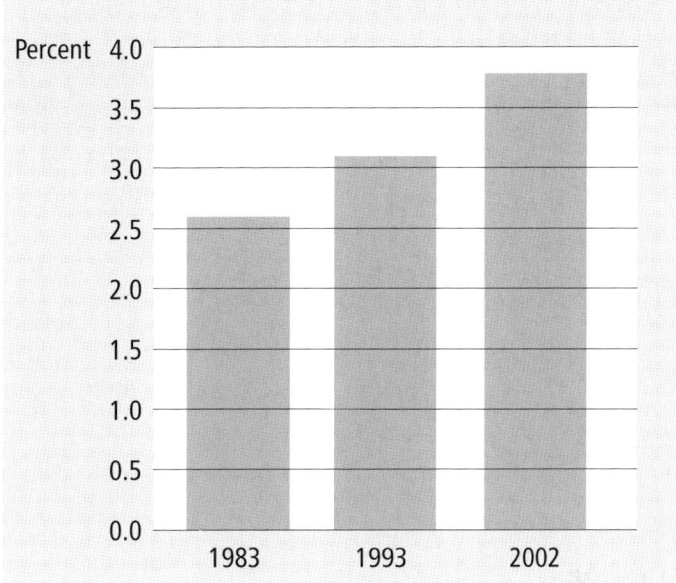

that permeate our media, conversations and daily life (Cossons, 1993; Millar, 1996). Science, it is argued, is a way of knowing in which knowledge is derived from, and checked against, empirical evidence. This form of knowledge, and the way it is derived, are a product of the Enlightenment. It is science that has led to the central commitment of democratic societies to evidence as the primary basis of views and actions. Hence, it is essential that schools offer young people not only an opportunity to acquire one of the main components of contemporary society's cultural capital but also an understanding of how this knowledge was derived, the hard-fought struggle this involved, and the great achievement it represents.

The democratic argument

This argument stems from the recognition that many of the dilemmas confronting society today are of a scientific and technological nature. What, for instance, are we to do about global warming? Should we commission more nuclear power stations? A core belief of democratic societies is that such disputes should be resolved by public debate with as many people as possible contributing. If, instead, decisions about such issues are taken only by experts, democracy is weakened. Hence, sustaining a healthy democracy requires as many individuals as possible to have at least a basic understanding of the underlying science, enabling them to engage critically and reflectively in a participatory debate. In addition, we need a way of holding scientists, like other members of a democratic society, to account for their actions. As a society, we provide large sums to fund and support their research. Should it be directed towards work that promises a material and tangible benefit, such as enhanced food production or a vaccine for malaria, or should we support work that has little obvious practical benefit, such as the construction of a new, orbiting space station? The resolution of such issues, it is argued, would benefit from greater public engagement.

The central tension in school science

The sociologist of science, Harry Collins (2000), has suggested that the demands made on the school science curriculum create not merely a dilemma, but a 'trilemma'. On the one hand, we want to teach that *science liberates from tradition and the "shackles of received knowledge"'* (p. 171), yet it can only work (ironically) within a tradition where it is taught as received knowledge. The third horn of Collins's 'trilemma' is that teaching consensually accepted, 'received' knowledge is no preparation for dealing with the open and unresolved issues raised by the current applications of science. It may even be harmful as the clash between science-as-it-is-taught and science-as-it-is-reported leads to confusion. All three strands of Collins's trilemma are apparent in the four arguments above. So can we resolve this tension, and perhaps use it productively – or are we attempting the impossible?

The place to begin, perhaps, is with the central tension faced by anyone designing a school science curriculum. This is between the kind of understanding of science that might be useful to people in the course of their everyday lives and the kind of understanding that they might need to progress to more advanced courses in science, perhaps eventually leading to a scientific job or one that requires science as a basis. The former we might call 'developing scientific literacy' and the latter 'pre-professional training of scientists'. Courses that attempted to develop 'scientific literacy' would be an education *in* and *about* science. They would have to develop some understanding of some of the major explanatory ideas of science such as the germ theory of disease or the atomic/molecular model of chemical reactions, as it is not possible to imagine a form of 'scientific literacy' without this. But they would also have to develop an understanding of science itself – both as a process and as a product. This would involve an understanding (or at least an awareness) of critical 'ideas-about-science', by which we mean ideas about the nature of scientific knowledge, the processes of scientific enquiry, the role of the scientific community in checking and refining knowledge claims, and the issues that can arise when we apply scientific knowledge in practical ways. These ideas are tools for analysing issues raised by specific applications of scientific knowledge; they help students understand *how* we know the things we claim to know and how sure we can be about them. They enable young people to become more critical consumers of scientific knowledge, and less intellectually dependent on experts. McComas and Olson (1998) have shown that there is a broad international consensus for such an emphasis in science curriculum documents. We found a similar consensus in a three-phase questionnaire study of 23 influential scientists, science educators, philosophers, sociologists and teachers of science (Osborne *et al.*, 2003). Likewise, when 250 eminent scientists were asked what was the one thing they would like to convey about science the principal answer was an understanding of the scientific approach to enquiry and of the methods employed.

In contrast, science courses whose principal aim is to educate the next generation of scientists involve an immersion in the foundations of the discipline, the acquisition of a lot of detailed factual knowledge, and practice in using standard approaches and solutions to problems of certain kinds. These are what Thomas Kuhn (1962) called 'paradigms'. Kuhn argued that science is taught and learned through immersion in these paradigms. The aim is to teach current understandings and ways of solving problems, not to open up discussion and debate about alternatives. We should not duck the implications of this. In Collins's (2000) words, *'it is romantic nonsense to imagine that potential science specialists can learn all the science they need without a lot of routine learning and practice along with indoctrination into traditional ways of thinking'* (p. 171). Inevitably, a science course entirely of this sort neglects wider aims and concerns.

This tension, between the pre-professional training of future scientists and the 'scientific literacy' of all, can be clearly seen in the history of the school science curriculum (see Chapter 3). In England prior to 1989, when science was optional beyond the age of 14, curriculum content at every stage was based on the needs of those who might progress to the next stage above. So undergraduate science courses were planned to train future researchers, A-level courses were designed to prepare students for undergraduate science, and GCSE (or before it, GCE O-level) to prepare students for A-level. With the introduction of the National Curriculum and compulsory science for all, this design principle became no longer defensible. The result, however, was not a complete rethink and overhaul, but rather a series of attempts to modify the existing curriculum to meet a broader range of needs. The outcome was a 'one size fits all' course that was a weaker foundation for aspirant scientists, but could not be said to have produced a measurable improvement in 'scientific literacy' for the majority.

Resolving the dilemma

The series of seminars that led to the report *Beyond 2000: science education for the future* (Millar and Osborne, 1998) highlighted this central tension within the science curriculum, and explored ways of resolving it. The report argued that the primary goal of science education should be to provide an education *in* science and *about* science, which could enhance the 'scientific literacy' of all students. 'All' here, of course, includes future scientists. Scientists increasingly work in narrower and narrower specialisms. Outside their own discipline they are often no more 'expert' than a non-scientist. Future scientists also need to have a good understanding of how science works. Consequently, the principal focus of any GCSE course should be on developing students' 'scientific literacy' rather than on training future scientists.

This does not, however, mean that school science should neglect the process of preparing some students for careers in science. As a society we need a steady supply of able students wanting to study more advanced science. The science curriculum should provide access to more advanced courses, in both 'pure' and applied science, for those who wish to take them. The challenge is finding a way to do this, without having it become the sole aim.

In England, the new National Curriculum programme of study for key stage 4 (ages 14–16) from 2006 recognises the breadth of aims of the science curriculum, perhaps for the first time. It has been designed to provide the flexibility needed to address the multiple purposes of the science curriculum and the diversity of students' needs and interests.

Science education in the 21st century

The *Beyond 2000* report goes on from diagnosis of key problems and issues to outline a possible solution. In essence, it is to separate the science curriculum into two strands, one designed to promote 'scientific literacy' and a second to prepare young people for more advanced study. The differences between programmes with these two purposes – in choice of content, depth of treatment, and overall style and approach – are so great that any single course is inevitably an uncomfortable, and ultimately a less than successful, compromise. The 'scientific literacy' strand would be studied by all, and would aim for a qualitative and descriptive grasp of 'big ideas' that would not lose learners in the detail, and an understanding of important 'ideas-about-science'. In addition, students could opt to take additional science, designed either to provide a basis for further academic study or to provide insight into applied science.

This is not, however, a tried-and-tested solution: it is a hypothesis about what might work better than what we have had in the past. The *Twenty First Century Science* project (*21st Century Science* project team, 2003; Burden, 2005) can be seen as an experiment to test this model, to check that it is feasible, to see whether teachers feel it offers possibilities that the previous structures did not, and to find out whether it leads to improved student learning and interest in science. *Twenty First Century Science* is a pilot study, commissioned by the English Qualifications and Curriculum Authority (QCA). The teaching materials to support the new approach have been developed by the University of York Science Education Group and the Nuffield Curriculum Centre. The specification and examinations have been developed and managed by the awarding body, OCR.

The pilot began in September 2003 and will run for three school years, with two cohorts completing the pilot course. Evaluation studies, focusing on students' learning and attitudes to science, teachers' and students' views of the approach, and the teaching demands it makes, have been commissioned and are in progress. Final reports on these will be available in Summer 2006, when the pilot ends. So it is too early to make a final judgment. What can be said at this point, though, is that it is feasible to design a key stage 4 science curriculum using the core + additional model, and that it can be successfully implemented in schools. Many pilot schools report improvements in students' interest in science and in their responses to it, welcoming in particular the closer and more apparent links between the science learnt about in school and the science students read or hear about outside school through the news media and elsewhere. Teaching that involves more discussion, sometimes of open issues to which there is no single right answer, poses new challenges for many science teachers. The core science component has also helped to show what a 'scientific literacy' emphasis might look like in practice. As some science educators have pointed out, 'scientific literacy' is not a clearly defined term (DeBoer, 2000; Norris and Phillips, 2003). This is discussed in Chapter 24. Trying to design a course whose aim is improve 'scientific literacy' is one way of clarifying its meaning. *Twenty First Century Science* is not the only way to teach for scientific literacy, but it does set out one possible way in detail. This lets us see more clearly the implications of a focus on scientific literacy, and so takes debate about the content and emphasis of the science curriculum forward. The next few years will provide much more evidence about the effectiveness of the *Twenty First Century Science* approach. The issues involved are of very wide interest in many countries throughout the world, but there are few examples anywhere of such courses being implemented and evaluated, and none (known to us) within the compulsory phase of education.

Whatever emerges from the *Twenty First Century Science* pilot, the underlying issues are ones that we cannot avoid. All students, both future scientists and non-scientists, are citizens who need some understanding of science to participate fully and 'feel at home' in the kind of society in which we live. Some students also need broader and deeper understandings to pursue their career aspirations or their specific interests. The curriculum must provide adequately for both – without letting the needs of one overwhelm the other. Twenty years after making science a core subject of the curriculum, we are perhaps beginning to see how this might be done.

References

21st Century Science project team (2003) *21st Century Science – a new flexible model for GCSE science. School Science Review*, **85**(310), 27–34.

Burden, J. (2005) *Twenty First Century Science. Education in Science*, **213**, 10–12.

Collins, H. (2000) On *Beyond 2000. Studies in Science Education*, **35**, 169–173.

Cossons, N. (1993) Let us take science into our culture. *Interdisciplinary Science Reviews*, **18**(4), 337–342.

DeBoer, G. (2000) Scientific literacy: another look at its historical and contemporary meanings and its relationship to science education reform. *Journal of Research in Science Teaching*, **37**(6), 582–601.

High Level Group for Human Resources and Technology (2004) *Increasing human resources for science and technology in Europe*. Brussels: European Commission.

Kuhn, T. S. (1962) *The structure of scientific revolutions*. Chicago: University of Chicago Press.

McComas, W. F. and Olson, J. K. (1998) The principal elements of the nature of science: dispelling the myths. In *The nature of science in science education: rationales and strategies*, ed. McComas, W. F. pp. 53-69. Dordrecht: Kluwer.

Millar, R. (1996) Towards a science curriculum for public understanding. *School Science Review*, **77**(280), 7–18.

Millar, R. and Osborne, J. F. ed. (1998) *Beyond 2000: science education for the future*. London: King's College London, School of Education.

National Science Board (2004) *Science and Engineering Indicators*. Washington: National Science Foundation.

Norris, S. and Phillips, L. (2003) How literacy in its fundamental sense is central to scientific literacy. *Science Education*, **87**(2), 224–240.

Osborne, J. F., Ratcliffe, M., Collins, S., Millar, R. and Duschl, R. (2003) What 'ideas-about-science' should be taught in school science? A Delphi study of the 'expert' community. *Journal of Research in Science Teaching*, **40**(7), 692–720.

Chapter 2

Turning purpose into practice in science education

One of the purposes of education is the promotion of the intellectual, personal and moral development of children. This chapter focuses on the contribution that science education can make to the general development of children and considers the ways in which such purposes are achieved in practice. It examines the links between curriculum and pedagogy, the pressure of assessment on the curriculum, and the links between pedagogy and assessment.

Paul Black

Taking purposes seriously

It is not inevitable that science be given the high priority that it now enjoys in the school curriculum, nor even that it be a subject at all. A case could be made out, for example, for medicine or politics being essential components. Thus one priority in a discussion of purposes is to justify the place of science in schools. Why, for example, should science be required in both primary and secondary stages, rather than, as for languages, at secondary only? Does it have to be a separate subject when other aspects of education are deemed worthy only of cross-disciplinary or extra-curricular attention, notably personal, social and health education and environmental education?

The issue of purposes should be discussed to frame answers to two questions:

- What contribution can science education make to the general development of children?

- What are the purposes that are specific to science education?

This chapter will focus mainly on answers to the first question, concentrating on the aim of promoting the intellectual, personal and moral development of children and on those purposes which may be achieved in several subjects but which transcend their individual boundaries. Its main concern will be with the ways in which purposes are achieved in practice, the argument being that such achievement depends on far more than a clear statement of what is desirable. So the next section sets out a model to highlight interactions between curriculum, pedagogy and assessment. Subsequent sections deal in turn with the implications for practice of different purposes, by examining in turn the links between curriculum and pedagogy, the pressure of assessment on the curriculum, and the links between pedagogy and assessment. The various threads will then be drawn together in the concluding section.

The triangle

Any commitment to purposes is pointless without a matching commitment to achieving them. Moreover, striving to achieve them may alter the purposes or the way one understands them. A more realistic view of a complex picture may be achieved by close examination of the links between a curriculum and the pedagogy through which it is implemented. This pedagogy is itself powerfully affected by both summative and formative assessment. Figure 2.1 represents these three elements and the interactions between them in a simple way.

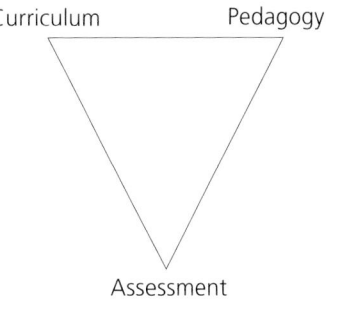

Figure 2.1

Two features are central in determining these interactions. For the first, assumptions about how pupils may learn best will underpin the ways in which those involved develop the interactive links: this will be true whether or not the learning theories held are made explicit. What is involved here is more than just theories of memory and understanding. The growth in the motivation, self-esteem and self-confidence of pupils are also powerful factors, and constitute a set of purposes in their own right. (These matters are discussed in other chapters.)

The second feature is the way in which those involved see their own roles, as teachers or as learners. Those teachers who focus on 'delivery' of the curriculum and strive to meet external test requirements will teach very differently from those whose central purpose is striving for the development of the potential of all pupils. The latter group see outside prescriptions as constraining their aims. Similarly, pupils may see themselves as passive recipients or as active and responsible learners.

Changing curriculum, changing pedagogy

A discussion of the purposes and aims of science education is outside the scope of this chapter. (These are discussed in Chapter 1.) The focus here is on the relationships within the triangle. What is relevant to this focus is the effect of different types of curriculum purpose on both pedagogy and assessment. One example is the purpose of involving pupils actively in their own investigations in or about science. If this calls for work with equipment, then teachers need, in addition to suitable skills and facilities, the pedagogic skills to handle open-ended practical investigations. The teacher might have to tolerate uncertainty rather than tidy closure, and provide feedback that encourages and guides pupil initiatives. This calls for skills and attitudes rather different from those usually deployed in conceptual learning or in routine laboratory exercises. If the purpose calls for library or Internet research followed by composition of an essay, the pedagogic skills needed are different again – more akin to those exercised by teachers of English than those usually needed in the science classroom. In both possibilities, assessment could hardly be by written examination, and would have to be based on teachers' assessments of selected products, combined with inter-teacher moderation.

The challenges are different again if pupils are to engage in study of the social implications of the achievements of scientists. Such engagement calls for participation in open debate, whereby implicit assumptions and differences in beliefs and values on social and moral issues must come into play. The pedagogic skills required may then be more akin to those needed by teachers of religious education or history, whilst assessment will involve looking for quality in oral or written argument rather than for correct answers.

Pressures on curriculum and assessment

The need for a national curriculum arose from a culmination of longer-term political and social trends. (Historical influences are discussed in Chapter 3.) Public and political interest in education continues to be strong. Such interests are heightened by a growing emphasis on the need to expand numbers in tertiary education and by pressures from business, industry and environmentalists. It seems that political control over the curriculum, far from leading to stability, is leading to more questioning of school practices and to temptations to exert power to 'improve' as soon as difficulties are publicised.

Thus, the determination of purposes and priorities for the science curriculum is, like other social issues, an essentially political struggle between competing traditions, perspectives and interests. However, whilst schools are not in full control of specification, they have very strong control over implementation, so that their own priorities, and their views of the priorities of others, will continue to be of outstanding importance.

The instrument that politicians use to hold schools 'accountable' to the public, the 'bottom line' for most teachers, is the system of tests which are organised outside the control of schools. This could be, in principle, a benign way of reinforcing the implementation of the purposes of the nationally agreed curriculum. However, a recent study of the effects of the current system of external testing on the work of teachers concluded that:

> As currently constituted external assessment in school science education
> would appear to have a malign effect on the teaching of science,
> encouraging teachers to teach by transmission which, in turn, results in
> negative student attitudes towards school science. Too often assessment in
> school science supports a practice which sees science as a body of
> knowledge to be learnt rather than as a way of knowing which has
> transformed the world in which we live. (Black et al., 2004, p. 2)

Such concerns apply to two kinds of tests: written tests for which the limitations of cost and administration constrain both the testing time and the scope of the aims that they can assess; and, at secondary level, teacher-based assessment of practical work, where the rules of examining agencies have so constrained teachers' judgements that they produce stereotyped work that does positive harm to the learning of science.

In technical terms, the accountability system is invalid, that is, it does not measure what it should. Added to this is the evidence that short written tests cannot measure with adequate accuracy the limited range of goals that they do measure, that is, they are not sufficiently reliable for their purposes. For example, an analysis of key stage 3 tests shows that it is likely that the proportion of pupils misclassified by at least one level is at least 24 per cent, and might well be over 35 per cent (Wiliam, 2001). Another example concerns the 11-plus selection tests in Northern Ireland, analysed by Gardner and Cowan (2000). Of the 18 000 children tested every year, between 6000 and 7000 succeed; yet analysis of the reliability of the tests shows that about 3000 entrants will be wrongly placed, some gaining places when they should not have, and some failing when they should have succeeded.

The only way to escape the cul-de-sac in which present practice is trapped is to place far more reliance on teachers' own assessments, which some other countries seem able to do. Both Scotland and Wales have policies that are moving in this direction. However, such a system could not command, or deserve, public confidence in England without a large investment in teachers' assessment skills.

Assessment and pedagogy

There are two reasons why pedagogy is relevant to a consideration of the purposes of science education. The obvious one is that it is the means by which the purposes are achieved in practice, so the purposes and the practice have to be moulded to form a consistent relationship. The more subtle purpose is that the way a teacher teaches gives pupils both models of learning and knowledge of themselves as learners. Enabling young people to learn to be effective learners in the future is a central aim of school education, and, in so far as science is one of the powerful modes of learning, becoming effective learners in science is an important aim for all pupils.

For pedagogy aimed at helping pupils to develop as learners, formative assessment is central. What is fundamental to it is the development of two-way feedback interactions between pupils and teachers. Such development requires that pupils' ideas be elicited with care, that they be encouraged to express these orally and in writing, that teachers respond to what pupils express by affirmation, challenge and guidance, and that pupils learn to collaborate with one another and to take responsibility for their own learning. The details of such pedagogy are explored in Chapter 22. What is important here is that the ways in which teachers interact every day with pupils be based on basic principles of learning, namely that effective teachers should:

- start from a learner's existing understanding;
- involve the learner actively in the learning process;
- help the learner to understand the learning aims and the criteria of quality, so enabling self- and peer-assessment;
- support and guide social learning, i.e. learning through discussion.

A pedagogy of science education based on these principles will serve to enhance the general personal and intellectual development of the pupils. It is through personal involvement in discussion that pupils may gain experience in using assumptions, models, evidence and argument to reach conclusions.

Good learning should explore the conceptual, the cognitive, the epistemic and the social dimensions of knowledge creation in science. Two quotations from Driver, Newton and Osborne (2000) express the implications for classroom work. On the conceptual aspect:

> It is our view that conceptual change is dependent on the opportunity to socially construct, and re-construct, one's personal knowledge through a process of dialogic argument. (p. 298)

On discussion about the nature of scientific knowledge:

> The teacher then has the demanding task of orchestrating a reflective discussion in which the different positions are explained, then compared and contrasted, and decisions are made as to which offers the best interpretation. (p. 300)

The emphasis here on the importance of dialogue in science education is echoed in many studies of learning in general. For example, in these quotes from Mercer (2000):

> in normal human life, communicative activity and individual thinking have a continuous, dynamic influence on each other. (p. 9)

> language provides us with a means for thinking together, for jointly creating knowledge and understanding. (p. 15)

Studies of classroom practice have shown that many science classrooms fall far short of achieving fruitful learning dialogue with and amongst pupils. (Chapter 20 discusses the importance of dialogue.) The following extract from the report of Driver, Newton and Osborne (2000) illustrates this point:

> Our observations and interviews with science teachers suggest that few teachers have the necessary skills to effectively organize group and class discussions and, hence, they lack confidence in their ability to successfully manage sessions devoted to argumentation and discussion in the classroom. Consequently, such activities rarely, if ever, take place. (p. 309)

All of this bears on learning seen only as a cognitive activity. However, there is far more involved. The way in which pupils are treated in learning has powerful effects on their motivation and self-esteem, which are powerful determinants both in their learning and in other aspects of their personal development. One type of evidence arises from studies of different ways of giving feedback on written work. From such a study, Butler (1987) concluded that those given feedback as marks are likely to see it as a way to compare themselves with others ('ego-involvement'), while those given only comments see it as helping them to improve ('task-involvement'); the latter group outperform the former.

Such differences have important effects on the development of the potential of pupils to achieve. Extensive research by Butler (1987), Dweck (2000) and others led Dweck to conclusions that can be summed up as follows:

● With ego-involvement, both high- and low-attainers are reluctant to take risks and react badly to new challenges, and failure simply damages self-esteem.

- With task-involvement, learners believe that they can improve by their own effort, are willing to take on new challenges and to learn from failure.

Such issues are far-reaching and fundamental. A school and classroom culture that emphasises competition, by responding more to those quick to answer in classroom dialogue, by highlighting marks and grades for every piece of work, and by giving praise and prominence to those who do best, is creating a culture of winners and losers. Such effects, in common with the practices of setting and streaming, are damaging overall. The winners gain little, whilst the losers come to believe that they are inherently unable to learn and often cease to participate. If schools are to develop the potential of every pupil, they must replace the culture of competition with one in which all pupils are encouraged, so putting into effect a principle that everyone can make progress in reaching targets that are appropriately challenging in relation to their progress to date. (This is discussed further in Chapter 18.)

Making it happen

As schooling in general and science education in particular are inevitably subject to frequent change, purposes have to be re-examined. In such scrutiny the most important and over-arching purposes must be kept in focus. For primary children, these are the need to develop their power for thoughtful argument and reflection, their developing grasp of the ways in which science contributes to human knowledge, and their enthusiasm for the exploration of science. For secondary pupils, there should evolve, in addition, a critical understanding of the strengths and limitations of science in guiding personal and social life, and a deepening understanding of science, which might inspire and guide the desire to study it further.

Above all, in the face of well-intentioned but sometimes misguided external pressures, science education must hold on to and amplify its contribution to the personal development and self-confidence of all pupils, so that all can leave school as competent as possible in their own capacity to learn, and confident that they can always, by their own efforts, develop their understanding of both familiar and new issues.

The continual effort to achieve such purposes ought to be guided by attention to the framework suggested by the triangle model. This implies that attention must be focused on:

- **curriculum renewal** – and the changes in pedagogy and assessment that such renewal requires;
- **renewal of assessment**, both in public policies for summative assessment so that it can have benign, rather than harmful, effects on pedagogy and on curriculum aims, and in school practices in formative assessment to help all to become better learners;
- **development of teachers' skills** so that they can better meet all their curriculum purposes.

The issues that lie at the core of this triangle, and which determine the positive interplay between its nodes, are the principles of learning that should underlie all three, and the ways in which both pupils and teachers understand their roles in the school enterprise. Experience in the development of formative assessment has underlined this issue of role change, both for pupils (see e.g. Cowie, 2005; Mercer *et al.*, 2004) and for teachers (see Black *et al.*, 2003, Ch. 6, pp. 80–99). The literature on professional development of teachers shows how difficult and delicate such development can be.

But it must never be forgotten that the underlying value that should be treasured and nurtured in any systemic programme of renewal of purposes is the personal potential and dignity of the pupils. Such nurture is expressed in the way in which teachers treat their pupils. As Stephen Norris (1997) expressed it:

> To ask of other human beings that they accept and memorise what the science teacher says, without any concern for the meaning and justification of what is said, is to treat those human beings with disrespect and is to show insufficient care for their welfare.
>
> It treats them with a disrespect, because students exist on a moral par with their teachers, and therefore have a right to expect from their teachers, reasons for what the teachers wish them to believe.
>
> It shows insufficient care for the welfare of students, because possessing beliefs that one is unable to justify is poor currency when one needs beliefs that can reliably guide action. (p. 252)

References

Black, P., Harrison, C., Lee, C., Marshall, B. and Wiliam, D. (2003) *Assessment for learning: putting it into practice*. Maidenhead: Open University Press.

Black, P., Harrison, C., Osborne, J. and Duschl, R. (2004) *Assessment for learning 14–19*. London: Royal Society (www.royalsoc.ac.uk/education).

Butler, R. (1987) Task-involving and ego-involving properties of evaluation: effects of different feedback conditions on motivational perceptions, interest and performance. *Journal of Educational Psychology*, **79**(4), 474–482.

Cowie, B. (2005) Pupil commentary on assessment for learning. *The Curriculum Journal*, **16**(2), 137–151.

Driver, R., Newton, P. and Osborne, J. F. (2000) Establishing the norms of scientific argumentation in science classrooms. *Science Education*, **84**(3), 287–312.

Dweck, C. S. (2000) *Self-theories: their role in motivation, personality and development*. Florence, KY: Psychology Press.

Gardner, J. and Cowan, P. (2000) *Testing the test: a study of the reliability and validity of the Northern Ireland transfer procedure test in enabling the selection of pupils for grammar school places*. Belfast: Queen's University of Belfast.

Mercer, N. (2000) *Words and minds*. London: Routledge.

Mercer, N., Dawes, L., Wegerif, R. and Sams, C. (2004) Reasoning as a scientist: ways of helping children to use language to learn science. *British Educational Research Journal*, **30**(3), 359–377.

Norris, S. P. (1997) Intellectual independence for non-scientists and other content-transcendent goals of science education. *Science Education*, **81**, 239–258.

Wiliam, D. (2001) Reliability, validity, and all that jazz. *Education 3–13*, **29**(3), 17–21.

Chapter 3 | Schooling secondary science

Change has been the norm ever since science was introduced into English schools over 150 years ago.

Edgar W. Jenkins

The curriculum, teaching methods and cohort of eligible pupils have all been reformed in response to changing political priorities, developments in science itself and shifts in understanding of how children learn. Current science curriculum developments are the latest in this history of reform and this chapter allows them to be viewed in this wider perspective.

A struggle for recognition

Science did not secure a place in the curriculum of secondary education without a struggle. For much of the nineteenth century, the educational claims of science were opposed by those who equated science education with the teaching of facts. They argued that, unlike the classics, studying science could not promote the development of character and moral sensibility, then regarded as the principal purpose of a liberal secondary education. However, by the mid-nineteenth century, the nature of the debate about the inclusion of scientific subjects in the curriculum had begun to change and a greater perception of the complexity of the problems of curriculum reform gradually led to a broader and more rational analysis of the issues. In 1864, the Clarendon Commissioners, while emphasising the value of a classical education, acknowledged its contemporary shortcomings and described the exclusion of natural science from the education provided in public schools as a *'plain defect and a great practical evil'*. Only three years later, the British Association for the Advancement of Science, in its report, *On the best means for promoting scientific education in schools*, confidently, if over-optimistically, asserted that there was *'already a **general** recognition of Science as an element in liberal education'*.

The British Association report of 1867 was widely publicised, and it remained an important point of reference for advocates of scientific education for over half a century. The case for teaching science in secondary schools was said to rest on several grounds. Science offered an excellent means of mental training by *'providing the best discipline in observation and collection of facts, in the combination of inductive and deductive reasoning, and in accuracy of both thought and language'*. The inclusion of science within the curriculum could appeal to those upon whom the usual non-scientific studies provided *'very slight effect'*, as well as adding a valuable element for those whose interests lay principally in *'literary culture'*. No one who claimed to be educated could remain unacquainted with the methods and results of science. Science should also be taught because it *'affected materially the present position and future progress of civilisation'*, that is, because scientific knowledge was useful. This educational rationale was accompanied by the drawing of an important distinction between scientific information and scientific training. While both of these were regarded as important, the principal benefit of a scientific education was the development of a *'scientific habit of mind'*. This distinction between scientific 'content' and 'process' and the relative importance to be ascribed to them have continued to frame much of the discussion about science education to this day.

Implementing science in the curriculum

Moving from a persuasive rationale for science education to implementation in the school curriculum was far from straightforward, despite some isolated pioneering initiatives earlier in the nineteenth century. It was necessary to devise curricula and teaching methods, design and build teaching laboratories, write and publish textbooks, construct examinations and provide a supply of science teachers. Most of these problems had been addressed and substantially solved by 1902 when the state first became involved in funding a system of selective secondary (i.e. grammar school) education. The Secondary School Regulations issued two years later made science, including practical science, a compulsory component of the grammar school curriculum, reflecting the firmly established view that school science should be based on laboratory work: over 1100 school science laboratories were built between 1877 and 1902, often by adapting existing classroom accommodation.

The science curriculum consisted essentially of chemistry and elements of physics, the latter often taught as separate courses such as 'electricity and magnetism', 'heat, light and sound', and 'mechanics and properties of matter'. Chemistry courses emphasised the preparation and properties of elements and compounds, with more advanced work based upon volumetric and qualitative analysis. The teaching of biology was restricted to older pupils intending to study medicine, although botany featured prominently in the work of girls' grammar schools. Textbooks reflected the emphasis on the recall of knowledge and routine calculations required by an array of science examinations that was not systematised until the introduction of the School Certificate and Higher School Certificate at the end of the First World War. Manuals, written to support laboratory teaching, introduced strategies for writing up practical work, such as 'test, observation, inference' and 'aims, apparatus, method, conclusion', that were to become routine for many subsequent generations of pupils.

Teaching methods included teacher demonstrations, learning definitions, laws and principles 'by heart', and the use of laboratory work to help develop pupils' understanding of scientific concepts. While Armstrong's heuristic method, which sought to place the pupil in the position of an original discoverer, was widely known and vigorously promoted, especially by Armstrong himself, relatively few schools paid it much more than lip service. Even so, the approach was to endure in spirit if not in substance, and it resurfaced in the twentieth century in a variety of guises, such as 'teaching by discovery', 'guided investigation', 'process science' and 'scientific inquiry'.

General science for all

The role played by science in the First World War renewed the debate about the role of science in education. This led the government to appoint an inquiry into 'Natural Science in Education' under the chairmanship of J. J. Thomson. The Thomson report, published in 1918, set out a new vision for secondary science education and one which, to Armstrong's fury, was highly critical of the heuristic method. Science was to be taught, not to train pupils in scientific method or simply with future scientists in mind, but as a means of liberal education for all. School science was to be broadened, humanised and *brought into the homes of the people*. Moreover, science had a new 'learning theory'. The Thomson Committee, drawing upon the ideas of T. P. Nunn, detected *three conspicuous motives* of wonder, systematisation and utility in science itself and convinced itself that these were also present in the minds of pupils, although to different degrees at different ages. Henceforth, young children were not to be taught 'physical measurements' but topics such as nature study or astronomy presented in ways that appealed to the 'wonder motive'. Likewise, in the case of older pupils, Archimedes' Principle was to be taught not as a 'property of fluids' or as a method of determining specific gravity but as the principle that explained why ships are able to float. Moreover, the Principle was to be taught when pupils were most receptive to the 'utility motive'.

A new direction was clearly needed for school science and this took the form of 'General Science' for all, an initiative strongly supported by the Science Masters' Association (formed in 1919 from the Association of Public School Science Masters founded in 1901) and the Association of Women Science Teachers. In this context, 'all' referred only to those pupils attending public and maintained grammar schools. In the school year 1920–1921, there were 336 836 pupils attending 1205 grant-aided secondary schools in England and Wales. Most pupils were among the 5 933 458 who attended public elementary schools and were not considered in these discussions of science education.

By 1930, six of the eight examination boards in England and Wales offered a syllabus and examination in general science at School Certificate level. Six years later, there were only 4847 entries at this level in general science, compared with 21 676 and 29 975 in physics and chemistry respectively. However, the Second World War brought a surge in entries, partly because of the shortage of science teachers and resources, with general science always remaining more popular among girls' schools. Even so, underlying difficulties with general science remained. Was it a subject or a *miscellany of cigarette card knowledge* as some of its critics maintained? Did the unity of general science lie in 'scientific method' or in the way the subject was taught? These and other questions proved difficult to answer, the more so since textbooks bore titles such as *General science physics* and *General science chemistry*, and examination papers were often divided into sections clearly identified as physics, chemistry and biology.

The inclusion of biological topics in a 'general science' syllabus was particularly significant since it challenged the case for biology as a separate subject. By 1930, all eight examination boards examined biology at School Certificate level, although there was great diversity in the syllabuses and examinations, some of which had separate botany and zoology sections. This diversity reflected the relative immaturity of biology as a discipline and the lack of agreement among science teachers about what should be included in a school biology course. Among the members of the Science Masters' Association and the Association of Women Science Teachers there was particular sensitivity about the inclusion of topics such as heredity, sex education and dissection.

Although it survived until well after the Second World War, the demand for science specialists in the post-war world meant that general science could not hope to prosper within selective schools. After reprinting *The teaching of general science* in 1960, the science teaching organisations ceased to argue the case for general science. The attempt to engage science with citizenship represented by general science was to find a later expression in the Science–Technology–Society (STS) movement and, most recently, in *Twenty First Century Science*.

Redefining secondary science

The Education Act 1944 entitled all children to receive a free secondary education and it created three nominally equal types of secondary school to which children could be admitted by selection in accordance with their ability and aptitude. Only a minority of children moved to a grammar school rather than a secondary modern or secondary technical school. Unlike science teachers in the grammar schools, those working in secondary modern and technical schools could not call upon a well-established and familiar tradition of science education based upon an all-graduate profession, public examinations and close links with the universities. While they could call upon some examples of work done in the pre-war elementary, senior and modern schools, their work was inevitably shaped by the social functions attributed to the various types of post-war secondary education. Since, unlike their grammar school counterparts, secondary modern pupils were judged to '*have no profession in view*', secondary modern science courses eschewed an academic approach in favour of projects or schemes of work with titles such as 'Science in the home' or 'Science in our daily lives'. There were often close links to industry and commerce and an emphasis on providing the skills necessary for employment in the locality. In the absence of a national system of examinations for secondary modern school pupils, a multitude of science curricula emerged in response to the needs and opportunities of each school. These curricula frequently included little or no physical science, especially in the case of girls, and biological education often took the form of 'health education' or 'social biology'.

By the mid-1950s, it had become clear that secondary school science education was in need of major reform, despite the replacement of the group-based School Certificate examinations by the subject-based Ordinary and

Advanced level General Certificate of Education in 1951. Apart from the introduction of courses in general science and biology, grammar school science curricula, examinations and teaching methods had changed little since 1918. Examination questions set in the 1920s were still being set in 1956, little having changed save the replacement of Imperial units by the cgs system. Chemistry courses focused attention on the preparation and properties of elements and compounds, and school physics remained confined to the world of classical physics, both having failed to respond to the major developments that had taken place in science during the twentieth century. School biology was still dominated by the 'type system' and by attention to anatomy, physiology and plant morphology, and, at sixth-form level, by the requirements for entry into the medical schools. The mechanism of the much-needed reform and the resources needed to bring it about in a decentralised system of education were by no means obvious.

In April 1962, the Minister of Education, Sir David Eccles, told the House of Commons that the Nuffield Foundation had decided to make £250 000 available towards the cost of a long-term development programme to improve the teaching of school science and mathematics. It was an announcement that witnessed the beginning of a curriculum development era, characterised by worldwide attention to the reform of school science education. In the UK, the outcome of the Nuffield Science Teaching Project was envisaged as a coordinated set of up-to-date curriculum resources, including apparatus, film-loops and other teaching aids and textual material that teachers could use as they wished. Initially, attention was focused upon physics, chemistry and biology for 11–16 year-olds in grammar schools and streams, but these O-level projects were quickly followed by several others at A-level and by a Secondary Science Project intended for pupils of average ability and below. All the projects emphasised 'learning by doing' and sought to engage pupils in so-called 'guided discovery'. In each case, science teachers were the focus of the development process and were supported by the activities of a large number of science teachers' centres, many of which were set up within, or in close association with, institutions of higher education.

Science teachers in secondary schools of all types in the 1960s and 1970s were able to work within something of an educational free market. They were free, at least in principle, to choose from a range of syllabuses and examinations, and to adopt, adapt, ignore or select from a growing range of textual and audio-visual material and apparatus produced by a number of curriculum projects. There were unparalleled opportunities for professional development as science education became institutionalised as a field of teaching and research within higher education. Many schools made use of project materials, including apparatus, without wishing to enter pupils for the special project examinations, and the more traditional O- and A-level syllabuses and examinations were reformed in response to the demand to modernise school science education. Apparatus and equipment that had been the staple of grammar and public school science teaching since the nineteenth century, such as Fletcher's trolley, Kipps' apparatus and dip circles, were all discarded, only to surface later in antique shops or the catalogues of specialist dealers.

The Certificate of Secondary Education examination, introduced in 1965, was available in three modes, the third of which allowed teachers, subject to external moderation, to devise their own syllabuses, examine their own pupils and award appropriate grades. Secondary modern schools and the rapidly growing number of comprehensive schools took full advantage of the science curriculum opportunities available to them under these new and flexible examination arrangements, and devised large numbers of new courses and examinations that they judged best met the needs of their pupils.

Legislating practice?

A belief that the key to improving school science lay with science teachers themselves was at the heart of the Secondary Science Curriculum Review established in 1981, partly in response to the shift to a comprehensive system of secondary schooling. Like earlier attempts to effect change, the Review was underpinned by ideas about how children learn and thus how they can best be taught, in this case by a 'constructivist' approach. Although the work of the Review had a significant impact on a government policy statement for school science published in 1985, the political climate towards education was already changing. Between 1977 and 1985, a succession of official documents gradually made clear the direction of official thinking. Concerns about standards, teaching methods, wasteful duplication, gender inequity and a lack of agreed objectives all pointed towards the need for a national curriculum entitlement, planned as a continuous and coherent whole throughout compulsory schooling and, in the case of science, based upon the notions of breadth and balance.

The Government's intentions were made clear in the Education Reform Act 1988 and the subsequent National Curriculum and its associated assessment strategies in England and Wales. Not surprisingly, it proved much easier to establish by legislation the principle of a national curriculum than to define its substance, implement it in schools or develop a clear and satisfactory relationship with teachers and their work. Throughout the 1990s, science teachers struggled to give substance to the Government's prescription. The first attainment target (AT1/Sc1), a codification of the investigative element of Armstrong's heurism and the science curriculum projects of the 1960s, was a source of particular and enduring difficulty, despite a series of major revisions. The statutory creation of a new school subject 'science' from an amalgamation of scientific disciplines with different curriculum histories, methodologies and pedagogies, led to a rapid decline in entries in physics, chemistry and biology in the GCSE examination that had replaced CSE and O-level in 1988. It also highlighted the growing mismatch between the needs of the schools and the output of specialised science graduates from higher education.

Despite the succession of major reforms that have followed the Education Act 1988, it is clear that many problems remain, notwithstanding the fact that more teachers are teaching more science to more pupils than at any time in history. Many school science teaching laboratories and the equipment in them seem increasingly remote from the world of twenty-first century science, and the content of the National Curriculum is widely seen as failing both to reflect the role that science has come to play in the modern world and to engage the interests of pupils. A broad, balanced and compulsory science curriculum has not led to increased numbers of pupils studying science beyond the age of 16;

nor has it mitigated the long-standing unpopularity among girls of physics as an A-level subject. In addition, for some teachers, National Curriculum science has been a demoralising experience that has undermined their professional expertise and confronted them with questionable notions of generalisable 'good' or 'evidence-based' practice that hints at a 'national pedagogy'. They also judge that the National Curriculum has diminished their pupils' enjoyment of science, and narrowed the range of laboratory work undertaken.

Change has been the norm for school science education and further changes are as unavoidable as they desirable. At the time of writing, many changes are already underway, including *Twenty First Century Science*, GCSE and A-level Applied Science, and the reduction in the statutory requirements of the science component of the National Curriculum for 14–16 year-olds. As always, fundamental questions about the aims, form and content of secondary school science remain and it is the task of each generation to provide answers that make sense in a contemporary context. Nonetheless, most of the day-to-day work of science teachers remains that of teaching groups of 15–30 young people in classrooms or laboratories. To this extent, school science education in the opening decade of the twenty-first century has something in common with the way in which science was taught over a century ago. It remains to be seen how long this will continue to be the case.

Further reading

Donnelly, J. F. and Jenkins, E. W. (2001) *Science education: policy, professionalism and change.* London: Paul Chapman.

Jenkins, E. W. (1979) *From Armstrong to Nuffield: studies in twentieth century science education in England and Wales.* London: John Murray.

Layton, D. (1984) *Interpreters of science: a history of the Association for Science Education.* London: ASE/John Murray.

Woolnough, B. E. (1988) *Physics teaching in schools 19860–85: of people, policy and power.* London: Falmer Press.

Chapter 4

What is good science education?

This chapter draws on the experience and reports of Ofsted inspectors in discussing the

Ian Richardson

meaning of quality in secondary science education and how to improve it. It summarises the extent to which science education has improved since 1998. Ofsted is a government department established to take responsibility for the inspection of all schools, and many other educational institutions, in England (see website). Nevertheless the points raised are relevant to practice in all countries of the UK and beyond.

So what is quality?

'*Quality hits you in the face*' is a memorable phrase used by a science adviser grappling with the issue of standards. The quote is a précis of a view that is certainly pithy but not particularly helpful to those striving for quality. We can become more specific by looking at the reports of inspectors who regularly visit classrooms and evaluate the quality of what they find. High standards and high levels of engagement are seen in lessons where the teacher is enthusiastic and has high expectations of the pupils. Some key aspects are listed in Box 4.1. Good practice includes teachers pointing the way to further involvement in science, either in the next key stage, in post-16 education and training or as adults in a technological society.

Later, in Box 4.4, we show that the quality of provision has increased since 1998. But it is clear from inspectors' reports that much can still be improved. In the following sections some key areas for improvement are discussed.

Good teaching

At the heart of what teachers do is the pursuit of good outcomes for pupils. When teaching is good, learners make good progress and show good attitudes to their work, as a result of effective teaching. The teachers' good subject knowledge lends confidence to their teaching styles, which engage learners

Box 4.1

Some key aspects of good practice

The elements coming together to make science engaging and enjoyable include:

- effective planning
- good subject knowledge
- science enquiry
- clear objectives
- lively and energetic teaching
- good classroom management
- a variety of activities including ICT
- appropriate pace
- challenge and differentiation
- involvement of pupils in decisions
- effective feedback to pupils

and encourage them to work well independently. Any unsatisfactory behaviour is managed effectively. The level of challenge stretches pupils without inhibiting their learning. Based on thorough and accurate assessment that informs learners about how to improve, work is closely tailored to the full range of learners' needs so that all can succeed. Learners are guided to assess their work themselves. Teaching assistants and other classroom helpers are well directed to support learning. Pupils with additional learning needs have work well matched to their needs, based upon a good diagnosis of them. Good relationships support parents and carers in helping learners to succeed.

Teachers' knowledge and understanding of science

Science makes high demands on teachers' subject knowledge and in some lessons misunderstandings are evident and pupils' misconceptions about science go unchallenged. In the secondary phase teachers are often teaching science in areas other than their subject specialism. For example, many biologists are teaching physics and need the support of specialists and advice on how to teach particular issues. It is difficult to generate engaging and relevant contexts for science that you have not studied in depth. Schools therefore need to make every effort to identify opportunities for professional development.

Leadership and management

Leadership and management of science can be evaluated by the impact they have on achievement and standards. Good leadership of science is successfully focused on raising standards and promoting the personal development and wellbeing of learners. It creates a common sense of purpose among staff.

A well-managed science department:

- engages in effective self-evaluation, which takes account of the views of all major stakeholders, so that heads of departments have a good understanding of strengths and weaknesses within the department and have a good track record of making improvements, including dealing with the issues from the last inspection;
- has a central vision of inclusion of all learners and is effective in pursuing this and dismantling barriers to engagement;

- is well organised on a day-to-day basis;
- uses resources well, including out-of-school opportunities, to improve learners' outcomes and to secure good value for money;
- applies robust monitoring procedures for all adults who work in the department;
- promotes good links with parents, carers and outside agencies to support its work.

The impact of good management is seen in good progress made by most learners, in their sense of security and wellbeing, and in a department's deservedly good reputation. The leadership and management provide the department with a good capacity to improve.

School self-evaluation

It is not the sole prerogative of an inspectorate to use such criteria as those above. It is teachers who are best placed to use the evidence available to them to evaluate standards. Such criteria provide a common 'language' which can be used by teachers, school managers and external inspection agencies. The clear implication of this is that teachers need to take a lead in establishing standards through effective self-evaluation. These matters of standards need to be part of professional discussions and dialogues in schools.

In the early days of Ofsted inspections there were many accounts of stony-faced inspectors observing lessons and giving teachers very little feedback. Teachers often demonstrated a belief that they were like specimens being observed and they did not see themselves as active participants in the process of inspection. Although practice varies across countries of the UK, teachers are increasingly recognising that they have the evidence needed to evaluate standards and quality. It is teachers who are best placed to give an account of the standards in their school. Inspections should begin with the school's self-evaluation, which is the subject of Chapter 12.

Improving management

The importance of leadership and management to promoting effective teaching of science has been commented on in reports from Ofsted. Unsatisfactory and inconsistent teaching is often associated with weaknesses in the management and leadership of the subject. In four-fifths of schools, reports indicate that the management and leadership of science are good or better, a slight increase since 1998. Attention needs to be given to developing the management role, which might be expected to include the following:

- monitoring teaching and evaluating the standards of pupils' work and achievement;
- a programme of in-house training, with a focus on those aspects of science that teachers find most problematic;
- the development of a science handbook, which includes guidance on the principles of good teaching and learning, and policy and procedures for assessment to inform planning and target-setting;
- creating a scheme of work in which a good range of learning activities and the development of skills in science investigation play a significant part.

Improved assessment practice

Science departments in secondary schools have a relatively good record of effectiveness in monitoring performance data and reviewing patterns of performance. However, they are less successful at responding to individual pupils' needs. In too many departments, assessment is confined to testing at the end of a teaching sequence to yield data on attainment. The data gathered are often inadequately used to inform planning, analyse the success of teaching or provide individual pupils with information and advice on how to improve. Even when there are policies on marking and written feedback to pupils, there is often too much variation in practice, which is not picked up by consistent monitoring. The most successful assessment is guided by policy and procedures that focus on assessment for learning (see Chapter 22). Box 4.2 provides an example of this practice.

Box 4.2

An example of successful assessment practice

In one school, test measures are used to identify the learning style of pupils on entry and are taken account of in the way learning activities are then differentiated. The school and the science department work from the belief that knowledge of the learning mode preferred by pupils is a significant contributory factor to teachers' ability to improve teaching and learning. Another good feature is the extensive use of peer-assessment, with partners marking each other's work, followed by whole-class discussion of the key points. The self-assessment carried out by pupils is based on declared end-of-unit, end-of-year and end-of-key-stage targets. On this basis, at regular intervals pupils reflect on their progress, consider their next target and write down what they need to do to improve. Each pupil has a chart for plotting their own progress as a record of these reflections. This understanding of learning and of assessment has put pupils in a situation where they can also reflect on their own learning style and challenge the provision of suitable materials and activities in lessons. Teachers are supported by a key stage 3 scheme of work in which all lessons have a section on methods of assessment to provide formative information for pupils. End-of-unit plenary sessions are planned to provide an assessment opportunity during which misconceptions can be identified. The head of department and deputy head of department monitor assessment and offer support and advice.

Pupils as assessors

My son was awarded 8 out of 10 for his plum crumble in food technology. Setting aside fatherly feelings and partiality, I thought it was a pretty good plum crumble and my son could not explain how he could have got 10/10. The poor lad was commissioned to ask teacher why 8 out of 10. The answer? Nothing is perfect so we do not give 10/10 and he did not put his spoon away properly. This bizarre reasoning would not have been exposed had he not asked: how would he ever have known about spoon management if his teacher had not been gently challenged? The criteria for success had not been made clear and the assessment was delivered starkly as a verdict but without a rationale.

Assessment needs to be understood by pupils if they are to benefit fully from it, and teachers are not the only source of assessment information. When pupils are set a particular task they need clarity about the objectives of the activity to do it well. The standard of work that follows can be assessed against the objectives and when these have been clearly expressed and explained pupils are well able to evaluate the work of other pupils. Chapter 23 discusses pupil self- and peer-assessment in more detail.

Planning for scientific enquiry

Scientific enquiry is an aspect of the subject that makes particular demands on teachers' subject knowledge. Schools are, however, adopting a stronger focus on learning through investigative work. This has a very positive impact on pupils' understanding and enjoyment of science.

The highest standards seen are often in schools where the scheme of work includes well-integrated experiences of scientific enquiry. In these schools, pupils are involved in planning and carrying out regular science investigations, so that they understand the processes involved. It is this combination of both procedural and conceptual knowledge that promotes effective learning in science.

Without such regular involvement in scientific enquiry, pupils are unable to participate and learn actively. For example, where practical work is simply directed by the teacher, without pupils making their own contribution to the planning, learning is less effective and pupils show less evidence of developing both their skills and knowledge. Enquiry work can lead to high levels of motivation and engagement. Pupils need to participate in all aspects of investigation, forming hypotheses, planning, carrying out and evaluating. Pupils only carrying out instructions from worksheets to complete a practical activity are limited in the ways they can contribute and how they benefit. The present arrangements for assessment of scientific enquiry at GCSE have led to the same set-piece practical activities being carried out across the country. Too often, the scientific enquiry component of key stage 4 becomes limited by schools simply rehearsing practical assessments.

Engagement and enjoyment

It is a privilege to go into classrooms and see the business of education transacted. It is exhilarating to see young people engaged in their work, hear the buzz of discussion, and recognise the satisfaction that comes through understanding and new knowledge.

Since the National Curriculum was introduced teachers have had the freedom to select appropriate knowledge and understanding from the Programme of Study. The Programme of Study has set out the 'what' of science education but not the 'how'. If teachers do not select appropriate work this results in pupils being taught the same content, often in the same way, as they learned in the previous key stage. This is demotivating for pupils and is a poor use of teaching resources, not the least of which is time. Demotivation leads to disengagement and to a depressing of standards.

Too often teachers have felt they have to teach didactically to get through the content of programmes of study or awarding body specifications. In the worst cases this is so that they can say they have taught it, regardless of whether

Box 4.3

An engaging science activity

Year 8 pupils (12/13 year-olds) were completing a unit of work on acids and alkalis that had involved them in research on the effect of acid rain on limestone. Pupils had presented the outcomes of their research to the class in the form of high-quality *PowerPoint* presentations. Discussion with pupils showed how varied these presentations were. Pupils working in groups had also planned investigations effectively and carried out the practical work. At the end of the last presentation the teacher invited the year 8 presenter to stay at the front and use the computer to gather the data from the investigations. Using wireless laptops each group transmitted its tabulations of data to the teacher's computer and the pupil displayed these on the interactive whiteboard. As soon as data started appearing pupils began to spot anomalous figures, compare patterns of data, summarise trends, account for differences, evaluate data, and suggest improvements. There followed a rich time of discussion and clarification that allowed pupils access to the ideas and work of others to build their own knowledge and understanding, not only of the chemistry but of the way science works.

pupils have understood or learned effectively. In the best practice, teachers use assessment to ascertain how learning is proceeding and use the assessment outcomes to modify planning and to inform pupils of how they can improve.

Pupils' involvement is the key to their engaging with science. Group work and class discussion need to be well organised if they are to challenge pupils sufficiently. The pursuit of scientific enquiry makes a significant contribution to the excitement of science, as illustrated in Box 4.3, or it can do if not hidebound by stereotyped and repetitive contexts and routines.

Identifying progress

If teachers' activities match the quality criteria discussed above, the outcomes are likely to be reflected in their pupils' attainment and achievement. Attainment outcomes are clearly important in keeping track of standards, but on their own they do not say how much benefit individuals have received from their education. In order to check that pupils are learning as effectively as possible we need to consider achievement, that is, to what extent pupils have shown increased knowledge, understanding and skills. The scale of pupils' achievement needs to be judged by considering their starting point and whether the progress they make is suitably matched to their capability. Put simply, an able pupil attaining grade C at GCSE has not shown as much achievement as a lower ability pupil attaining grade C, that is, the same outcome but a 'different distance travelled'.

When achievement is good:

- the outcomes are likely to compare well with those from similar schools;
- learners meet challenging targets and, in relation to their capability and starting points, they achieve high standards;
- most groups of learners, including those with learning difficulties and

Box 4.4

Changes since 1998 – an overview based on a review by Ofsted subject inspectors

As shown in Figure 4.1, pupils' achievement in key stage 3 science (ages 11–14) has risen since 1998, with a 20% improvement in the proportion whose achievement is good or better. This is almost twice the increase seen in key stage 4 (ages 14–16).

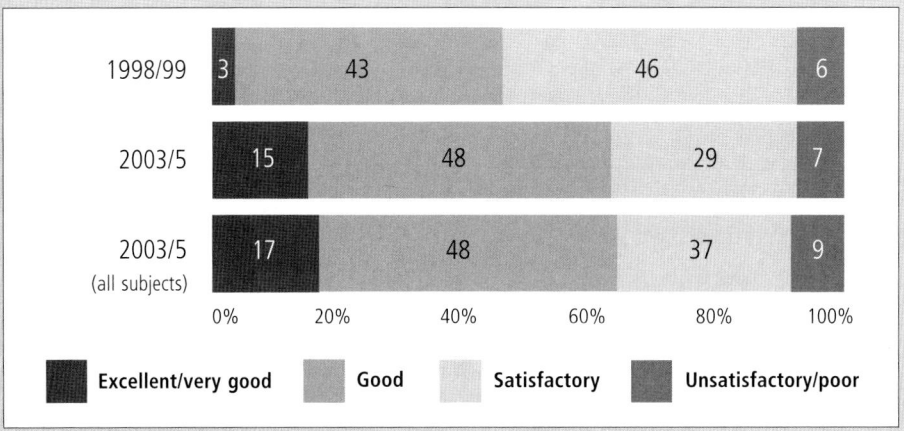

Figure 4.1 **Changes in achievement in science at key stage 3 (ages 11–14) in secondary schools, between 1998/99 and 2003/05.**

The strength of key stage 3 science is confirmed by international comparisons. Year 9 pupils (age 13/14) show attainment significantly higher than the average in the sample of 46 nations participating in an international survey in 2003, with only four countries outperforming England (see TIMSS website). However, recent Ofsted data show that achievement in key stages 3 and 4 has now reached a plateau. The improvement in achievement, up to now, can be linked in part to the dissemination of the Key Stage 3 Strategy, but there are also other factors at work. For example, Ofsted reports since 1998 have highlighted the need for key stage 3 teachers to take account of the science learned in primary school. This situation has now substantially improved. with schools working more effectively with associated primary schools to improve transition.

Quality of teaching has improved in all key stages since 1998, as shown in Figure 4.2. In 1998 teaching was good or better in under two-thirds of schools and in 2005 teaching of this quality is seen in nearly three-quarters of schools. The proportion of less than satisfactory teaching has hardly changed (around one in twenty). Teaching now is more varied in the approaches used, and planning and assessment practice has improved. Learning has risen in line with teaching.

Assessment practice has improved since 1998, with 16% more schools having good or better practice in key stage 4, and around 30% more having good or better practice for assessment of post-16 work. During this time, vocational courses such as GNVQ and the introduction of AS/A2 GCE qualifications have required a more systematic and thorough approach to the management of assessment, including the need to

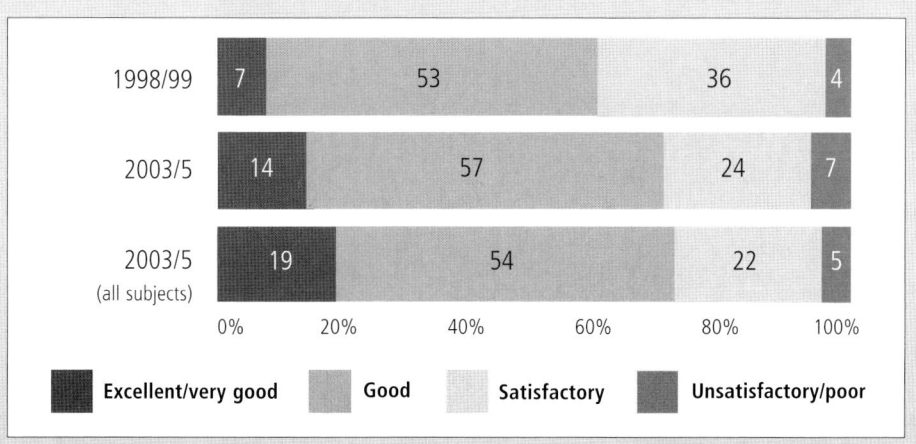

Figure 4.2 **Changes in quality of teaching in science in secondary schools between 1998/99 and 2003/05.**

meet tighter timescales for school-based assessment and to prepare for frequent external assessment of unitised courses. Although much time and effort has been expended by science departments on summative end-of-unit tests, the outcomes have not been used effectively to inform planning or to inform pupils of what they need to do to improve. Key stage 3 and 4 pupils' understanding of how they can improve is a good feature in only two-fifths of schools. On post-16 courses, the situation is much more positive with around three-quarters of students understanding well how they can improve.

The breadth of the curriculum has generally improved. Particularly on post-16 courses, teachers have introduced better contextualised work of greater relevance to students, within *Curriculum 2000* developments. At key stage 4, as well as improvement in existing courses, there has been significant curriculum development in new courses. These include *Applied Science* and *Twenty First Century Science*, promoting a vocational aspect to learning and science for public understanding respectively. The new Programme of Study has a smaller core and allows a wider range of content and ways of learning and assessing to be accommodated.

Resources have improved at a quicker rate than accommodation, but whereas two-fifths of schools now have good resources, they are unsatisfactory in one-tenth. A greater selection of ICT resources has promoted interactivity and enabled higher levels of pupil engagement. Well-deployed ICT has brought about a broadening of pupils' experiences in science.

disabilities, make at least good progress and some make very good progress, as reflected in value-added measures;

- learners gain knowledge, skills and understanding at a good rate across all key stages.

Websites

Ofsted: http://www.ofsted.gov.uk/
TIMSS (Third International Maths and Science Survey) 2003 report: http://timss.bc.edu/timss2003i/scienceD.html

Chapter 5

Values and ethics in science education

Some teachers may consider that values and ethics are not really a part of science education. Yet every classroom, including the science classroom, is value-laden. If a teacher presents science as a value-free pursuit of objective truth, that in itself is a value position and conveys a particular view of science to pupils. This chapter examines whether science education should include issues of values and ethics and how teachers of science might explore values and ethics in their lessons.

Mary Ratcliffe and **Michael Reiss**

The meaning of values

In this chapter we adopt a standard working definition of values used by many in the field of values education:

> *principles, fundamental convictions, ideals, standards or life stances which act as general guides to behaviour or as reference points in decision-making or the evaluation of beliefs or action.* (Halstead, 1996, p. 5)

In a science classroom, at least three such guides to behaviour might be present (Figure 5.1):

- How teachers are guided by the values embedded in the science curriculum.
- How teachers are guided by the values of science and how these are conveyed, explicitly or otherwise, and interpreted by pupils.
- How teachers are guided by the values of individuals and society when considering the implications of science.

Teachers usually do not recognise that these values are operating in their

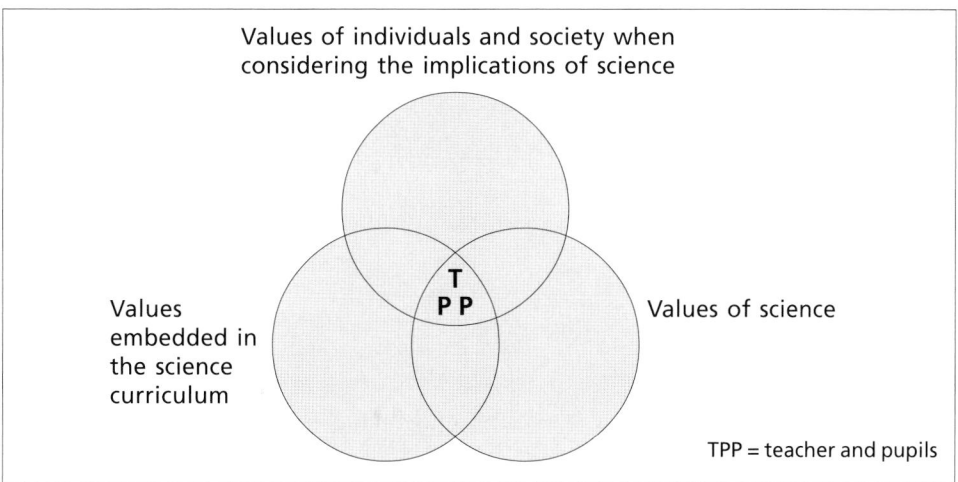

Figure 5.1 **Interpretation of values influencing science classrooms.**

lessons. In a survey of secondary science teachers *'Almost half of the science teachers interviewed feel that their teaching of science should be "value-free", that it does not yield issues that have social or ethical implications'* (Levinson and Turner, 2001, p. 7). Yet if a teacher presents science as a value-free pursuit of objective truth, that in itself is a value position and conveys a particular view of science to pupils (Layton, 1986).

Science teachers have values that relate to their general role as teachers as well as ones that are important in the context of teaching science. There are values embedded in the science curriculum itself. For example, at key stage 3 the current science National Curriculum for England says of pupils that:

> *They think about the positive and negative effects of scientific and technological developments on the environment and in other contexts.*
> (DfEE/QCA, 1999)

However, the purpose of this chapter is not to explore the nature of the science curriculum as this is discussed in Chapters 1 and 2; here we focus on teachers' actions and the implications for pupils.

Values of science

We start by looking at the range of values that could be presented about science and how they relate to contemporary views of the nature of science. Some aspects of terminology related to the nature of science are worth exploring here. Nott and Wellington (1993) developed a useful exercise for teachers to allow them to reflect on their view of the nature of science. In this exercise, agreeing or disagreeing with such statements as *'There is such a thing as a true scientific theory'* and *'Human emotion plays no part in the creation of scientific knowledge'* allows teachers to draw a profile of their own views to compare with those with others. Underpinning this exercise are a number of dimensions along which teachers position themselves, reflecting some of the terminologies and concepts relevant to the nature of science and its teaching (Figure 5.2).

In reading these dimensions, teachers may reflect on their own position and understanding of the nature of science. Some of the terminology may be

Positivist

Holds that science is the primary source of truth. The laws and theories generated by experiments are descriptions of patterns in a real, external **objective** world.

Relativist

Holds that judgements as to the truth of scientific theories vary from individual to individual and from one culture to another, i.e. truth is **relative** not absolute.

Inductivist

Holds that scientists generalise from a set of observations to a universal law, inferring from the particular to the general. Scientific knowledge is built by induction from a secure set of observations.

Deductivist

Holds that scientists form hypotheses that are not determined by the empirical data but may be suggested by them. Science then proceeds by testing the observable consequences of these hypotheses, so that observations are theory-laden.

Decontextualist

Holds that scientific knowledge is **independent** of its cultural location and sociological structure.

Contextualist

Holds that the truth of scientific knowledge and processes is **interdependent** with the culture in which the scientists live and in which the science takes place.

Realist

Believes that scientific theories are statements about a world that exists in space and time **independent** of the scientists' perceptions. Correct theories describe things that are really there, independent of the scientists, e.g. atoms.

Instrumentalist

Believes that scientific theories are fine if they work, that is they allow correct predictions to be made. These theories are instruments that we can use but they say nothing about an independent reality or their own truth.

Content is important

Thinks that science is characterised by the **facts and ideas** it has and that the essential part of science education is the acquisition and mastery of this 'body of knowledge'.

Process is important

Sees science as a characteristic set of identifiable **methods/processes**. The learning of these is the essential part of science education.

Figure 5.2 **Some dimensions and terminology relating to the nature of science** (summary from Nott and Wellington, 1993).

very well known; other aspects may be unfamiliar. Although there is no one correct view of the nature of science, some views are widely regarded as having greater validity than others. For example, a mature understanding of the nature of science recognises that while some scientific knowledge is extremely secure, some is more tentative.

A near consensual view of the nature of science can be summarised thus: science is a creative, collaborative and culturally bound activity in which reliable knowledge is generated through diverse but rigorous methods, albeit knowledge that could be subject to change depending on the collection of further evidence or reinterpretation of evidence (McComas and Olson, 1998; Osborne *et al.*, 2003).

What is more contentious is the extent to which what is accepted as valid scientific knowledge varies from culture to culture. At its simplest, cultures vary in what they expend their scientific efforts on. For example, in the early days of genetic engineering relatively little research was done into the possible harmful ecological consequences of genetically modified (GM) crops. The common assertion from companies involved in these technologies, that GM crops had no harmful effects on the environment, was therefore of little scientific value, since the hypothesis 'GM crops have no harmful effects on the environment' had not been tested. It is worth emphasising that, in this sense, scientific knowledge is *produced*: it does not simply sit around waiting to be discovered in an unproblematic manner.

Although the science curriculum has a strong influence on what is taught and how it is taught, the science teacher's views on the nature of science and the importance, or otherwise, of ethical aspects will bear on the detail of classroom interactions. Box 5.1 gives an example of a teacher's efforts to focus on the nature of science – in this case an experienced teacher, Judith, who participated in a research project to look at the barriers and opportunities in teaching 'ideas-about-science' (Bartholomew, Osborne and Ratcliffe, 2004).

Box 5.1

Focusing on the nature of science

Judith set up a lesson in which the learning outcomes were to '*know that scientists often work collaboratively and make hypotheses and predictions*'. She presented pupils with a cube, five sides of which were shown with BAT, CAT, FAT, HAT and MAT on them. Pupils were then asked to work out what they thought was on the sixth (covered) side. (This task was developed by Lederman and Abd-El-Khalick (1998) to support teaching of scientific creativity and pattern-seeking.) The pupils were initially perplexed but once they understood that they had to reason for themselves they engaged in the activity with growing confidence, each group making predictions based on what to them was logical reasoning. The nub of the lesson came when Judith asked about their predictions. The following report is from field notes:

When they report back Judith calls on each group in turn to give their answer and reasoning – though most groups are still discussing and haven't reached consensus. Some groups who were beginning to think about patterns in the alphabet revert to their earlier ideas when reporting back. One pupil explains to the class that she thinks the word is PAT and gives an explanation based on the fact that B and C (BAT and CAT) are next to each other, F and H have one letter between (FAT and HAT), and M and P have two letters between. Judith says that this is the right answer and she goes over it again, explaining that BAT and CAT are opposite each other, FAT and HAT are opposite each other and there is nothing opposite MAT.

This vignette conveys a crucial point in science teachers' normal pedagogy, seen many times in the research project but illustrated here succinctly. The pupils had been encouraged to consider their reasoning, but the teacher and class were dominated by the imperative to get 'the right answer'. Judith embraced the research project's aims of explicit teaching of 'ideas-about-science', through evaluation of evidence, and showed a reasonably sophisticated understanding of the nature of science. However, her actions show how strong was her need, whether through long-engrained habit or her underlying values, to arrive at fixed scientific knowledge. This lesson would have conveyed very different messages to pupils about the nature of science if the reporting back stage had allowed for:

- pupils to develop their own and challenge each other's ideas;
- the possibility of there being more than one right answer;
- a much greater acknowledgement of the ways in which theories are generated, tested, rejected and refined.

Ethical aspects of science

Whereas science can tell us what we can do, ethics, as a discipline, helps us decide what we ought to do. Just as teachers may have different views on the nature of science, they may also hold views as to whether social and ethical aspects of science should be pursued within the science curriculum (Reiss, 1999). Whatever stance one takes, to ignore the ethical dimension of the pursuit and applications of science is to sell pupils short in their appreciation of the issues of contemporary science.

There are ethics involved in the *conduct* of science as well as in considering the *implications* of scientific advancements. So, for example, when pupils at key stages 3 and 4 ensure that the data they collect are accurate and impartial, objectively report findings that contradict what they expected to find, and strive to be open-minded, for instance by considering alternative explanations for their findings, they are developing the habits of good scientists that help ensure that scientific knowledge is reliable.

Many advances in science raise ethical issues in their implications. Ethical issues in genetics, for example, are increasingly recognised within the science curriculum. But how can science teachers, who may have had little or no training in ethics, address ethical issues? One response is to leave these issues to be discussed in religious education or personal, social and health education (PSHE). While this response solves certain problems, we should be aware of the messages it can convey about school science: does it reinforce a view that school science is remote and irrelevant to everyday life?

Lack of discussion of socio-scientific issues in science classrooms could lead pupils to ignore the scientific evidence behind a problem and see science as a sterile pursuit unconnected with modern societal issues. Many societal issues arise precisely because of advances in scientific knowledge. If pupils were the ones who determined the content of the science curriculum, social and ethical issues would definitely be included as they are seen to be important for their future and very motivating (Cerini, Murray and Reiss, 2003; Haste, 2004).

However, consideration of socio-scientific problems can raise issues for the teacher. From a year-long study of classroom discussions of socio-scientific issues (Ratcliffe and Grace, 2003), we recount in Box 5.2 one particular interaction which shows the dilemmas for teachers.

The exchange in Box 5.2 shows, perhaps unsurprisingly, that these 15-year-old boys are very egocentric. It also illustrates the dilemma in which science teachers can find themselves. Should this teacher persist with exploring the environmental impact arising from consumer choice? Should he try to impose his own views? Should he act as devil's advocate or as neutral chair? Should he spend time clarifying the individual and societal values that impact on such decision-making?

Of course, a humanities teacher might be asking what all the fuss is about.

Box 5.2

An ethical teaching dilemma

The lesson was about what material you would use for replacement window frames – and it could just be done from the point of view of examining the advantages and disadvantages of the properties of softwood, aluminium, hardwood and uPVC as materials. However, the teacher gave the pupils opportunities to clarify their views on the issue. This extract is from his summary at the end of the lesson:

Liam: *Well, we thought we'd go for uPVC 'cos it's quality and if you buy the softwood you've got to keep up the maintenance. It would cost more and you'd probably end up paying as much as you'd pay for the uPVC anyway – so you might as well buy that.*

Teacher: *Did the environmental effects have any bearing on your decision?*

Mike: *A little bit.*

Keith: *Yeh, a little bit, [very quiet] just a tad.*

Teacher: *So that helped sway you away from hardwood?*

Keith: *Oh yeh, but we still think just cutting down one more tree for our bedroom window's not going to make that much difference.*

Teacher: *OK. Do you all agree with that?*

Liam: *Yeh.*

At this point the teacher does not pursue the conversation further.

Social science lessons thrive on discussion, exchange of opinion and evaluation of evidence – clarification of values being a strong feature. And here's the paradox: despite science being an evidence-based discipline, at its frontiers full of controversy about competing theories and models, many pupils in science classrooms do not normally engage in discussion and argumentation, either of scientific controversies or of socio-scientific issues. This seems to be mainly because for so long school science has been seen as a body of accepted knowledge – which of course most of it is; but a body of accepted knowledge to be learnt and regurgitated in exams, not to be interrogated for its evidence base. Teachers who see their role entirely as helping pupils understand the way the natural world works – mastering explanations of scientific concepts that are often counterintuitive – may not wish to engage in value-laden discussions. Such teachers are understandably often less confident and skilful in dealing with controversy in the classroom.

Approaches to handling controversial issues

Given the dilemmas science teachers may face in dealing with socio-scientific issues in the classroom, what is there to guide them in their role? The Crick Report (Advisory Group on Citizenship, 1998, p. 59) acknowledges three general approaches adopted by teachers in handling controversial issues: the 'neutral chair', the 'balanced' and the 'stated commitment' approach:

- In the role of **neutral chair** the teacher acts as facilitator in encouraging pupils to explore the issue and express their opinions fully. Teachers do not declare their own views.
- The **balanced** approach assumes that teachers will ensure that all different aspects and views are covered. They will discourage discussions which only concentrate on one particular viewpoint, acting as 'devil's advocate', if necessary, to counter one-sided arguments.
- In the **stated commitment** approach the teacher declares his or her own views at the outset, encouraging pupils to disagree or agree on the basis of their own reasoning.

Each of these three perspectives has advantages and disadvantages. The 'stated commitment' approach allows pupils to recognise teachers as authentic beings with their own perspectives on an issue, yet *'carries the risk that teachers who use it may well be accused of bias and attempting to indoctrinate those whom they are teaching'* (Advisory Group on Citizenship, 1998, p. 59). The reality that individual teachers hold views is ignored in the 'neutral chair' and 'balanced' approaches, though these approaches have the advantage of encouraging open discussion. However, the plurality of views encouraged by both these approaches may prevent pupils from developing the critical skills needed to judge the worth and validity of different solutions. The teacher in the extract in Box 5.2 is, to a certain extent, combining elements of these three perspectives in a commonsense approach – a stance that is encouraged by the Crick Report to dispel fears of indoctrination and insensitivity.

Whichever approach is taken, a great deal can be achieved by teachers encouraging pupils to reflect on the reasons for the ethical views they hold. At its simplest, gently asking *'Why do you think that?'* can be effective. Furthermore, encouraging pupils to think about the implications of their views for others as well as for themselves, is very productive. And 'others' doesn't just mean 'other humans': it can mean other animals and even the environment.

References

Advisory Group on Citizenship (1998) *Education for citizenship and the teaching of democracy in schools: final report* (The Crick Report). London: The Stationery Office.

Bartholomew, H., Osborne, J. and Ratcliffe, M. (2004) Teaching students 'ideas-about-science': five dimensions of effective practice. *Science Education*, **88**, 655–682.

Cerini, B., Murray, I. and Reiss, M. (2003) *Student review of the science curriculum: major findings*. London: Planet Science. www.planet-science.com/sciteach/review/findings.pdf (accessed 24 May 2005).

DfEE/QCA (1999) *Science: The National Curriculum for England.* London: Qualifications and Curriculum Authority.

Halstead, J. M. (1996) Values and values education in schools. In *Values in education and education in values*, ed. Halstead, J. M. and Taylor, M. J. pp. 3–14. Lewes: Falmer Press.

Haste, H. (2004) *Science in my future: a study of values and beliefs in relation to science and technology amongst 11–21 year olds.* London: Nestlé Social Research Programme.

Layton, D. (1986) Revaluing science education. In *Values across the curriculum*, ed. Tomlinson, P. and Quinton, M. pp. 158–178. London: Falmer Press.

Lederman, N. and Abd-El-Khalick, F. (1998) Avoiding de-natured science: activities that promote understandings of the nature of science. In *The nature of science in science education*, ed. McComas, W. F. pp. 83–126. Dordrecht: Kluwer.

Levinson, R. and Turner, S. (2001) *Valuable lessons: engaging with the social context of science in schools*. London: The Wellcome Trust.

McComas, W. F. and Olson, J. K. (1998) The nature of science in international science education standards documents. In *The nature of science in science education: rationales and strategies*, ed. McComas, W. F. pp. 41–52. Dordrecht: Kluwer.

Nott, M. and Wellington, J. (1993) Your nature of science profile: an activity for science teachers. *School Science Review*, **75**(270), 109–112.

Osborne, J., Ratcliffe, M., Collins, S., Millar, R. and Duschl, R. (2003) What 'ideas-about-science' should be taught in school science? A Delphi study of the 'expert' community. *Journal of Research in Science Teaching*, **40**, 692–720.

Ratcliffe, M. and Grace, M. (2003) *Science education for citizenship: teaching socio-scientific issues*. Maidenhead: Open University Press.

Reiss, M. J. (1999) Teaching ethics in science. *Studies in Science Education*, **34**, 115–140.

Chapter 6

Continuing professional development: enhancing professional expertise

The nature of teaching in all subjects, but particularly in science, changes constantly, bringing a

Derek Bell

continuing need for teachers to update their subject knowledge, understanding of learning and application of new approaches and technologies in teaching. This chapter considers what we mean by continuing professional development (CPD), provides an overview of the variety of CPD opportunities that exist to enhance professional expertise, and sets out some of the initiatives that are being put in place to improve access to and recognition of CPD for science teachers. It also discusses some of the tensions that exist for science teachers in trying to enhance their professional expertise and ensure their own professional development.

Why do we need CPD?

Without question teaching is a complex process. We only have to look at the standards that have been produced to provide benchmarks for gaining qualified teacher status (such as those for England and Wales by the TTA/DfES, see website) to appreciate the wide variety of skills, knowledge and understanding required. However, a newly qualified teacher still has much to learn and becoming a good teacher is more than simply ticking off a series of tasks or achievements. Furthermore, the subject matter we teach has moved on, understanding of approaches to teaching, learning and assessment has developed, and the curriculum and the context in which we work have changed. In other words, 'what we learnt in college' is not enough. We need to keep updating our skills, knowledge and understanding if we are to teach effectively in order to continue providing high-quality learning opportunities for pupils. Also, for our own benefit and interest, we need to keep learning, exploring and enhancing our own expertise and enthusiasm.

For science teachers there is a particular imperative to keep up to date for three key reasons. The first is the need for updating of subject knowledge in order to help keep abreast of at least some of the new developments and levels of understanding in science. The second relates to the demand for new teaching approaches to accommodate different learning styles, not only to meet the needs of those pupils who will continue to study sciences through to university but also to develop all pupils' scientific literacy to enable them to engage with issues they will meet in their lives. Finally, there is a need to be able to apply principles of formative assessment to science lessons and to use information and communication technology (ICT) effectively to enhance the teaching of science.

What do we mean by CPD?

CPD is a term used in a variety of contexts but often referring to different things. In some situations it relates to courses; in others it means engaging in research, reading articles and books; in yet others it refers to attending conferences and in others to a variety of informal means of gaining new ideas. More recently, use of the World-Wide Web and the Internet for gathering information, contributing to electronic discussion groups and engaging in on-line courses has added yet another area of activity referred to as CPD. In fact, CPD is not any of these individual things but is a complex amalgam of them all, plus others. Thus, finding a definition of CPD is not a straightforward task. Rather we need to build up a model of CPD that is applicable to a range of circumstances but at the same time sets out key features of what it means both generally and with specific reference to science teaching.

The term CPD is said to have been coined in the mid-1970s in relation to training for the building profession because 'it did not differentiate between learning from courses and learning "on the job"' (Leaton Gray, 2005, p. 5). In her review of research relating to CPD, Leaton Gray highlights the positive benefits of sustained collaborative professional development (see EPPI, 2003) and the potential impact of longer award-bearing schemes with a subject focus (see Soulsby and Swain, 2003). She also notes the change in terminology from In-service Training (INSET) to CPD which, she argues, 'signifies a shift in emphasis away from the provider and/or employer, towards the individual. In other words, the individual is now responsible for his or her lifelong career development, under the umbrella of the school or schools that employ the teacher' (Leaton Gray, 2005, p. 5).

This shift reflects a much wider debate about CPD, both in the UK and internationally, that is trying to address the question 'What do we mean by CPD?' and, importantly, how to embed CPD into the culture of schools, colleges and the profession more widely. The Training and Development Agency (formerly The Teacher Training Agency, TTA) for England and Wales proposed that the term CPD should be used to refer to:

> a planned and sustained series of activities, designed to improve a teacher's knowledge and skills. In this usage, CPD is not to be viewed as a 'bolt-on' or a short-term experience, but as a continuous exercise in addressing individual teacher's needs and in supporting improvements in their professional practice over time. (TTA, 2005a, p. 5)

A wide range of activities can contribute to professional development. These include: accredited and non-accredited courses, studied at centres or on-line; school-based courses; action research; mentoring; exchanges, placements and sabbaticals; award schemes; and peer networks. There are also a large number of sources that might provide training, help, advice and guidance. These include: local education authorities or boards; higher education institutions; national strategies; small and large independent providers; professional bodies and subject associations such as the Association for Science Education. Some of the activities take place in-house while others require time to be spent off-site. The important thing is that provision for CPD needs to be relevant and build on existing understanding, knowledge and skills so that it can be used to enhance practice. Principally this should be related to teaching and learning but it will also include other aspects of professional expertise such as interpersonal, leadership and management skills.

Provision of CPD

Frameworks for professional development

In recent years the interest in CPD has increased significantly and extensive advice and materials are available. In particular, the General Teaching Councils for England, Scotland and Wales (GTCE, GTCS, GTCW) have each identified it as a priority. In Scotland its importance was highlighted in the McCrone Agreement (Scottish Executive, see website). In England the Training and Development Agency (TTA, 2005b) is now responsible for, among other things, developing, coordinating and putting in place standards for CPD. Importantly, there is recognition that CPD is not separate from initial training so that already there are mechanisms in place for improving support for individuals in their first year of teaching. These include career entry profiles and entitlements for induction (TTA, 2005c). Further developments are being undertaken to provide improved continuity and coherence to the overall framework of professional development for teachers in the UK. Beyond these generic approaches there has been a great deal of development work to provide a framework in which professional development for science teachers can take place.

ASE Certificate of Continuing Professional Development

One such framework is provided by the ASE Certificate of Continuing Professional Development. Originally aimed at individuals in the early years of teaching, this approach has been found relevant at any stage in a career, and is equally applicable to both primary (see Haigh, 2003a) and secondary (see Haigh, 2003b; Haigh and Reece, 2003) teachers. The approach is firmly based on the needs of individual teachers and their schools and encourages them to explore seven areas of development:

- Subject knowledge and understanding.
- Pedagogical content knowledge: how to present the subject matter to different learners.
- Development of teaching and assessment skills.
- Understanding teaching and learning.
- The wider curriculum and other changes affecting teaching.
- Management skills: managing people.
- Management skills: managing yourself and your professional development.

The process involves an audit and self-review against these elements which contribute to professional expertise, and then the identification of a programme that ensures academic, pedagogic and professional rigour. Support and monitoring of progress involve a mentor and tutor providing advice and encouragement. An important element of this process is the need to think about how different activities (e.g. attending courses, making presentations to colleagues, writing schemes of work and personal reading and research) can all contribute to professional development in a focused and coherent manner. Importantly, this involves evaluating the impact that there has been on practice.

Science Education Forum framework for professional development

Building on the work of the ASE Certificate of CPD and working closely with science teachers, the Science Education Forum (SEF) task group has developed a subject-specific framework for professional development. The SEF framework consists of 12 elements (Box 6.1). Each element has several sub-elements, with statements at three stages of development which indicate the progression steps that might be expected as individuals enhance their professional expertise. (At the time of publication we are awaiting display of the complete framework on the SEF website.)

National network of Science Learning Centres

The issue of CPD for science teachers has been under discussion for some time and several reports have been published (e.g. Dillon *et al.*, 2000; Roberts, 2002) that have argued the need to strengthen subject-focused CPD and recommended that Government should be involved in improving CPD opportunities for science teachers.

This resulted in the announcement in October 2003 of the setting up a network of Science Learning Centres as a joint initiative funded by The Wellcome Trust and the Department for Education and Skills. The purpose of the national network of Science Learning Centres is to offer high-quality professional development principally for those involved in science education including secondary and post-16 science teachers, primary teachers, technicians and teaching assistants. The overall aim is to improve science teaching, raise morale in the teaching profession and through their teachers to inspire pupils with a more exciting, intellectually stimulating and relevant science education, enabling them to gain the knowledge and the understanding they need – both as the citizens and as the scientists of the future.

The network is made up of nine regional centres in England (see Figure 6.1) and the National Science Learning Centre based in York, which has a remit to

Box 6.1

SEF framework for professional development: the 12 elements

Professional knowledge and understanding

Elements 1–3 relate to **teacher knowledge** – these elements focus on your knowledge about science, about the teaching of science and about the pupils you teach. They form the underpinning knowledge base for your practice.

1 Having a broad knowledge of science and science curricula related to the nature of their teaching.

2 Having a broad and current knowledge of teaching, learning and assessment in science.

3 Knowing your students well and understanding the influence of cultural, developmental, gender and other contextual factors on your students' learning.

Professional practice

Elements 4–9 relate to aspects of the **teaching and learning processes** – these are essentially 'can do' statements describing what you do in all aspects of the teaching/learning process. These are the core elements of your work as a science teacher.

4 Planning coherent sequences of lessons appropriate for your students' needs and interests.

5 Creating and maintaining intellectually challenging, emotionally supportive and physically safe learning environments.

6 Engaging your students in generating, constructing and testing scientific knowledge by collecting, analysing and evaluating evidence.

7 Continually looking for and implementing ways of extending your students' understanding of the major ideas of science.

8 Developing in your students the confidence to use scientific knowledge and processes to understand the world around them and to make informed decisions.

9 Using a wide variety of strategies, coherent with learning goals, to monitor and assess students' learning and provide effective feedback.

Professional attributes

Elements 10–12 relate to **self-evaluation**, **collegial activity** and **involvement in leadership**. These are overarching principles that characterise your life as a professional.

10 Analysing, evaluating and refining your teaching to improve student learning.

11 Working collegially within your school community and wider professional communities to improve the quality and effectiveness of science education.

12 Being involved with leadership, management and development of science teaching.

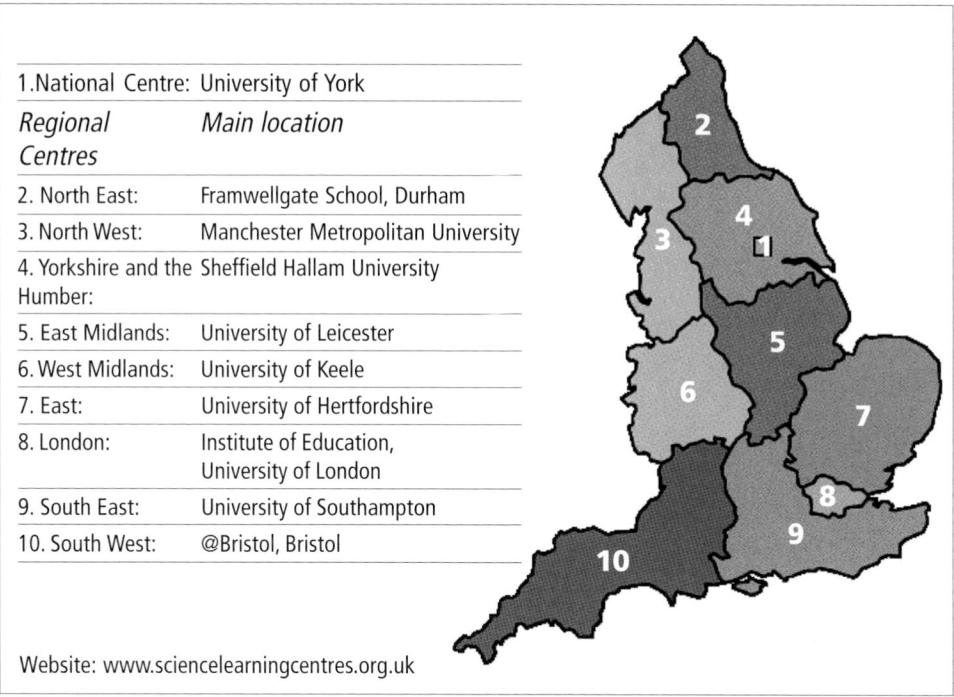

1.National Centre: University of York	
Regional Centres	*Main location*
2. North East:	Framwellgate School, Durham
3. North West:	Manchester Metropolitan University
4. Yorkshire and the Humber:	Sheffield Hallam University
5. East Midlands:	University of Leicester
6. West Midlands:	University of Keele
7. East:	University of Hertfordshire
8. London:	Institute of Education, University of London
9. South East:	University of Southampton
10. South West:	@Bristol, Bristol

Website: www.sciencelearningcentres.org.uk

Figure 6.1 **National network of Science Learning Centres in England.**

cover the whole of the UK. Discussions are taking place to develop complementary provision in Wales, Scotland and Northern Ireland, linking with the National Centre. Each of the centres is run by a consortium of partners, but with its own identity, and is working to develop programmes to meet the needs of the teachers, technicians and teaching assistants around its region and beyond.

Although each centre has its own character, by working together the synergies in expertise and facilities promise to make the impact of the network greater than the sum of its parts. Together with all their partners, which include the ASE, the centres are aiming to make available CPD that is:

- relevant to individual career development needs yet contributes to meeting the school priorities;
- up to date, reflecting new developments in scientific knowledge and tackling the moral and ethical issues that arise in contemporary society;
- practical, providing ideas that can be implemented in the classroom or laboratory yet give time to think more deeply about underpinning research and other evidence;
- high quality, in both the standards of the provision and the environment in which it takes place;
- reflective, providing time and opportunities to learn from other colleagues but with provision for personal follow-up and support.

Science Learning Centres Web portal

An exciting aspect of the national network is the development of the Science Learning Centres Web portal (SLC, 2005, see websites), which will provide not just details of the programmes and activities that are available with on-line booking, but on-going support for CPD. By building up a collection of materials for courses and other forms of advice and support this Web-based resource will be central to the way in which the Science Learning Centres support CPD for science teachers and technicians. A key element is the facility for each individual to have his or her own electronic CPD portfolio and web-space to store and record evidence of CPD activity, regardless of where it has been undertaken. Access to the portfolio is restricted to the individual, who has the power to make parts of it available to other people or to simply maintain it for personal use.

CPD recognition and reward

One of the issues that the Science Learning Centres, along with others, have been grappling with is how to acknowledge that someone has undertaken some CPD and how to give recognition to individuals who have continued to keep up to date. There are programmes available, mainly through higher education institutions, that give credit or qualifications for particular courses or research activity, but recognition for a wider range of activities is more difficult to achieve. The GTC in England (GTCE) has developed the Teacher Learning Academy, which provides a framework for recognising CPD. The GTC in Scotland (GTCS) has also developed a process by which teachers gain recognition for their CPD (see websites). Throughout the UK, the increased emphasis in performance appraisals on the quality of teaching and learning and their links with salary arrangements underline not only the need for teachers to engage in CPD but also for them to be able to demonstrate their commitment and have it recognised.

Having looked at other professions, some years ago the ASE started exploring the possibility of gaining a Royal Charter, which could allow the Association to offer a chartered designation for science teachers. The outcome of the discussions between the Science Council (see website) and the ASE is the development of a new designation of Chartered Science Teacher (CSciTeach). The ASE was successful in being awarded its Royal Charter in November 2004 (see Roberts, 2005; Bell, 2005; Lawrey, 2005) and is currently working with the Science Council to agree the detailed arrangements for CSciTeach.

The CSciTeach designation aims to recognise the unique combination of knowledge, skills and qualities demonstrated by good science teachers, who also show their commitment to maintaining their high-quality expertise through ongoing CPD. Apart from setting quality standards, a key feature of CSciTeach will be the requirement for it to be renewed every five years, thus ensuring that claims that individual's expertise is up to date can be substantiated in line with practice in other professions. Although the details have still to be agreed, the setting up of this charter designation is timely and, in the context of wider developments, provides a major opportunity for science teachers to enjoy recognition, and possibly reward, for their professional status. Further information will be posted on the ASE website (see websites) as and when it becomes available.

CPD entitlement and responsibility

For the most part the argument about the importance of CPD has been won and much progress has been made in developing CPD for science teachers.

There also seems to be willingness at all levels of government and throughout the profession to make this work. However, the practicalities can get in the way of turning all the theory and good intentions into reality. Inevitably there will be difficulties, but with appropriate leadership and careful management at all levels much can be achieved.

From the important perspective of the individual, there needs to be scope for negotiation with head teachers, subject leaders and colleagues in order to work towards an overall balance of professional development. Developing appropriate transparent mechanisms for identifying and meeting CPD needs is fundamental to reducing the tensions, as is a common understanding of entitlements and responsibilities.

Few people would disagree with the idea that CPD should be an entitlement for all teachers and should be planned with personal and organisational needs in mind. Hand in hand with the idea of entitlement goes the matter of responsibility of both the organisation and the individual. The organisation has a responsibility for making sure that CPD opportunities are available for individuals and teams so that they are able to develop their own professional expertise, which contributes to school improvement. The organisation is also responsible for ensuring that any specific entitlements (e.g. the arrangements for support, guidance, and funding for teachers in their induction year) are provided. Individuals have responsibility for keeping up to date, developing new skills and maintaining the highest possible professional standards in everything they do. This includes thinking ahead to possible future developments and preparing for them in appropriate ways.

A third dimension to the area of responsibility is that to the profession, ensuring that science teaching generally is of the best possible quality and contributing to raising the status of the profession as a whole. Although it may not be a day-to-day priority, the way in which science teaching is perceived in the wider community makes an important contribution to the confidence that parents, industry, business and government have in the science education available to our students.

References

Bell, D. (2005) Achieving chartered status. *Education in Science*, **211**, 10.

Dillon, J., Osborne, J., Fairbrother, R. and Kurina. L. (2000) *A study into the views and needs of science teachers in primary and secondary state schools in England. Final Report to the Council for Science and Technology.* London: King's College London. Summary available at: www.cst.gov.uk

Haigh, G. (2003a) The ASE's continuing professional development programme. *Primary Science Review*, **79**, 11–12.

Haigh, G. (2003b) The focus of teachers' in-service training. *Education in Science*, **202**, 24–25.

Haigh, G. and Reece, M. (2003) Integrating CPD into your practice: linking the ASE cCPD and developments at key stage 3. *Education in Science*, **205**, 24–25.

Lawrey, K. (2005) Incorporation by Royal Charter: value, significance and responsibility. *Education in Science*, **211**, 11.

Leaton Gray, S. (2005) *An enquiry into continuing professional development for teachers.* London: Esmée Fairbairn Foundation. Available at: http://www.esmeefairbairn.org.uk/grants_reports.html

Roberts, G. (2002) *SET for success: the supply of people with science, technology, engineering and mathematics skills.* HM Treasury. Available at: www.hm-treasury.gov.uk

Roberts, G. (2005) SET for success: a key role for Chartered Science Teachers. *Education in Science*, **211**, 8–9.

Soulsby, D. and Swain, D. (2003) *A report on the award-bearing INSET scheme*. Available at: http://www.teachernet.gov.uk/docbank/index.cfm?id=4129

Websites

ASE (The Association for Science Education): www.ase.org.uk

EPPI (Evidence for Policy and Practice Information and Co-ordinating Centre) (2003) *The impact of collaborative CPD on classroom teaching and learning. How does collaborative Continuing Professional Development (CPD) for teachers of the 5–16 age range affect teaching and learning?* Available at: http://eppi.ioe.ac.uk/EPPIWeb/home.aspx?page=/reel/reviews.htm

GTCE (General Teaching Council for England). Continuing professional development: http://www.gtce.org.uk/cpd_home/

GTCS (General Teaching Council for Scotland). Continuing professional development: http://www.gtcs.org.uk/gtcs/cpd.aspx?MenuItemID=111&selection=5

GTCW (General Teaching Council for Wales). Continuing professional development: http://www.gtcw.org.uk/cpd/information.html

Science Council: www.sciencecouncil.org

SEF (Science Education Forum): http://www.scienceeducationforum.org.uk/

Scottish Executive: *A teaching profession for the 21st century: agreement reached following recommendations made in the McCrone Report*. Available at: http://www.scotland.gov.uk/library3/education/tp21a-03.asp#4

SLC (Science Learning Centres) (2005) Web portal: http://www.sciencelearningcentres.org.uk/

TTA (Teacher Training Agency) (2005a) TTA's expanded CPD remit: response from the TTA to the Secretary of State; covering letter (MS *Word* file 30 KB) and detailed report (MS *Word* file 78 KB). Available at: http://www.tta.gov.uk/php/read.php?sectionid=371&articleid=2385

TTA (2005b) *Expanded remit for the Teacher Training Agency*. Available at: http://www.tta.gov.uk/php/read.php?sectionid=284&articleid=1945

TTA (2005c) *Induction for newly qualified teachers (NQTs)*. Available at: http://www.tta.gov.uk/php/read.php?sectionid=188&articleid=1311

TTA/DfES (2002) *Qualifying to teach: professional standards for qualified teacher status and requirements for initial teacher training*. London: Teacher Training Agency. Available at: http://www.tta.gov.uk/php/read.php?sectionid=108&articleid=456

Chapter 7

Science education across and beyond the United Kingdom

When teachers spend time teaching in schools overseas, their most common response is that they have learned more about

Alan Peacock, Lynne Symonds and **Andrew Clegg**

our own system in the UK through having to make comparisons and to think about why we do things the way we do. This chapter looks at how some issues relating to the teaching of science are dealt with in some different regions of the globe. It begins near to home with the differences across the countries of the UK and then gives a glimpse of what is going on in Europe, North America, Africa, India and China. Finally, some points are brought out that show what we have to learn from taking a wider perspective of ways of implementing science education.

Science, globalisation and environmental awareness

The ease with which we can now link with other countries has the potential to affect science education throughout the world. For science teachers in Britain, it presents a rich, exciting and ever-changing menu of resources, ideas, inspiration and learning opportunities. Opportunities to develop a global perspective include school linking, teacher exchange, project sharing, collaborating through the Association for Science Education's *Science Across the World* website (see websites) and considering the current realities of science education in societies that, at least on the surface, are different from our own. We can benefit from this global perspective by identifying international trends, relating these to our thinking, and acknowledging what we can learn from other ways of doing things.

Variations in practice within the UK

We first need to look at differences within the UK, notably what distinguishes England from Wales, Scotland and Northern Ireland. Recent developments in these countries demonstrate that, in the primary phase, each is moving away from the heavily structured content focus that characterised the early years of the National Curriculum in England towards more generic thinking and learning skills within a 'real world' context. The Scottish Executive has National Guidelines for the 5–14 age range, of which one subject area is Environmental Studies, incorporating Society, Science and Technology (see website). This immediately sets science within an integrated approach that *brings together the main ways in which pupils learn about the world*, rather than seeing it as a subject with a separate identity. An important difference from the National Curriculum in England is that these guidelines are not mandatory: almost all teachers use them, but they do not have the statutory force experienced south of the border. Skills development focuses on the strands of *preparing* for tasks, *carrying out* tasks and *reviewing and reporting* tasks; this categorisation runs across the Environmental Studies framework, and is not specific to science. Science shares many learning outcomes with history and geography and, like these subjects, embraces the importance of *'active citizenship, the central concept of equity'*. When it comes to post-14 in Scotland, however, the majority of pupils study separate sciences; they must study at least one subject from science, biology, physics or chemistry.

In Northern Ireland, science is part of a curriculum area called *The World Around Us*, which incorporates science and technology, history and geography. Changes to the assessment system proposed by the Council for Curriculum Examinations and Assessment (CCEA, see website) will increase the emphasis on teacher reporting; as in Scotland, science is not formally tested. In Wales, too, there has been a movement towards active teacher assessment using skill profiles and away from formal testing, in the hope that, as in Scotland and Northern Ireland, these moves will help free up the science curriculum for more creative teaching and learning. So far England has not been willing to abandon National Curriculum tests at ages 11 and 14.

Across the UK, there have been attempts, so far less effective in England than in the rest of the UK, to change the post-14 science examinations and curricula. The aim is to combat the decline in candidates choosing science, through such initiatives as *Twenty First Century Science* (see Chapter 1), offering shared and coordinated teaching approaches across GCSE science subjects, with new options such as *Environmental and land-based science*, a wholly e-assessed qualification offering units in agriculture, horticulture and conservation. The intention is to cater for those who want to work or study in a wider range of fields, rather than becoming 'academic' scientists post-16. In Scotland, national qualifications at Access and Intermediate level, designed originally for the 16+ group of students, are increasingly being offered to 14–16 year-olds as alternatives to the traditional Standard grade.

Trends in Europe

Science education tends to reflect the educational priorities of a country. However, at the same time, representatives from different systems are increasingly coming together to share and cooperate in a desire to improve the attractiveness of school science and tackle the universal problem of the rejection of science by adolescents as a preferred field of study. In the recent past, science teaching in secondary schools across Europe tended to be didactic and theoretical, whilst at the same time, in many countries, science hardly existed at all as a subject in the primary phase. What science there was at primary level tended to be subsumed within study of the natural environment – weather, local habitats, conservation, pollution, the earth, living things. There was a marked absence of emphasis on the 'big ideas' of science, such as energy, forces, photosynthesis, particle theory or chemistry concepts, in the primary phase. As a consequence, learners in many countries experience a relatively abrupt transition on first encountering science in high school, as examples below will demonstrate.

In Europe, projects such as SCIENCEDUC (see website) have brought together teachers and trainers from various countries, as the basis for a wider collaboration in the future. Initially, the countries involved were Estonia, France, Hungary, Portugal, Sweden, Germany and Italy. The programme was seen as contributing to a reduction in inequality through science education by combining the rich diversity of European tempers, education styles and innovations. Several European countries have been following such guidelines to improve science teaching across the primary and lower secondary age ranges. Where implemented, they allow pupils to use thinking skills, ask questions, make hypotheses and conduct experiments to verify them, while learning how to work in groups and respect each other, thus preparing for active citizenship in the future.

Science educators in many countries, therefore, are no longer concerned with simply getting some 'real' science into the primary curriculum but with the quality of science learning. This often means setting up systems to provide professional development and other support to ensure initiatives that have been successfully implemented in particular localities can be 'scaled up' to take root nationally. In France, for example, teachers are progressively implementing such hands-on principles in their classes. *La Main à la Pâte* (see website) sets out to improve science teaching in primary schools through a focus on experimentation, observation and questioning. It promotes school twinning through e-learning, around shared scientific and technological projects. Several countries are also adopting *Science and Technology for Children* (STC), a structured enquiry-based programme originating in the USA (see below), for example Sweden, where it is known as *Science and Technology for All*.

Developments in the USA and Canada

Increasingly in the USA the Internet is being used to give wider access to materials both for the classroom, as in the WISE (Web-based Integrated Science Environment) project, and for professional development (see website). The STC approach has also led on to a matched version for middle schools (STC/MS) (see website). These programmes are tightly structured by UK standards, although they do promote progression in scientific skills and processes as well as ideas. Transition to middle school in the US (at grade 6, age 12) is well managed in this scheme: the curriculum focuses on life and earth sciences on the one hand, and physical science and technology on the other. But it is important to remember that, beyond this stage, many states do not have mandatory national curricula for science, and science is frequently taught in high schools as separate disciplines, and often in separate years, thus limiting continuity and integration.

Canadian science education exemplifies some of the points emerging above. Provincial curricula vary widely: in Ontario, for example, primary science (grades 1–8, ages 6–14) is based on five themes (life systems, matter and materials, energy and control, structures and mechanisms, and earth and space). Grades 9–10 (ages 15–16) then focus on ecosystems, matter and energy, the universe and electricity, as 'academic' and 'applied' strands. From grade 11 (age 17), the curriculum reverts to conventional biology, chemistry and physics. In Quebec, however, the curriculum is structured very differently. At primary level, science and technology is one 'subject area' required to link with 'broad areas of learning' including 'environmental awareness and responsibilities', through 'cross-curricular competences' which cover many skill areas. From grade 9 onwards, however, the curriculum is structured into life sciences, chemistry, physics, and earth and space sciences. In both provinces, applications have been given as much emphasis as the subject matter of science.

So a key question raised by the above is: does a skills-based, integrated approach in primary schools prepare children for specialisation in the secondary phase? Should it? Or should the post-primary sector build on the strengths of the primary approach, to overcome the decline in pupils' interest in science?

Africa – the problems and progress

Science Teacher Associations in Africa report problems associated with enormous populations of often poorly trained teachers lacking access to information or professional development. The main problems facing science teachers relate to the lack of adequate funds and materials, overcrowded classrooms, administrative failings, low salaries and consequent lack of teacher motivation, overloaded curricula, and the pressures of recall-focused testing systems. Yet changes and improvements are taking place.

Southern Africa (Botswana, Lesotho, Mozambique Namibia, South Africa and Swaziland) can be taken as an example. Schooling tends to be divided into four phases: lower primary (3 years), upper primary (4 years), junior secondary (2 years) and senior secondary (2 years). Access to junior secondary schools varies from mandatory (Botswana) to less than 20 per cent in some other countries. Science is not compulsory in senior secondary in most of these countries, but is likely to become so within the next few years. None, however, has yet embarked on the development of appropriate science curricula for senior secondary schooling. Science is taught as a single subject in most countries in primary schools: via the mother tongue in lower primary, and then in English at upper primary level. It is then split into two subjects (in Namibia and South Africa) for junior secondary: in other countries the split comes at senior secondary, usually into the three traditional subjects. Science curricula at all levels tend to be conventional, reflecting closely their colonial predecessors that catered to a selective minority. Most have statements regarding the acquisition of skills as well as knowledge and understanding, but these are not yet reflected in teaching.

Throughout the region, science lessons rarely include practical work; there is widespread evidence that simply placing equipment in schools does little to bring about a change in science teaching. Despite many African children's early involvement in real practical activity in the home and farm, with first-hand experience of collecting water, animal care, gardening, cleaning, preparing food and cooking, there is little tradition in schools of using everyday equipment to teach science. Nor is it often realised that using everyday items in this way is actually quite a high-level skill, for which most teachers have to be trained. Similarly, little opportunity has been taken to develop an environmental science focus based on pupils' experiences. The main problem is that teachers are often conditioned to value a traditionally 'academic' science curriculum aimed at test success and therefore do not enable pupils to see the significance of science in relation to their daily lives.

One positive feature of science education in the region is the rise in both quantity and quality of the research and development that is being carried out in the tertiary institutions (mainly in South Africa), a good deal of which is finding its way into science teacher education programmes. The Southern African Association for Research in Maths, Science and Technology Education (SAARMSTE) is in a healthy state and holds a large annual meeting.

An increasing minority of secondary schools in the region have computers: data-logging equipment exists in the region but as yet is used rarely, as most science teachers are not yet computer literate. All this is beginning to change dramatically throughout the region, by circumventing software licence costs through the use of Open Source software, negotiating favourable educational Virtual Private Network (VPN) rates, and wireless Internet connections for schools without telephone lines. There is a lack of good local e-learning materials in science but this issue too is being addressed.

A recent study of promising practices in science education across Africa has shown that the key element in improving practice has been teachers' professional development. In French-speaking West Africa, for example, the use of an Internet-based support system that involves several countries has diminished science teachers' sense of isolation, and enabled them to learn from each other through sharing of ideas and attending distance-learning seminars, supported by materials and tuition provided in collaboration with a university in France (see RESAFAD website).

Health education forms a significant part of basic science education, particularly HIV/AIDS education. The Science Teachers' Associations of Nigeria and Ghana work together and with the ASE and CASTME (Commonwealth Association of Science, Technology and Mathematics Educators) to improve their capacity for reciprocal learning. Science teachers from Cameroon and Gambia have carried out some effective work in HIV/AIDS education, extending far beyond the schools.

Developments in China

Basic science is part of Chinese pupils' primary school studies, but often they do not realise that this is science. The curriculum includes the study of 'Nature and Work', which includes simple biology, as well as measuring shadows, simple circuits, etc. In primary school, the teachers focus on identifying strengths, so that pupils are 'selected into science' on the basis of internal tests. Many schools still have very large classes, where the teaching approach is characterised by the teacher reading from the text, then demonstrating an activity and finally testing pupils' recall. There is, however, a strong emphasis on the environment: teachers take pupils out of the classroom to make observations, for example to study insects in their habitats. After primary school, however, science becomes much more prominent in the curriculum, being taught as separate subjects or as combined science, depending on location. Whilst science equipment itself is sparse, ICT provision is definitely generous, even in the large schools of central China, where computer suites are standard. Video is also often used as part of lessons. There seems also to be a relatively smooth transition from primary to secondary science programmes, something not well achieved in most other parts of the world.

India

In India, there is still a high degree of Eurocentric textbook content, despite the large contribution of India to scientific knowledge. Teachers and pupils perceive science as imported ready-made knowledge, and science is presented in an authoritative manner in the classroom, so that pupils take the role of passive receiver rather than creator of knowledge. A new approach to the curriculum developed by the National Council for Educational Research and Training (NCERT) sets out to encourage the teaching of science in such a way that pupils acquire scientific and technological literacy and understand how basic scientific principles are applied in finding solutions to problems in agriculture, weather, energy, health/nutrition, industry, defence, etc. The curriculum also stresses that science teaching should focus on processes such as experimentation, observation, data collection, classification, analysis, making hypotheses, drawing inferences and arriving at conclusions for objective truth (see NCERT website).

Disparities between states are still great. Despite all the difficulties, and often only a poorly surfaced chalkboard and at best a few textbooks as resources in overcrowded classrooms, an impressively high degree of attentive learning still takes place. Pupils are often keen to learn, listening carefully, valuing their lessons and their teacher. They work hard for their exams, and families must budget carefully to pay the exam fees. In much of Africa and Asia science is seen as a good thing, beneficial to society and enabling progress in many fields.

Implications and ways forward

It would seem that for many years, teachers in many parts of the world have not been at ease with science, especially in the primary phase. They fear to say *'I don't know'* to children, when being 'stuck' is often the starting-point for real science. They are often reluctant to do practical work, and are discouraged by obstacles that are put in their way, such as punitive inspections, endless tests, rapidly changing administrative requirements, health and safety directives and the introduction of new technologies. One effect of this has been to discourage teachers from working not only outside the assessed curriculum but also outside the classroom, in the everyday world of learners. Fieldwork is harder and harder to justify, teachers say; hence the environmental awareness that many curricula emphasise is harder and harder to achieve.

Yet this glimpse of science in some other countries indicates not only that things are improving in many areas, but also that we can learn from how science is taught in other countries. Botswana, whose main exports are diamonds and cattle, has built agriculture and earth sciences into the secondary curriculum, and has led the way in tackling AIDS education in primary schools. Kenya has done a great deal of work on identifying the pre-vocational skills needed by school leavers in the informal and tourist sectors of their economy, such as in food preparation, hairdressing, stone carving or metalworking, and has begun to redevelop the science curriculum to incorporate these. Some highly creative and successful teachers, who take problem-solving literally and organise their curriculum around it, are to be found in rural schools in Kenya. It may not be appropriate for UK children to design and build windmills to saw wood, or to collect, test and identify insects causing skin lesions amongst children, for instance, but we should value the skill and confidence of those teachers who are prepared to take greater ownership of what and how they teach, in order to meet their pupils' needs. In many ways, we in England do things differently; but we often fall short of what we hope to achieve, particularly in the way we manage such matters as the impact of testing, the use of published materials, generating a sense of purpose and relevance for young learners and the transition from primary to secondary science.

So how might we, as part of the international science education community, contribute to the improvement not only of science education but also of its image, which is currently a fairly negative one among learners in many countries? One key way would be to sustain and develop even further the international perspective of our publications, journals and web-based materials such as *Science Across the World*, and to find ways to make these more widely available. Another would be to use publications and web-based professional development to encourage and support teachers and children working practically outside the classroom, so that they can become confident and skilled in 'making science real', in order to develop greater environmental awareness. A third focus might be on the way different countries manage the link between primary science and secondary science, where there is still a hiatus that affects children's positive image of the subject by turning it into something that seems no longer to have relevance to their lives. And finally, we might look for ways of helping less well-resourced countries to develop their own materials to reflect the needs, cultures and languages of their children, materials that teachers will have the confidence to allow children to use themselves. Nothing less, in the end, will be effective.

Websites

ASE (Association for Science Education) *Science Across the World*: www.scienceacross.org
CCEA (Northern Ireland Council for Curriculum Examinations and Assessment): www.ccea.org.uk
La Main à la Pâte: www.inrp.fr/lamap/-
NCERT (National Council for Educational Research and Training): http://www.ncert.nic.in/ sites/publication/schoolcurriculum/ncfr.htm
RESAFAD (Réseau Africain de Formation à Distance): www.sn.resafad.org
SCIENCEDUC: www.cienciaviva.pt/projectos/scienceduc.asp?accao=changelang&lang=en
Scottish 5–14 guidelines: http://www.ltscotland.org.uk/5to14/guidelines/index.asp
STC/MS (Middle Schools Science Technology for Children): www.carolina.com/stc/
WISE (Web-based Integrated Science Environment): http://wise.berkely.edu

Chapter 8

Science education 14–19

Government bodies, prestigious organisations and students themselves have questioned the **Martin Hollins**

appropriateness of the existing science curriculum for 14–19 year-old students in the UK. This chapter outlines the current and forthcoming changes to the curriculum menu at both 14+ and 16+ and to its assessment. It concludes with the need to review this phase in relation to the prior science curriculum and to future scientific developments.

Why 14–19?

> *Today, as the frontiers of scientific understanding continue to expand, reaching down into the molecular machinery by which living things assemble themselves, it is ever more important to have a scientifically informed citizenry. If not, it will be difficult to conduct the democratic debates we need to have about which doors to open and which to leave closed, be they about stem cell research or designer babies or topics yet unglimpsed.* (May, 2004)

This quote, from Lord Robert May, president of the Royal Society, presents science education with a fundamental challenge. How do we ensure that science education provides all future citizens with the ability to take part in debates on topical scientific issues, as well as preparing future scientists to explore those topics yet unglimpsed?

There have been significant advances in science education in UK schools in the past twenty years. The National Curriculum has ensured that all pupils must study science from age 5 to 16 in maintained schools in England, Wales and Northern Ireland, and in Scotland curriculum guidelines have brought about similar developments. But problems are manifest at post-16 when students specialise and fail to choose science in significant numbers. This is part of a wider problem in that the UK compares poorly with its economic competitors in the proportion of the population that continues in education and training beyond the statutory leaving age of 16. To ensure economic development, the demand for those with higher qualifications in science and science-related subjects is predicted to rise. The Government's Treasury review (HM Treasury, 2003) for 2004–2014 recommends urgent action to remedy the deficiencies in uptake of further and higher science education.

Since there is a very marked drop-out from science at age 16, an obvious way to address this problem is to consider an integrated approach across the two phases of 14–16 and 16–19. This involves looking at the nature of science education at key stage 4 (14–16) and post-16 and at the curricular, assessment and institutional implications of linking them more strongly. Other chapters in this book explore these aspects of the science curriculum in general terms; here we examine those related to this issue.

Students' views of science

In the *Student review of the science curriculum* (Science Museum/NESTA, 2003), post-16 students in England conducted a survey into the attitudes and experiences of GCSE science of their fellow science and non-science students. Although the findings were not particularly negative, a useful insight is that many students were not engaged fully by the science they had studied. They recommended more time for practical work and for discussion and consideration of topical issues of everyday life, particularly those that may be controversial – such as those referred to by Lord May. Too many felt that there was too much content for in-depth treatment and nearly half felt that their curiosity was not encouraged in studying GCSE science.

There has been belated recognition of the fact that students need to feel they have ownership of their studies and, under the heading of 'personalised learning', there have been initiatives that encourage this in the choice of curriculum topics, teaching and learning approaches, and at the level of course planning.

Work-related learning

British education suffers from a difference in status between academic education and education that is more focused on work-related activities. This can be one of the reasons for students giving up science at 16. They may choose those academic subjects at which they have shown most aptitude (and, if none, may drop out of education), rather than consider more applied or vocational approaches. Economically, there is a particular need to increase the number of technically qualified people.

Since 2004 the National Curriculum in England has required students at key stage 4 to be offered work-related opportunities throughout their studies. This course-enrichment can include visits and work experience as well as classroom-based activities. It is hoped that this will enable students to see more relevance in their studies, compared to a more academic approach. Schools have often found it difficult to offer challenging alternative courses to students for whom the academic route seems unattractive. Further education colleges are better resourced to do this. Developments designed to improve communication between schools and colleges help to ensure that students are well informed.

Centres of Vocational Excellence (CoVEs) have been designated and funded to disseminate their good practice to other institutions. Learning and Skills Councils have the job of reviewing provision and progression opportunities at 16 in their local areas, and of ensuring that these are widely known. Some local education authorities are now implementing institutional collaboration between all the providers of 14–19 education, which is clearly the most effective way to ensure that the learner is able to access the widest range of opportunities.

Reforming the system

While the central issue of increasing the uptake of science courses by students beyond 16 has been recognised for some time, solutions have been hard to find. One approach is to disseminate good practice, and this can be seen in, for example, Ofsted reports and Qualifications and Curriculum Authority (QCA) publications. There have been institutional changes to foster this approach: Science Learning Centres (see Chapter 6) and the Secondary National Strategy: Science (see Chapter 9) for improving teachers' professional development; Specialist Science Schools and Advanced Skills Teachers with remits wider than their own school improvement. Increasingly, however, it has been recognised that the current system of curriculum and assessment, in particular the qualifications framework, needs to change. There have been frequent policy reviews from the Department for Education and Skills (DfES). *Opportunity and excellence* (2003) commissioned work by QCA on work-related learning (see above), and on science at key stage 4. This resulted in the new key stage 4 curriculum for 2006. The DfES also set up a two-year review of 14–19 education under the chairmanship of Sir Mike Tomlinson, whose report (DfES, 2004) presented radical proposals. The Government's response was provided in the White Paper *14–19 Education and skills* (DfES, 2005).

These documents have identified the following aspects of the system that need reform:

- The curriculum needs modernising to offer a more realistic account of science in contemporary life.
- Teaching methods need to take more account of new understanding about learning, in particular how to engage students.
- Assessment burdens need to be reduced; new methods should make use of ICT.
- The qualifications system is complex and lacks flexibility; it perpetuates the unhelpful academic/vocational learning divide.
- A wider range of learning opportunities needs to be offered to provide for the diversity of interest and aptitude, with clear progression routes to ensure that learners do not spend time on inappropriate courses.

What there has been disagreement on is the nature and extent of the changes needed to provide these desirable outcomes. Most of the radical proposals from the Tomlinson review were shelved by the DfES, wary of the destabilising effect of change and mindful of the damaging 'A-level grading' crisis of 2002, which accompanied the last major change. The DfES plans, which can be seen as a more cautious approach towards achieving the same goals, are reviewed in a later section.

What science at 14+?

Changes to the system arrive first for 14–16 year-olds (key stage 4 in England, Wales and Northern Ireland). The programme of study for science has been substantially changed, following a QCA-sponsored development programme, which included widespread consultation and a pilot GCSE suite called *Twenty First Century Science* (see Chapter 1). At the heart of the new curriculum is the recognition that after ten years of compulsory science it is time to give pupils a choice. Since surveys of pupil attitudes have shown a lack of engagement for a substantial proportion, the hope is that this may be addressed if they can choose which science to study.

However, there are some constraints on a free choice. A core has been identified which includes the kind of science that all future citizens will find useful, whether as scientist, technician, householder, consumer or citizen. In the new National Curriculum for 14–16 year-olds in England this is called '*How science works*' and emphasises the process of science rather than the content (although approached through selected content areas). It is much wider than the 'Sc1' which it replaces, and includes the four strands shown in Table 8.1.

The other requirement of the programme is called the '*Breadth of study*' and is a selection of key ideas from across the sciences: biology, chemistry, physics, astronomy and earth and environmental sciences. The selection builds on the work in key stage 3 and is seen to be of current relevance – to pupils' personal wellbeing, their everyday life and the technological world they inhabit. These requirements are expressed in less detail than the previous versions of the National Curriculum, so that those devising qualifications can provide their own detailed treatments of the content.

To meet the needs of those who intend to progress in their science studies beyond 16 and beyond 18/19 there is a range of additional courses. For example, single science courses in biology, chemistry and physics, which, taken together, cover the core requirements and provide access to advanced-level sciences,

Table 8.1 **The four strands of 'How science works' (see Box 24.1 for full version).**

Strand of *How science works*	Elements of study
1 Data, evidence, theories and explanations	What is distinctive about scientific understanding
2 Practical and enquiry skills	Ranging from technical skills with apparatus to planning procedures and evaluating evidence
3 Communication skills	Using scientific, technical and mathematical language and ICT tools to interpret and present scientific findings
4 Applications and implications of science	The benefits, drawbacks and risks of scientific and technological developments and the role of the scientific community

with a character that emphasises the investigative and theory-making aspects of science. Additional science, as a single course, may also have this character, or could take an applications approach, for example through health, making materials and using electricity. In order to allow scope for some in-depth work-related learning in the technical applications of science, there are double-award GCSE applied science courses which cover all the core requirements. Apart from these, all other GCSEs are single award, to encourage wider choices. The Government has, however, indicated its intention to ensure that this does not result in less science being studied:

> Every young person will have a statutory entitlement to science study leading to two GCSEs and we expect that, as now, at least 80% of students will continue to take at least two science GCSEs, with many progressing to science courses at higher levels. We will take further action, if necessary, to maintain the numbers of young people taking two science GCSEs. (DfES, 2005)

In other words, the message to pupils is 'We'll give you choice, but if you don't choose enough science, we may find a way of making you do it!'

Although the main qualification at 14–16 will continue to be GCSE, there are also developments at entry level (Certificates of Achievement), and schools and colleges will increasingly offer courses leading to BTec and other vocational qualifications. There will be schools that offer AS, and other qualifications usually taken post-16, as a way of promoting continuity across the 16 age divide.

What science at 16+?

At 16+ students have their first opportunity to stop studying science, and the problem is that very many make that choice. The changes pre-16 are intended to leave students with a more positive attitude to science and a clearer idea about what further science-related study would be useful to them, and therefore encourage more to continue. The Tomlinson proposals included a compulsory core of key skills in literacy, maths, and ICT but not science. The reforms of pre-16 science have arisen partly because of the problems of a large compulsory core of content, so it is unlikely that it will reappear post-16.

It is at this stage that the academic/vocational divide asserts itself. Tomlinson proposed that all existing qualifications be incorporated in a single diploma system, with only levels to differentiate achievement. The Government is currently not prepared to risk losing the 'gold standard' of A-levels when standards of achievement are so politically sensitive. The 2005 White Paper proposes some changes to the AS/A system and the development of a range of new diplomas that could bridge the academic/vocational gap. For example, an engineering diploma is to be piloted that will occupy a substantial proportion of a student's time and cover a range of subjects including a core of 'functional' maths and English.

A distinctive feature of the post-16 curriculum for most students in England, Wales and Northern Ireland, compared to other countries, is the narrowness of the specialisation. The development of the current AS/A system was intended to broaden the curriculum as additional AS subjects would be taken in the first year. This has had some effect, though the majority of students take only one or two extra, commonly complementary rather than contrasting, subjects. It was also intended that choice would increase. There have been a small number of new AS courses, notably *Science for Public Understanding* and the pilot *Perspectives*, which covers the history and philosophy of science. However, there has not been a growth in alternative or optional units in existing A-level courses, denying students the opportunity to study areas of cutting-edge research such as neuroscience, nanotechnology and cosmology. There have been some substantial recent innovations such as *Salter's Nuffield Advanced Biology* and *Advancing Physics* from the Institute of Physics. Generally, though, curriculum innovation has been inhibited by the system's changes and caution over comparability of standards.

It is significant that the 2005 DfES White Paper is entitled *14–19 Education and skills*. The attempts to unify the system across the academic and vocational routes is likely to lead to a focus on key skills and a minimal core of content that can be used in a range of different contexts according to the choice of courses. In this, post-16 science may well follow the lead of the new key stage 4 changes – but this will not happen soon!

Assessment, qualifications and accountability

International comparisons show that UK countries have amongst the highest amounts of publicly accountable assessment in the world. This is because of regular National Curriculum tests and major qualifications at both 16 and 18/19. Scotland avoided the NC tests and Wales and Northern Ireland plan to reduce these in the near future. One major advantage of considering 14–19 as a continuum is the possibility of reducing this so-called 'excess assessment burden'. If most students continue post-16, then qualifications at 16 are less important as a measure of an individual's achievement. The problem is that the results are used to measure the success of the institution, and this accountability seems ever more important. Even worse, not all qualifications have counted in ratings, with the vocationally oriented ones often being ignored. Work to remedy this has raised the sensitive issue of 'standards'.

The framework of qualifications for 14–19 allows for levels: entry, 1 and 2 (GCSE), and 3 (A-level). The scope is being extended to bring adult qualifications at these levels (mainly vocational) into the 'Framework for achievement'. It looks complex, for example with BTecs, which are variously the size of one, two or three A-levels, and there is the added difficulty of comparing standards across different subjects. The 2000 revision of A-levels brought in unitisation of qualifications; AS and A2 each have three assessment units, making 6 for a full A-level. The advantage is that students and their teachers can monitor their progress by assessment units taken through the course. This also reduces the stress of end-of-course examinations. It has, however, increased the total amount of assessment and there are currently plans to reduce the number of units.

Another concern related to the assessment burden is the internal assessment by the teacher, often called coursework. A climate of high accountability puts pressure on students and teachers to put a lot of work into ensuring the grades achieved are as high as possible – and can raise conflicts of interest between teacher as tutor and as assessor. The Tomlinson proposal for an extended project post-16, borrowed from the Baccalaureate examinations, is currently being consulted on, prior to piloting and its possible introduction as a free-standing qualification. This, it is argued, is both motivating for the student who gets to choose the project, and can also reduce the need for extensive coursework elsewhere. At GCSE, there is to be a review to see how the demands of assessment and coursework in particular could be reduced in extent – though not in standard.

Keeping science under review

The 14–19 phase builds on a substantial foundation of compulsory science education. The changes that are being implemented at 14–16 and developed at 16–19 prompt a review of those foundations. If there is to be more choice and flexibility post-14, what are the implications for early secondary and even primary science? Are there successes at these phases that should inform the later ones? QCA is beginning a review of key stage 3 in England to try to answer these questions.

Many of the changes that are being planned for the next few years will be about systems – of monitoring criteria, assessment methods, qualifications framework, progression routes, entry points for higher education, and so on. All these are necessary for fairness of access and equality of opportunity, but they are not sufficient to ensure that the country educates the scientists it, and the world, needs.

The choices offered during the 14–19 phase need to inspire young people with the excitement of contemporary scientific discovery and application. This science education will use the media, include new technology, and support students' engagement with the issues and choices that science throws up. At present these include cloning, global warming and mobile phone radiation, but the curriculum needs to be constantly under review to incorporate future developments.

References

DfES (2003) *Opportunity and excellence*. London: Department for Education and Skills.
DfES (2004) *Tomlinson 14–19 Final report*. London: Department for Education and Skills.
DfES (2005) *14–19 Education and skills*. White Paper. London: Department for Education and Skills.
HM Treasury (2003) *Science and innovation investment framework 2004–2014*. London.
May, R., Lord (2004) Communal connections. *Times Higher Educational Supplement*, 6 August, p. 23.
Science Museum/NESTA (2003) *Student review of the science curriculum*. Summary available at: www.planet-science.com/sciteach/review/findings.pdf (accessed 7 November 2005).

Websites

DfES: http://www.dfes.gov.uk/
QCA (for programme of study for key stage 4 and *Twenty First Century Science*): www.qca.org.uk/science
For details of GCE, GCSE and other specifications see websites of awarding bodies: AQA, CCEA, Edexcel, OCR, WJEC.

| Chapter | 9 | The Secondary National Strategy: Science |

The Secondary National Strategy: Science

The Key Stage 3 National Strategy was, and continues to be, about raising standards by improving teaching and learning in England. Consideration of its progress and success so far provide pointers to the possible application of this model of development beyond the English context. The model of continuing professional development used by the Strategy, including science, is described in this chapter, with information about its development into the Secondary National Strategy to include key stage 4. The Strategy has provided a significant opportunity for a large number of science teachers to hear and talk about the teaching and learning of science.

Phil Bunyan

In the beginning

The Key Stage 3 National Strategy in England began in 2001 with a focus on developing English and mathematics, following on from the successful literacy and numeracy strategies at primary level. Science was introduced as a pilot in 2001 and was extended to all schools from Easter 2002.

Although initially the Strategy provided support for schools through subjects (called 'strands'), as it developed there was a need to provide additional support for whole-school improvement of teaching and learning which could not be confined to subjects. Currently the Secondary National Strategy (SNS) operates through the strands, of which science is one, and through whole-school initiatives (assessment for learning; ICT across the curriculum; literacy and learning; leading in learning (developing pupils' thinking skills); improving generic teaching and learning skills).

The original focus on key stage 3 was because it was acknowledged that this had become something of a 'forgotten key stage'. It was seen as an interim time between the crucial end of key stage 2 and the clearly important GCSE years. It was widely recognised that pupils often did not make as much progress in their learning in key stage 3 as in key stages 2 and 4. In fact, pupils often appeared to fall back in their attainment during the early part of key stage 3:

> Standards in key stage 3 do not yet reflect the great strides made in primary science. By the end of the key stage pupils are spread across levels 3 to 7 of the National Curriculum Order; up to a third have not progressed beyond the expected level for 11 year olds, this gives cause for concern. (Ofsted, 1999)

The Strategy set out to improve the progress that pupils made at this stage. From the beginning there were four elements to the Key Stage 3 Strategy:

E **Expectations:** raising teachers' expectations of pupils and pupils' expectations of themselves;

P **Progression:** improving progression from KS2 to KS3, within KS3, from KS3 to KS4 and within KS4;

E **Engagement:** increasing pupils' engagement and participation in their lessons and their learning;

T **Transforming:** teaching and learning.

These four elements (EPET) remain crucial to the work of the Strategy and underpin all the development work:

> The Key Stage 3 Strategy is about classrooms and what goes on in them. It puts learners at its heart. Each aspect of the Strategy is only of value if it benefits the learners. (DfES, 2003)

Supporting teachers and schools

The Strategy provides a mix of national and local support. The science strand, as with other strands, uses national reports to identify issues for development that are common to schools across the country. Locally, education authorities employ consultants, all experienced and enthusiastic teachers, many of whom are former leaders of science departments. Under the management of the local education authority adviser (often an adviser for science), they work with teachers in schools, using nationally developed support strategies and materials. They adapt and develop the national support to tailor it as closely as possible to the needs of individual schools in their local area.

Support in science includes:

● The *Framework for teaching science: years 7, 8 and 9* (DfES, 2002) which sets out some of the main ideas and principles and identifies five key scientific ideas (cells, interdependence, particles, forces and energy) with scientific enquiry as a sixth theme. Each of these has some agreed teaching objectives which should be taught by the end of each year during key stage 3.

● A programme of core and optional high-quality continuing professional development (CPD) training that could be attended by one teacher from every department who would be responsible for disseminating ideas among colleagues in school.

● Follow-up support in departments and classrooms by consultants. This support should be matched to the school and department improvement priorities and will include coaching teachers, team-teaching, giving demonstration lessons and providing materials to help plan the science curriculum and individual lessons.

- Some materials for use in lessons to illustrate ideas about teaching and learning.
- Intervention materials for use with pupils whose progress is less than expected.
- Booster materials illustrating lessons that can be used to help prepare pupils for the end-of-key-stage tests.
- The promotion of locally identified leading science teachers and departments who are keen to develop their practice and share it with other local schools.

For the purposes of the Strategy, England is divided into nine regions, each of which is supported by a science regional adviser who is a member of the science strand national team. The CPD materials are produced by the national science team, drawing on their own expertise and experiences and that of others within the science education community. The regional adviser works with consultants supporting CPD training, helping to lead local meetings, or visiting schools where such visits are seen as useful. Regional advisers also survey schools and meet with local advisers to gauge the impact and appropriateness of developments.

The science national team provides regular regional briefing and training for consultants once or twice per term. These meetings are used to:

- discuss science issues that are important nationally;
- explain and take consultants through newly written science CPD units and other materials that they will use locally with groups of teachers;
- explain and discuss any science-specific elements to whole-school training;
- update consultants on wider aspects of the Strategy;
- provide opportunities for consultants to share effective practice that they have developed;
- gain feedback from consultants about the effectiveness of Strategy support and further development needs in science.

In addition to being used by consultants and local authority advisers, the well-researched training guides and accompanying materials for teachers to use in school have been taken up and used by those in initial teacher training. All science materials, including those for CPD, were given to initial teacher training institutions, along with briefings to support their use. This has meant that all trainee teachers are at least familiar with the priorities of the Strategy and their implementation in schools.

A wide range of CPD units has been produced, focusing variously on aspects of pedagogy, teaching strategy, teaching key scientific ideas, scientific enquiry, etc. Each unit is designated as either core or optional training. Core training is viewed as essential and was accompanied by specific funding for schools to release teachers, often the head of science or the key stage 3 science coordinator. Some funding was also provided to release teachers to attend optional training when it met the identified needs of the department or individual teachers.

Consultants have run the CPD as off-site training courses and have also delivered bespoke training to individual science departments. Sometimes consultants use a complete CPD unit but often individual sessions from units have been used to provide very focused and timely support to departments.

The major developments in science education

Ongoing development and support through the Strategy are focused on many of the issues discussed elsewhere in this book and aim to:

- improve planning for progression in learning across the key stage, making use of the five key scientific ideas and scientific enquiry;
- improve progression between key stages 2 and 3, and latterly between key stages 3 and 4, so there is less disruption in learning;
- bring about more specific teaching of scientific enquiry including that for ideas and evidence;
- structure lessons so that objectives and outcomes are clear and shared with pupils, and lessons include opportunities for teachers and pupils to reflect on their learning;
- widen the repertoire of teaching and learning approaches so as to give pupils as many opportunities as possible to engage with enjoyable learning;
- widen the range of assessment strategies that can be used to judge ongoing progress by both teachers and pupils and to set pupils targets for improvement;
- broaden individual teacher's knowledge of science including identifying pupils' common misconceptions in science and how to overcome them;
- improve pupils' literacy (reading, speaking and writing) in science;
- help teachers make more use of contemporary science and those issues that are relevant to pupils' lives;
- move on pupils' learning from simply remembering, which is characteristic of National Curriculum level 4, to explaining appropriate concepts and ideas, which is characteristic of level 5, and to applying those concepts and ideas, which is characteristic of level 6;
- help science departments to identify the strengths and weaknesses in teaching and in pupils' learning, to prioritise and plan to tackle the weaknesses, and to monitor and evaluate progress with the planned actions.

The intended outcomes for pupils correspond to these focuses, including, for example, to recognise links with pupils' previous science work and build on it and on their developing science knowledge and understanding from year to year.

How much progress have we made?

The CPD was very well received by all science teachers whatever their position of responsibility within a department. Consultants were excited by their own training and discussions in meetings, and transferred this enthusiasm to teachers both during CPD sessions and when working in schools. Teachers found that the CPD allowed them to review their own teaching and at times

Box 9.1

Teachers' comments during and after CPD training

'It's been a very long time since we were able to talk about science and teaching.'

'It has made me realise why some of my pupils have difficulty with this topic. I will certainly change the way I teach it in future.'

'I can use some of the ideas in my teaching this week.'

'I shall reconsider why and how we use topic tests and maybe introduce some other forms of assessment like those we talked about today.'

'I've learned to use models... now I can teach electricity.'

'I've used the planning tool on the CD-ROM with my department to map scientific enquiry through the whole of year 7.'

(DfES, 2005)

challenged some long-standing practices. Many left their CPD sessions invigorated by intensive professional discussions and enthusiastic for change (Box 9.1)

However, change is not always easy to bring about, particularly the task of helping colleagues in the department to have the insights and discussions that were available during the training sessions away from school. Many departments found it difficult to identify time for discussion and the dissemination of ideas, but others have refocused department meetings on discussions of teaching and learning rather than routine administrative tasks, which are now dealt with through more efficient, e.g. written, communications. Other significant changes include:

- Teachers make much more use of objectives and outcomes in their lesson planning and teaching.
- Pupils have a greater involvement in their science learning.
- More lesson time is spent in pupils discussing scientific ideas and less on copying notes.
- Teachers use a wider variety of types of assessment to identify how well pupils are learning and what they need to do next.

The provision of local consultants is a crucial element in the success of the Strategy. Consultants are able to maintain contact with schools, to support dissemination of CPD ideas, to plan support that matches department-identified needs and to review with the head of department and school senior managers the impact that these planned developments are having. Head teachers, heads of department and class teachers routinely praise and value the support that consultants provide (Box 9.2).

In recent reports, HMI have identified that the Strategy is having an impact on the way science is taught and learned. In addition, they recognise the beneficial impact on science lessons of Strategy whole-school initiatives such as assessment for learning (Box 9.3).

Box 9.2

Comments by science subject leaders following an initial audit of their departments

Some subject leaders found the audit challenging, but achievable because the consultant was able to work alongside them:

'I found the audit process quite daunting as I had never been asked to comment on the quality of teaching in the department before. The consultant and I undertook some joint lesson observations. This gave me a fascinating insight into what was actually going on in classrooms; having the consultant there too had a mediating effect on my judgements. As a result of this we regularly undertake peer assessments now which has had a very positive effect on the quality of teaching in the department.' (Science subject leader of 8 years)

'As a result of doing the audit I found action planning for the department much easier. I was able to highlight a couple of middle-attaining year 8 sets who were not being stretched and target the consultant to work with a small group of teachers to improve the scheme of work for this group.' (Science subject leader of 15 years)

Consultants have helped teachers to identify pupils' weaknesses and also whether they are making the expected progress. For those who are not, consultants can work with the teacher to make the best use of the science intervention materials:

'Early in September the consultant showed us how to analyse last term's completed test papers for some borderline (level 4/5) year 9 pupils. To be frank, I thought it would be a waste of time as these pupils had now moved in to year 10. However, I was amazed to find that there was clearly an issue with the way these pupils had tackled the chemistry questions, which helped to explain why they are having so much difficulty with the GCSE particles module. If I'd done the analysis earlier I'd have known this was going to be an issue and taken some remedial action.' (New science subject leader)

'Our consultant helped us identify a group of pupils in year 9 who would benefit from an intervention programme. He helped us plan the programme and came and demonstrated some lessons for the other staff to follow.' (Key Stage 3 science coordinator)

What's coming

Those improvements to teaching and learning that have begun to work successfully in key stage 3, will also work in key stage 4. Teachers are already transferring many of the ideas into their GCSE work. The Key Stage 3 Strategy has, therefore, evolved to become the Secondary National Strategy (SNS) covering both key stages 3 and 4, with a remit to support school improvement.

The SNS will support this and will aim to:

- help establish for both teachers and pupils explicit and recognisable progression in scientific knowledge, understanding and skills through secondary schooling;
- support lessons that continue to engage pupils with both science and their

Box 9.3

Comments from Her Majesty's Inspectorate

'The Strategy is having beneficial effects on curriculum planning and teaching in science and its emphasis on audit and action planning has led to a significant improvement in departments' evaluation of their strengths and weaknesses. (Ofsted, 2004)

'Teaching and learning are better in key stage 3 than in key stage 4, and there is evidence of science departments taking improvements in teaching and learning initiated by the Key Stage 3 Strategy and transferring them into practice in key stage 4.' (Ofsted, 2005)

'The Key Stage 3 National Strategy continues to have a positive impact on teaching and learning.' (Ofsted, 2005)

'Lessons start promptly with good use of starter activities and a brisk pace is maintained throughout. Clear lesson objectives are spelled out and form the basis of learning and assessment. Teachers are doing more to build on pupils' prior experiences, most often through questioning.' (Ofsted, 2004)

learning of it, leading to greater attainment and sense of achievement;
- help teachers and pupils better assess attainment and use this to plan for further progress;
- help maintain and develop pupils' interest in and enthusiasm for science.

The advent of the SNS coincides well with the changes to the National Curriculum programme of study for science for key stage 4 and the accompanying developments in GCSE syllabuses. Their aims match closely those of the science strand and together they provide an almost unique opportunity to promote, support and develop teaching and learning in key stage 4 science to meet the needs of pupils in the 21st century. The innovations at GCSE are discussed in Chapters 1 and 8. At heart these changes, though, are about teaching and learning which is where the Strategy began and continues.

The SNS is also developing new ways to support teachers. The most substantial developments in teaching and learning are those that teachers prioritise themselves. Therefore, the SNS is making all its CPD and other materials available electronically to teachers to use when they are ready. The materials will be reformatted to support self-study by individuals or groups of teachers who may also enlist the help of local science consultants. Science materials will integrate with and draw on related whole-school support materials, enabling schools to develop teaching and learning in ways that best match their needs and circumstances.

Consultants will support science subject leaders through regular local network meetings, which will provide a forum for sharing ideas and learning more about local and national priorities. Consultants will also continue to provide support within schools to meet identified needs and with a particular emphasis on coaching teachers and supporting them to coach their colleagues.

The science strand of the SNS is well placed to build on early developments in order to meet the aspirations originally described by EPET. The work continues to receive widespread support and encouragement from the science education community, who look forward with the Strategy to the achievement of its ambitions.

The Key Stage 3 and now Secondary National Strategies apply only to state schools in England, although there is much interest in other parts of the UK and indeed in countries beyond the UK. The Strategy approach to supporting school improvement may well be applicable and successful elsewhere.

References

DfES (2002) *Key Stage 3 National Strategy: Framework for teaching science: years 7, 8 and 9.* Ref. 0136/2002. London: Department for Education and Skills.

DfES (2003) *Key Stage 3 National Strategy: Pedagogy and practice, key messages.* Ref. 0125/2003. London: Department for Education and Skills. Available at: http://www.standards.dfes.gov.uk/keysatge3/downloads

DfES (2005) *Moving forward with teaching scientific enquiry and intervention.* CD. Ref. 0196/2005. London: Department for Education and Skills.

Ofsted (1999) *Standards in the secondary curriculum, 1997/1998.* London: Ofsted.

Ofsted (2004) *The Key Stage 3 Strategy: Evaluation of the third year.* Available at: http://www.standards.dfes.gov.uk/keystage3/respub/ks3eval_ofsted

Ofsted (2005) *Subject reports 2003/04: Science in secondary schools.* London: Ofsted.

Website

DfES Standards website: www.standards.dfes.gov.uk/keystage3

Section 2 School level: Policy and practice

Chapter 10

Effective primary/ secondary transfer

Easing the transfer of pupils from primary to secondary education has been the subject of concern

Roger Mitchell

and is fraught with many challenges. This chapter discusses ways in which the essential mutual understanding between primary and secondary teachers can be reached, transfer smoothed and continuity in pupils' curriculum experiences facilitated. It concludes by outlining some structured science transition projects.

The concerns and the challenges

Discontinuity in educational experiences as pupils move from primary to secondary school has been blamed for the dip in achievement that is found in the years after transfer, which is more marked in science than in maths and English (Galton, Gray and Ruddock, 1999). Pupils' enjoyment and concentration also decrease more in science, where they meet much repetition of content and experiments (see Chapter 25) and teacher language that does not recognise their prior knowledge and experience (Peacock, 1999). Many of the curriculum and pedagogic issues at this important transition stage are common across the curriculum and easing of the transition needs to be addressed at whole-school level; others are specific to science.

Regardless of the context, it is important that we think of the apparent barriers to success as 'challenges' rather than 'problems' or 'dilemmas'. Once this is established, it is easier to think about 'strategies' and 'solutions'. It is useful to establish a working group of colleagues from both phases and to brainstorm all the perceived challenges in a particular setting. Some of the most common challenges that have been identified are listed in Box 10.1.

Box 10.1

Challenges to effective transfer

- Providing a time and venue for all parties involved to be present, which is more challenging the more schools there are involved in the process.

- Knowing (and trusting) the experiences that the pupils have had previously.

- Being aware of the expectations of the school and phase to and from which the pupils are transferring.

- Deciding how much information is to be passed on, what type, and how useful it is.

- Reaching agreement in the teacher assessments of the pupils' abilities and levels of attainment.

- Implementing planned transfer projects, e.g. visits by teachers and pupils, teacher exchanges, curriculum-based bridging or transition units, joint activity planning.

Once the list of challenges has been compiled it then needs to be refined by identifying any factors that teachers cannot influence and those where it is possible to provide strategies that will have the most positive impact. This refined list will provide the working group members with a coherent set of criteria on which to base their judgements of the best way forward.

Although the main focus will inevitably be identified as those year groups that directly border the transfer point, the outcomes of such discussions should also take account of the bigger picture. Embedding the transfer process in the culture of the whole school will allow the good practice identified to be disseminated to a wider staff group. For example, the nature of science concept acquisition allows us to operate a spiral curriculum in which areas of enquiry skills and knowledge and understanding are revisited at appropriate levels throughout a child's education. So if we are looking at a specific skill or area as the focus for a transition project that will feed through from primary to secondary, it is worth considering building directly on work undertaken by pupils in earlier years – and being explicit about this with both colleagues and pupils. This will give the transition unit greater value and provide opportunities for all teachers involved to become more aware of the expectations at different levels of education.

Strategies for success

Once partner schools have established their requirements in relation to primary/secondary transfer they need to think about how these requirements can best be met. Two key factors will influence the success of any emerging projects. Firstly, it is important that the head teachers of all partner schools are committed to the project, as this level of leadership and its protocols will be necessary for sustainability. Secondly, the schools involved should try to use existing structures to facilitate the promotion of any new partnership projects. For example, an established cluster group of schools may have regular meetings programmed into their academic cycle, which can be used. Other categories of practice that have been identified in secondary comprehensive

Box 10.2

Categories of current practice in tackling transfer

Bureaucratic
- Meetings between managers, heads of year and subject leaders from primary and secondary schools.
- Exchanges of information, e.g. pupil data and records of pupil work.
- Parents' evenings.

Social and personal
- Induction days for year 6 pupils.
- Special visits by year 6 to use specific facilities, including science.
- Open evenings.
- Parent or pupil 'buddy' guides for new entrants.

Curriculum
- Secondary teachers teaching in feeder schools.
- Joint projects, e.g. a science project started in primary school and completed at the start of year 7.
- Summer schools.
- Joint training days.

Pedagogic
- Joint programmes to share teaching skills.
- Co-observation, and debriefing, of teaching approaches, e.g. the Children Challenging Industry (CCI) project in Humberside and West Yorkshire.
- Teacher exchanges.

Managing learning
- Extended induction programmes to develop pupils' cognitive abilities (reflecting on methods by which they handle information, developing study skills, etc.).

(From Braund *et al.*, 2003, adapted from Galton *et al.*, 1999)

schools for tackling transfer are listed in Box 10.2 (note that school years are identified here in terms of the English education system, where year 6 is the final year in primary education).

Developing mutual understanding

Common challenges affecting successful transfer are, on the part of secondary schools, knowing (and trusting) the experiences that the pupils have had previously, and, on the part of primary schools, being aware of the expectations of the school and phase to which the pupils are transferring. It is also important to develop consensus in respect of teachers' assessments of the children's attainment. Some activities that can be undertaken by schools to assist in developing the mutual understanding needed are now outlined.

Reciprocal teaching

Secondary science teachers often visit, observe, and sometimes teach in, their feeder schools. Funding was provided for this in the Key Stage 3 Strategy in England, but was not extended to the reciprocal arrangement. Yet it is equally valuable for primary teachers to visit secondary science departments and to participate in the teaching. In both cases it is important to make time for the partner teachers to discuss the impressions arising from visits, and to identify issues of curriculum continuity and pedagogy arising from them.

Identifying the course of progression

Many clusters of feeder schools and their secondary school put aside one of their annual in-service training days for a joint event, as an opportunity to develop a better mutual understanding between colleagues from all schools and phases involved in transfer. Box 10.3 gives an outline of one activity that can be useful in breaking the ice and promoting relevant discussion. This activity allows what is a fairly low-key task, if such units are used in isolation, to become more revealing, with reference to the other linked units within the same key stage and to the linked units from other key stages. This may be the first opportunity that colleagues have had to get a full picture of this area of science in such a holistic way. Consequently, the feedback will often be very enlightening.

The same type of task as in Box 10.3 can be undertaken with respect to enquiry skills, using the same materials or using the progression of enquiry skills in the primary years suggested in books such as Goldsworthy and Feasey (1997) and Harlen and Qualter (2004). The expectation for enquiry skill development across the primary phase can be used as a starting point for

---

Box 10.3

Developing mutual understanding

Units from the QCA schemes of work for key stages 1 and 2 (years 1–6) and for key stage 3 (years 7–9) (see websites) for a particular area of science can be presented to mixed groups of teachers from different key stages. For example, a group could look at the theme of electricity in year 2 (unit 2F – *Using electricity*), year 4 (unit 4F – *Circuits and conductors*), year 6 (unit 6G – *Changing circuits*) and year 7 (unit 7J – *Electrical circuits*). Key questions should be provided for the groups to consider, such as:

- What do you notice about the pupil expectations for each unit?
- What do you notice about the expected level of scientific vocabulary for each unit?
- How do you think this contributes to continuity and progression in the teaching of this area of science?
- Is there anything that surprises you about the content of the units?
- Is there anything that doesn't surprise you about the content of the units?

discussion as to how this development is extended in secondary science. An important spin-off from this activity is the recognition of varied terminology in use with pupils and the need to develop a consensus language, or at least to acknowledge what the pupils are familiar with.

Developing consensus on assessment

The use of children's work in science from the partner schools, annotated with the age of the child and the key learning objective, can also be helpful when working in cross-phase groups. Such 'agreement trialling' leads to a better understanding of criteria used in teacher assessment. For instance, it is often the case that a piece of work that primary teachers identify as achieving a particular level is marked lower by secondary teachers. This difference appears to be because work that primary teachers see as providing a good *explanation* of a scientific concept is viewed by secondary teachers as providing a good *description* of that concept. It is these sorts of differences of viewpoint that need to be addressed if the teacher assessments that are transferred to secondary schools are to be trusted by those who receive them.

Structured transition projects

Although there are several transition projects available to schools, none will suit every circumstance. In undertaking such projects it is vital that the schools involved identify their unique needs and adapt materials and strategies to suit their specific requirements. This will allow the most relevant work to be undertaken and, more importantly, facilitate a greater ownership of the project for all of those involved.

As part of the Key Stage 3 Strategy (see Chapter 9), all schools in England were required to address issues of transfer between key stages 2 and 3. Consequently, many regional and local education authority (LEA) strategy coordinators initiated transfer schemes or adopted and promoted existing schemes. For example, the 'Bubbles' scheme, which originated in Cheshire (Cheshire LEA, 1997) several years prior to the Key Stage 3 Strategy, was taken up by other LEAs. The DfES Standards website (see websites) has a number of case studies of transition projects in science and other curriculum areas, including a successful science project based in South Gloucestershire and Bristol LEAs (McMahon, see websites).

The Welsh Qualifications and Curriculum Authority (ACCAC) has published a booklet, also available on their website, called *Bridging the gap* (see website). The booklet provides several examples of developing and using bridging units to support transfer between key stages 2 and 3, including some examples from science. In one example a cluster of partner schools produced a scheme of bridging work focused on investigative work and practical skills in science. Two investigations were undertaken: '*How does insulation make a difference?*' and '*How does a spring stretch?*' The equipment was supplied by the secondary school and secondary teachers went to observe and support the work. This was followed up in year 7 by pupils starting with a chapter on 'investigations' from a published scheme, and then undertaking the investigation '*Which crisp has the most energy?*' This time the primary teachers visited to observe. Although there is no doubt that the activities were of great value, opportunities may have been missed here with regard to fuller collaboration, for example team-planning and team-teaching by teachers from both phases in all of the investigations. In another cluster, primary and secondary teachers realised from their discussions that they had different ways of undertaking investigations. The teachers worked together to agree a common investigative approach and introduced this across both phases. This is a good example of how collaboration can aid continuity for pupils in the transfer process.

The Science Transition in Scotland Project (see website) also aims to support teachers to help pupils' science education through the transfer from primary to secondary school. This Web-based resource provides materials for use by clusters of partner schools. Every month a new experiment and newsletter are posted. The site provides resources that are easily adapted to suit particular clusters of schools. It also contains information and advice for cluster activities as well as case studies from successful projects. In addition, the Case Study Library is a useful forum for teachers to share experiences and information.

Much of the most significant work on primary/secondary transition has had major external funding. For example, starting in 2001, STAY (Science Transition AstraZeneca Science Teaching Trust York) was a three-year project of the AstraZeneca Science Teaching Trust, in partnership with York University, City of York LEA and 13 partner schools (Braund, 2004). The project developed bridging units in scientific enquiry based on two investigations, 'Fizzy drinks' and 'Bread'. Pupils were taught the year 6 part of the unit in the second half of the summer term, and the linked year 7 component when they transferred to secondary school in September. Lesson plans focused on the component skills of scientific enquiry, teaching these specifically and progressively. The project was disseminated to, and adopted by, all York schools in 2002. In 2003 the bridging units were used in East Yorkshire LEA, and to date there has been training and licensing of the project in over 50 LEAs and school clusters.

One of the most recent transition projects is the North Yorkshire AstraZeneca Science Pedagogy and Progression project (NYASPP, see website). Prompted by discussions of the need to concentrate on curriculum and pedagogical aspects in transfer work, the project is focused on teaching the process skills of scientific enquiry as this is work that underpins the science that pupils do either side of transfer, irrespective of the topic studied. This project built on earlier work which found that teachers from both phases:

- *value an improved understanding of the ways in which each other work including how the language of teaching and learning can be made more contiguous;*
- *are looking for ways of linking good quality opportunities for a range of types of scientific enquiry to their current schemes of work and to QCA units;*
- *are being focused on progressing pupils' learning from scientific enquiry by the changes in SATs;*
- *recognise a need for CPD in areas of scientific enquiry.*

(NYASPP website)

The NYASPP project addresses these issues through the development and teaching of pairs of practical tasks – one to be taught in years 5 or 6 in primary school and the other to be taught at some stage in key stage 3. Four such tasks have been produced which use pedagogical approaches that clearly show teachers and pupils the expected progression in knowledge, skills and challenge as they move from primary to secondary work. Key stage 2 teachers are encouraged to communicate to pupils how the work will be developed in the secondary school, and key stage 3 teachers are encouraged to recognise and build on pupils' previous achievements in the primary school. The NYASPP approach is the latest major project to provide support for primary/secondary transition work in science. Its flexible approach means that it is easily adaptable to the needs of different cluster groups.

A further simple strategy that has been employed by partner schools, regardless of the type of transition project undertaken, is the provision of exercise books by the secondary school to their feeder primary schools. These are used in the last half of the summer term in the core subjects and transfer with the pupils so they can continue to be used in the next school. There are several advantages to this as the exercise books provide clear evidence of the pupils' abilities to the next teacher, and also contain a teacher assessment commentary in the form of the previous teacher's marking of the work. Clearly this is easier to arrange when the majority of the pupils in the primary school transfer to the same secondary school. However, it is worth considering as it is relatively easy to facilitate and there are clear advantages for both pupils and teachers.

Finally, the ASE/Science Year *Science Passport* is described in Box 10.4. For the *Science Passport* to be of greatest impact, partnership schools need to work closely and look for opportunities to collaborate in both planning and teaching with the materials.

The *Science Passport* and its associated support materials are available to download free (see website). Further information about the *Science Passport*

Box 10.4

Science Passport

Developed as part of the ASE/Science Year CD-ROM initiative, the *Science Passport* is a template for successful bridging projects between primary and secondary schools. It is designed to resemble a real passport. There are six A4 pages that fold into an A5 booklet. Pupils have a section for a passport photograph and details about themselves, including primary and secondary school information. A personal section introduces the idea of inherited characteristics and there is space for information about investigations in years 6 and 7.

There is a choice of investigations with structured teacher notes as well as activity support sheets for pupils. Throughout these activities pupils can collect visas for skills and investigations to carry forward into key stage 3. These build for the children a reassuring link between their schools. There is also an apparatus checklist, vocabulary page and a final section where the pupils record the science centres they have visited. As a record of pupil achievements at key stage 2, the passport provides tangible information to key stage 3 teachers on which to build.

and its successful application in a transition project can be found in the case study 'Using the *Science Passport* for transition' (see website).

The pupils' view

Bridging projects look like an attractive solution to the challenge of curriculum continuity across phases. Yet Braund *et al.* (2003) caution enthusiasm for this route to the neglect of more careful curriculum design and transfer administration. Pupils may prefer 'curriculum discontinuity'; they may reject bridging work as something they did in primary school that they want to leave behind in the move to 'big school'. Bridging work needs to be carefully planned to challenge secondary pupils, while recognising and linking to their level of practical skills and concept learning from primary school.

References

Braund, M. (2004) Bridging work in science – what's in it for primary schools? *Primary Science Review*, **82**, 24–27. Available to ASE members at: http://www.ase.org.uk/htm/members_area/journals/psr/pdf/psr_82/pg-24-28.pdf

Braund, M., Crompton, Z., Driver, M. and Parvin, J. (2003) Bridging the key stage 2/3 gap in science. *School Science Review*, **85**(310), 117–123.

Cheshire LEA (1997) *Bridging the gap: KS2/3 liaison – Bubbles*. Winsford: Cheshire County Council.

Galton, M., Gray, J. and Ruddock, J. (1999) *The impact of school transitions and transfers on pupils' progress and attainment*. RR131. London: Department for Education and Employment.

Goldsworthy, A. and Feasey, R. (1997) *Making sense of primary science investigations*. Hatfield: Association for Science Education.

Harlen, W. and Qualter, A. (2004) *The teaching of science in primary schools*. London: David Fulton.

Peacock, G. (1999) Continuity and progression between key stages in science. Paper presented at BERA annual conference, University of Sussex.

Websites

ACCAC. *Bridging the gap*: http://www.accac.org.uk/uploads/documents/1515.pdf

DFES Standards site: http://www.standards.dfes.gov.uk/keystage3/casestudies/cs_sc_transition

McMahon, K. *Transition in science – South Gloucestershire LEA and Bristol LEA*: http://www.standards.dfes.gov.uk/keystage3/downloads/cs_sc_transition.doc

NYASPP (North Yorkshire AstraZeneca Science Pedagogy and Progression project): http://www.york.ac.uk/depts/educ/projs/STAY/NYASPPNov04.htm

QCA Key Stage 3 Scheme of work for science: http://www.qca.org.uk/9906_13181.html

QCQ Key stage 2 Scheme of work for science: http://www.qca.org.uk/9907_13180.html

QCA Key Stage 1 Scheme of work for science: http://www.qca.org.uk/9908_13179.html

Science Passport: http://www.sycd.co.uk/who_am_i/passport/activity.htm

Science Transition in Scotland Project: http://www.sciencetransitionscotland.org.uk/

Using the Science Passport for Transition: http://www.standards.dfes.gov.uk/keystage3/casestudies/cs_sc_transition_pass

Chapter 11 Learning science outside the classroom

Many organisations are expressing concern that 'fieldwork' of all kinds is being diminished. At the same time, these and other

Alan Peacock and **Mick Dunne**

agencies are doing a great deal to encourage teachers to get out more and take advantage of the resources available in the immediate locality of the school and further afield. This has relevance across and beyond the science curriculum, not being confined to ecological studies. This chapter begins by considering why we need to make provision for pupils to spend some time learning science outside the classroom. It looks at opportunities available in school grounds and in settings other than schools, and addresses the practicalities of taking pupils out, based on evaluations of out-of-school learning activities. It concludes by looking towards the future of education outside the classroom.

A growing concern

There is widespread concern that young people are distanced not only from the natural rural environment, but increasingly from any out-of-doors learning experiences (Rickinson *et al.*, 2004; DfES, 2005a; Growing Schools website). Concern about decreasing opportunities for learning outside the classroom was reported to the UK parliament by the Education and Skills Select Committee enquiry (DfES, 2005b). The Royal Society has reported data that suggest fieldwork is being diminished throughout the education system by a number of pressures on schools, colleges and universities. It has therefore established a working group to assess the apparent decline in the extent and type of fieldwork provision in science at all stages of education, from primary school through to degree level (see website). Reasons advanced for the decline in what can loosely be called 'fieldwork' are cost, health and safety, risk of litigation, time involved, pressures on teachers and the sense of being 'snowed under'. Despite all teachers being subject to similar constraints, historians, musicians, dramatists, linguists and particularly geographers use the outdoor classroom in greater numbers than scientists (Tilling, 2005).

However, schools in the UK have encouragement for this kind of activity from a number of official quarters (Ofsted, 2004). By the time this book is published, the Government Department for Education and Skills will have published its manifesto for education outside the classroom, developed in partnership with teachers and providers (DfES, 2005a). Already in existence, Growing Schools is a Government-funded programme that aims to harness the full potential of the outdoor classroom, both within and beyond the school grounds, as a teaching and learning resource for learning across the curriculum (see website). The Real World Learning campaign is a movement by a consortium of major environmental agencies to foster more out-of-school learning (see Field Studies Council website). Other agencies such as the Countryside Agency, English Nature and the Soil Association are also working closely with schools to this end.

A rationale

Well-organised education outside the classroom lets children explore science by using play and fun activities. Working outside the classroom provides experience of the physical, social, environmental and ecological aspects of the real world, and hence an expanded and purposeful science curriculum, enabling science learning to become embedded in meaningful contexts. It provides opportunities for novel, unique and exciting educational experiences, which are stimulating and motivate further learning. It fosters attitudes of awareness, interest, self-respect and respect for the environment. It provides opportunities to build closer relationships between children and their peers, children and teachers, and children and other 'expert' adults.

In terms of the objectives of the formal science curriculum, it enables pupils to practise and apply skills used in the classroom, with hands-on experience of careful observation and recording. It provides novel experiences that will raise questions to investigate, as well as opportunities to make hypotheses and predictions. These will often be the kinds of enquiries not feasible inside school, such as explorations, surveys, modelling and problem solving. Out-of-school work provides realistic, not contrived, data from first-hand observations and measurements, which pupils can then attempt to manipulate. This develops an appreciation that data from real contexts is 'messy' and complex. And while activities in the environment can develop pupils' autonomy, the informal talk with adults that arises allows the adults to identify pupils' misconceptions and to help clarify their ideas on the spot. In the long run '*it helps to train [potential] experts able to serve science and society through research; and to prepare citizens of the future for responsible management of their environment*' (Royal Society).

Opportunities in the locality

The majority of schools are in towns and cities but wherever a school is situated there will be opportunities to work outside, starting with the school grounds, which will include both natural and built environments. Even if there are only a few bushes around the school, a teacher can still use these to provide valid activities for children, such as the 'caterpillars' activity described in Box 11.1,

Box 11.1

Caterpillars

Cut pieces of wool of several different colours each into 10 strips, about caterpillar length, and scatter these in a bush. Let the children model being birds, and give them one minute to 'feed' and find as many caterpillars as possible. They will find the brightly coloured ones, but not the green/brown/yellowy ones! This activity can be adapted for any age and ability; for example, A-level students could apply statistical tests to the results of this model situation.

which develops the idea of camouflage. School buildings and walls can be used to do a study of materials and their properties, investigate habitats, enquire into the best places to grow pot plants (or for nails to go rusty!), survey pollution (by using lichens as indicators) and learn sampling procedures.

Beyond the immediate locality

Going slightly further afield, there will probably be a wildlife trust, wetland centre, city farm, museum, industrial heritage site, or similar venture not too far away. These are usually staffed by experts, many with a teaching background, who are keen to receive school groups. They have a wide repertoire of activities for children and many are able to help teachers by suggesting ideas for enquiries and explorations in locations near schools: a wood, pond, farm, disused quarry, hillside, stream, canal, seashore, or even a shopping mall. In addition, there are specialised field centres for biological, geographical and other environmental studies, managed by the Field Studies Council (see website), independent enterprises or local education authorities.

There is also a rapidly expanding network of major science learning centres across the UK, established deliberately with education in mind (see Box 11.2).

Finally, there are national agencies offering partnerships with schools that

Box 11.2

National centres providing experiences and activities for learning science
- Science Museum and the Natural History Museum (London)
- National Space Centre (Leicester)
- Magna (Rotherham)
- Eureka! (Halifax)
- Museum of Science and Industry (Manchester)
- Dynamic Earth (Edinburgh)
- At-Bristol (Bristol)
- Techniquest (Cardiff)
- Eden Project (Cornwall)
- Centre for Alternative Technology (Machynlleth)

All of these have websites that allow teachers and pupils to download materials, link the visit to the curriculum, plan a visit and support follow-up work. They, and others throughout the UK can be accessed from the 24 Hour Museum website (see websites).

take pupils out to work in the environment at venues such as National Trust properties (the National Trust Guardianship scheme, see Box 11.3) and organic farms (through the Soil Association and Farming and Countryside Education, see website); the Royal Society for the Protection of Birds, and events like 'Countryside Live!' sponsored by the Countryside Agency. Local authorities often run their own schemes such as the Somerset Waste Action Programme (SWAP), which allows schools to visit a working landfill site and recycling centre (Vrdlovçova, 2005). Recent evaluations of these show a striking success in terms of harnessing children's enthusiasm for science learning, and improving their behaviour, language and inter-personal skills at the same time.

Box 11.3

Examples of successful out-of-school learning

The National Trust Guardianship scheme involves partnerships between schools and properties in which children become involved in stewardship and conservation activity through regular visits to a particular site. Over 120 such partnerships exist around the country (see National Trust website). Here are two brief examples.

Pupils from The Abbey School, a Special School in Surrey, worked on several projects with the warden of Frensham Little Pond (see website). Some helped manage reed beds; others regularly litter-picked the area to ensure that the site was clean for visitors to enjoy, or helped build a new bench along the pond edge for visitors to watch the bird-life. The pupils felt it was important that the bench was accessible to all visitors to the pond. One pupil who is confined to a wheelchair advised on access and her suggestions for a path for wheelchair users were acted on. In their report on the school, Ofsted inspectors commended this care for the environment as a contribution to the pupils' moral education.

Every class from Ysgol Coed Menai (years 6 to 11) is involved with the Guardianship at Glan Faenol, near Bangor in Wales. Small groups of pupils visit each week during term time so there can be up to forty visits in a year. The work is highly practical and has included gate making, green woodworking, ivy clearance, path work, step making, track repair and bridge building.

Many other locations are appropriate for science visits, such as supermarkets, hospitals, manufacturing enterprises of various kinds, ports and harbours, power stations, sewage works, opticians; whatever is available in the school locality. Visits relating to environmental issues can focus on pupils' questions. For example, a visit to the glass treatment works, Rockware Glass (a subsidiary of British Glass), at Knottingley, West Yorkshire, can answer the question, '*What happens to the bottles we put in the bottle bank?*' (see Rockware Glass website).

Managing outside visits

Context and purpose

Despite many opportunities to engage in science education beyond the classroom, it is likely that the majority of schools do not maximise their educational potential. Many of the specialist centres provide a menu of age-range differentiated science activities that teachers are able to choose from and which are delivered by the specialist centre staff. However, teachers need to identify their particular requirements and the learning potential of a venue or activity as part of the normal planning process: context is crucial and preparation essential. Of critical importance is the match between the desired learning outcomes (the teacher's reason for going in the first place) and contextual considerations for the learning, such as issues of timing, group sizes, the use of activity sheets, and so on. At some centres, specialists are available (wardens, guides, explainers, farmers, education officers) who provide planning support as part of their general provision; this is far more effective when there is liaison with, and guidance from, the teacher. Centre staff see many different school groups: they rely on teachers to help them respond to specific needs, rather than providing an 'off the shelf' programme.

Teachers must also be very clear about their science objectives. For example, if the pupils are going to engage in a pond-dipping activity, should they concentrate on identifying and counting the plants and animals, or on simple relationships, or on the production of food chains and even food webs, or on adaptation? Perhaps the objectives are procedural: to generate a hypothesis, to understand sampling procedure, to learn appropriate recording processes, to identify patterns, or to evaluate evidence. Only the teacher knows what is appropriate for the pupils and must not be afraid of setting the agenda. Where no on-site assistance is available because of the nature of the venue then teachers must make a preliminary visit to devise tasks and activities that are not only designed to meet specific learning outcomes, but are also do-able on the day, which will depend on seasons, weather, time, and so on.

Continuity and curriculum integration

Children frequently perceive a visit to an out-of-school location as a 'day out' or a treat, rather than being particularly relevant to identified learning experiences. Multiple, linked visits for every pupil, say once a term, may be of much greater educational capacity than disconnected trips, although impracticable to organise for a large school population. Even if it is not possible for individuals to visit a site more than once, the school may compile records of the findings from each visit. This builds up a large bank of data, possibly over many years, which offers progressive insights into change over time. This bank can be used in preparation and follow-up work, including long-term projects.

The logistics and timing of visits can be seen as a challenge to curriculum integration (see Dillon *et al.*, 2005). For example, constraints can be experienced when visits take place after (rather than during) a related module of class work, when competing curriculum pressures limit extensive follow-up work, when not all members of a class or year group are able to take part, or when educators from the outdoor centres are not available for follow-up work in school (see 'Follow-up' below). Residential visits, of course, can mitigate some of these constraints.

Preparation

It is essential that adequate preparations are made for visits, and that they are followed up back in the classroom. Dillon *et al.* (2005) found that preparation of pupils tends to be limited to practicalities and logistics as opposed to curriculum issues. Teachers need to prepare the pupils to understand how the visit will enhance their science learning. Otherwise, work started by the pupils on the trip is likely to remain incomplete and not used to develop the pupils' knowledge and understanding when back in school. That out-of-school visits motivate and stimulate the vast majority of children is without question; but whether they are being taken to a local supermarket to look at a range of food types, to a sewage works or to a zoo, considerable effort is required before the visit, during the visit and after the visit in order to maximise the effectiveness of the learning experiences. The 'trip mentality' needs to be played down; at the same time, younger pupils especially need to know the time and place for ice-creams, lunch breaks and the gift shop, as these experiences do have a value in terms of social education. But by not having any food or drink for sale on site, for example, the 'Countryside Live!' days proved very successful in focusing pupils' attention on activities, in teachers' eyes.

Preparation involves not only preparation for pupils but also for all adults involved. Often, accompanying adults are preoccupied with behaviour management rather than with learning, but they have a key mediation role for learning during the visit. What are accompanying adults expected to do? What will they need to focus pupils' attention on? What kinds of questions are appropriate?

Another important planning decision relates to resources, both those provided by the centre and those that teachers prepare themselves. Evaluations (e.g. Peacock, 2004) suggest that the use of activity sheets on site is not helpful; they distract children from using their senses, and the dreaded clipboard becomes a handicap. Where the activity involves recording data on site, this can be done in groups with one scribe with a clipboard, or better still electronically.

Follow-up

Follow-up activities can take many forms and it is not unusual to see literacy considerations outweighing those of science. The class display, with word-processed 'newspaper articles' and digital snaps of 'our visit' may look good, but often the science ideas and skills can be lost as a consequence. Here again, serial work scores highly, as children can see that they are taking part in a longitudinal investigation that is accruing scientific evidence, as well as actively creating things, growing plants and conserving habitats. The pride that pupils take in talking about this kind of work often outweighs the value of writing about it. Some organisations not only provide web-based materials to assist with this kind of follow-up, but also offer outreach support, where their staff will visit schools to provide ongoing input. A powerful example of the success of this approach is the SWAP programme mentioned earlier (Vrdlovçova, 2005).

Health and safety

Appropriate management of health and safety is a major issue. Publication of *Health and safety of pupils on educational visits* (DfEE, 2000) has addressed many concerns. Specialist venues contribute to alleviating health and safety pressures on schools by providing comprehensive activity-specific risk assessments. The *Management of Health & Safety at Work Regulations* (1992) require employers to produce risk assessments and demonstrate how risk is managed. There is a duty on all teachers, therefore, to inform their employers of 'identified risks' – ignorance of this responsibility is no excuse! A complete risk assessment needs to be completed before each visit takes place (see Chapter 14). *Health and safety of pupils on educational visits* (DfEE, 2000) and local authority guidance should be consulted, as well as further sources referred to in these publications. Multiple copies of *Health and safety of pupils on educational visits* are available free from DfES Publications and from the DfES website which provides links to other relevant documents including: *Standards for adventures*; *Handbook for group leaders*; *Group safety at water margins*; and *Health and safety: responsibilities and powers*.

Parental concerns need to be addressed by schools. Many specialist centres produce videos specifically designed to support schools in tackling this issue. Children and parents who attended the same trip during the previous year provide useful advocates.

Assessing the learning

Inspectors have frequently praised the quality of schools' science work outside the classroom, particularly as it appears to enhance pupils' language and social skills as well as their science attitudes. But how should we assess this without spoiling the enjoyment and sense of achievement that children experience?

It is best to avoid too much of the kind of assessment that identifies the out-of-class work with testing and formal assessment. Using such work as a vehicle for extended writing should not be discouraged, as too few opportunities for this are taken in formal science lessons. A display of photographs of pupils working outdoors, with examples of environments observed or artefacts produced or used, can communicate very effectively the sense of achievement they experience. Alternative methods of recording, involving role-play, digital cameras and minidisk recorders, mapping techniques, cartoon strips, poster presentations or oral presentations, are popular. Learning with known and trusted adults helps develop those valuable one-to-one conversations that are important in the development and assessment of children's ideas. Evaluations of visits have indicated that children have many more misconceptions about the environments they encounter than we imagine (Peacock and Bowker, 2001).

The benefits of working in the environment

If we genuinely want children to make sense of their world, then working on science outside the classroom is essential. Our experience in a wide range of contexts shows us that the vast majority of children of all ages are enthusiastic about such ventures and apply themselves fully to this work. The educational benefits are huge, but there is a cost. There needs to be careful and focused planning to maximise learning, which should involve consideration of serial visits rather than 'one-offs' to make this type of experience work effectively. The question perhaps is not, 'What do we gain by going outside the classroom?' but 'What science are children missing by not having these experiences?'

References

DfEE (2000) *Health and safety of pupils on educational visits*. DfES publications (see DfES website.

DfES (2005a) Manifesto. Available at: www.teachernet.gov.uk/teachingandlearning/resourcematerials/museums/outsideclassroom/

DfES (2005b) *Education outside the classroom: House of Commons Education and Skills Select Committee report*. Ref. HC[2004-05]120. London: The Stationery Office (www.clicktso.com).

Dillon, J., Morris, M., O'Donnell, L., Reid, A., Rickinson, M. and Scott, W. (2005) *Engaging and learning with the outdoors – the final report of the outdoor classroom in a rural context action research project*. Available at: http://www.nfer.ac.uk/research-areas/pims-data/ outlines/the-outdoor-classroom-in-a-rural-context-action-research.cfm (links from various websites including http:/www.bath.ac.uk/cree/resources).

Ofsted (2004) *Outdoor education: aspects of good practice*. London: Ofsted.

Peacock, A. (2004) *Eco-literacy for primary schools*. Stoke on Trent: Trentham Books.

Peacock, A. and Bowker, R. (2001) Thinking of Eden. *Teaching Thinking*, **5**, 22–24.

Tilling, S. (2005) Outdoor science: in danger of extinction? *Education in Science*, **212**, 18–19.

Rickinson, M., Dillon, J., Teamey, K., Morris, M., Choi, M., Sanders, D. and Benefield, P. (2004) *A review of research on outdoor learning*. Shrewsbury: Field Studies Council.

Vrdlovçova, J. (2005) Waking up to waste. *Primary Science Review*, **86**, 8–11.

Websites

24 Hour Museum http://www.24hourmusem.org.uk

Abbey School NT Guardianship Scheme project: http://www.abbey.surrey.sch.uk/ National_Trust_Guardians.html

DfES heath and safety publications: http://www.teachernet.gov.uk/wholeschool/healthandsafety/visits/

Farming and Countryside Education: http://www.face-online.org.uk

Field Studies Council: http://www.field-studies-council.org/campaigns/rwl/index.aspx

Growing Schools: http://www.teachernet.gov.uk/growingschools/

National Trust Guardianship: www.nationaltrust.org.uk/.../learning/guardianship/

Rockware Glass: www.glassforever.co.uk

Royal Society http://www.royalsoc.ac.uk/page.asp?id=1991

Chapter 12 School self-evaluation of teaching and learning science

It has been many years since schools could be regarded as 'islands' within their communities, remaining **Lynne Wright**

largely unaccountable to them and to wider society. There is an increasing expectation that schools will share their philosophy, aims and approaches with the outside community. This chapter outlines those aspects that a science department needs to evaluate, not only for accountability, but to understand its own strengths, weaknesses and ways to develop. While the chapter is based on experience in England, similar aspects and procedures are applicable in Scotland and the same questions can form the basis for self-evaluation of schools within any system.

Why school improvement? Who is it for?

School improvement is now a permanent feature of school life, and there are tremendous pressures on schools, from many directions, to do ever better. This is one reason why the school development plan (SDP) is now often called the school improvement plan (SIP). Alongside a whole-school document there is normally a departmental development plan that indicates how the department contributes to the school plan. Although accountability to a wide range of stakeholders continues to put schools under pressure, it is right that they should demonstrate how well they are doing in helping each pupil to do his or her best.

To this end, it is very important that schools have as full a picture as possible of pupils' standards of *attainment* in science, as indicated by school and external tests and other performance data. Crucially, schools need some measure of the *progress* their pupils are making in science as they move through the school. However, accountability requires a much broader picture than this. It is necessary to look beyond the most easily measurable outcomes in order to gauge the effectiveness of science teaching in improving not only standards and achievement but pupils' attitudes to science and the school's partnership with parents and the community.

In England, external inspection seems to be a permanent feature of school life and has evolved through many manifestations, from 'we will tell you how well you are doing' to a more shared approach based on a school's own evaluation. Whilst external inspections are becoming shorter and more focused, crucially they are increasingly based on a school's own rigorous analysis of its data, both quantitative and qualitative. Even without this external pressure, it is in a school's best interest that its own analysis is ruthlessly honest and accurate. School self-assessment at any level, and for any aspect or subject, relies upon evidence collected by the school in a measured and planned way, rather than on assertions, expectations or hope! A helpful checklist, *Writing a subject evaluation that works*, in the same format as the self-evaluation form required for Ofsted inspections in England, has been produced by the National Advisers and Inspectors Group for Science (NAIGS) – see websites.

In Scotland, similar school self-evaluation is now necessary, with schools using *How good is our school?* (see HMIe website). This is a self-evaluation package asking three basic questions, relevant to any educational system: How are we doing? How do we know? What are we going to do now? and using a six-point scale of quality indicators.

Evaluating attainment

It is possible, but time consuming without a computer program, to analyse school data to build up a picture of the attainment of individuals or groups compared with national standards. An increasingly sophisticated array of software programs is available to help senior managers and heads of science to do this. Such analyses need to be very objective. Looking for reasons for particularly good performance is a positive experience, but it is less comfortable when there has been no, or only slight, improvement or even a downturn in performance. In these instances it is even more important to establish reasons for the results, rather than to provide excuses. Honest and objective explanations help to inform the next stage of the department development plan so that the strategic plan guides the actions of all concerned in the teaching of science. This plan must also take into account national and local priorities, as this is ultimately what schools are judged against.

It is important to look in depth at the attainment of different groups within a cohort. Do boys outperform girls or vice versa? Does this reflect the national trend? Is there a reason for this and is the school doing anything to redress the balance? How well are pupils doing who have special educational needs or are in the early stages of learning English (or whatever language science is taught in)? Is there a detailed picture of the attainment of pupils of different minority ethnic groups? Is the attainment gap wider for one group than another? If so, how does the school plan to narrow the gap? Is an increasing proportion of pupils achieving at higher levels? The answers to these questions give clear indications of the next steps in self-evaluation, and in the departmental action plan.

Where there are options between different courses in key stage 4 (or equivalent stages) the analysis needs to take account of the differences in national expectation between courses. Schools vary considerably in the groups of pupils entered for different courses, so careful interpretation is needed in comparing one school's attainment results with the national attainment in specific science courses and in what is called 'any science', for example, in Ofsted and DfES documents in England (see websites).

Evaluating achievement

By itself, pupils' attainment does not indicate successful teaching and learning. Pupils' prior attainment on entering the school must be considered. In England and Wales the end-of-key-stage 2 SAT results in English and maths as well as science indicate the level at which initial work for each pupil should be aimed. The effectiveness of a department's system for using this information needs to be evaluated. If other standardised tests, measuring different abilities, are used, it can be valuable to identify pupils who perform widely differently in different tests.

Attainment is often compared to attainment in similar schools, for example those where pupils had similar prior attainment. A particularly useful technique is the use of value-added graphs as in the DfES Pupil Achievement Tracker (see website). Value-added for individual pupils can be plotted on these graphs as well as averages for different courses, teaching groups, boys/girls, ethnic groups or any other relevant grouping. This is a very powerful tool in identifying strengths and weaknesses and is the only effective way of comparing different optional courses.

Analysing strengths and weaknesses

Although attainment and achievement can be judged in a global way by comparing test scores year on year this does not help the head of science to pinpoint areas of specific success or difficulty, which may highlight areas of good or weaker teaching. It is necessary to look beyond test scores to find out the detail of pupils' progress, both as a cohort and as individuals. How well are they applying their knowledge and understanding to new learning in new contexts? Do pupils use an increasing range of science terms correctly and with understanding? Do they conduct investigations in an increasingly well-organised and logical way and choose the most appropriate method of recording and displaying the results using increasingly precise measurements? How well do they make predictions based on their science knowledge and explain their findings in relation to their initial hypotheses? For key stage 3 SATs in England, support material from QCA and in the DfES Pupil Achievement Tracker can be used to identify areas of strength and weakness (see websites).

This level of analysis will enable the head of science to identify any areas in the teaching that need to become a priority in the science action plan. It will help teachers to identify which aspects are posing difficulties for individual pupils, so that science teaching plans can be amended to give extra support, or to provide extra challenge for those pupils achieving above the average.

Monitoring pupils' progress

Having found out the standards the pupils are reaching, it is essential that schools look at what progress groups and individuals are making in their science learning to find out which pupils are making the expected progress, which are achieving beyond this and which are not doing as well as anticipated against individual targets set for each significant stage. Targets for attainment in science need to reflect expected value-added plus a degree of challenge, taking into account teachers' knowledge of individual pupils and the impact of teaching and any planned intervention strategies during the key stage. The progress of those with special educational needs may be judged against special needs performance criteria and any specified in their individual education plans.

Supporting pupils by assessment

Support for pupils as partners in the learning process can only be really effective if there is consistency of teachers' judgements within a school and with national expectations. This is why the moderation and standardisation of the assessment of pupils' work is such an important process, and why portfolios of assessed and moderated science work are so useful. These exemplify to pupils and teachers why different pieces of work are of a particular standard. If end-of-topic tests are used, either school-produced or from published schemes, it is essential that they match national standards. The effectiveness of monitoring pupils' progress is totally dependent on the accuracy of this assessment. Once criteria are agreed and understood, pupils can be involved regularly in assessing their own work. The teachers' diagnostic comments, if they are sharply focused, help the pupils to see how they can improve. The pupils are better able to judge how well they are doing and, with practice, identify what they need to do to improve their work. Chapters 22 and 23 give details of such formative assessment.

In the face of the many pressures schools are under, this level of individual self-evaluation within the whole-school self-evaluation process is often overlooked. Through evaluating the level of support pupils are given in their learning, senior managers and the head of science are well placed to be even more accurate in their evaluation of the effectiveness of science teaching and its impact on standards and achievement.

Evaluating teaching and learning and pupils' attitudes to science

To establish effective self-review the senior management team and head of science need to have a clear picture of standards in teaching and how these link both to standards of attainment and achievement and to progress in learning. One of the most effective ways of doing this is to monitor science teaching by observing lessons. To do this objectively, and to provide the most useful information, the focus of the observation needs to be understood by, and shared with, all participants. It is desirable that the head of science takes

Box 12.1

Questions for self-evaluation of teaching

- Is the content of the lesson scientifically accurate?
- Has the teacher enough personal science knowledge and understanding to lead the learning of all groups of pupils forward at a good rate?
- Do teachers' plans provide for progress of all groups of pupils and those who need individual support?
- Do teachers share the objectives of each lesson with the pupils so that they have a clear idea of what they are expected to learn?
- Is a range of teaching styles deployed within a lesson or a topic sufficient to suit the preferred learning styles of all pupils?
- Are different methods of teaching, and of pupils' recording of their science learning, appropriate to the science content being taught?
- Are the different activities planned and organised for effective learning with appropriate consideration being given to health and safety?
- Are pupils given enough opportunity and time to think through, explain and explore their own science ideas using enquiry, investigation, research and discussion?
- Is marking regular and consistent?
- Is the department/school's marking policy followed?
- Does marking concentrate on what was planned for the pupils to learn?
- Does it correct misconceptions and inaccurate use of science terminology?
- Does the teacher ask questions which further develop pupils' thinking in science?

part in observing lessons but if all observations are undertaken by senior managers it is essential that the focus is on science as well as generic issues. Box 12.1 lists some questions that can guide the self-evaluation of teaching.

Observing science teaching gives the head of science a good idea of pupils' attitudes to science. It will enable a picture to emerge of whether they are enthusiastic learners or passive recipients of teaching and how much scientific curiosity they display. The sorts of questions they ask and their intellectual independence in pursuing scientific enquiry are also good indicators. Their ability to work cooperatively, to organise themselves and to behave well under all circumstances is not only another indicator of their attitudes but further evidence of the quality of teaching. All these are an integral part of self-evaluation.

In addition to lesson observations, scrutiny of pupils' work in science can give a lot of valuable information. One of the best ways of establishing pupils' attitudes to science and the effectiveness of teaching and learning is talking to them! This can be done both formally through individual reviews or informally in small-group discussions.

Experience across the UK shows that observing teaching helps identify where professional development is needed to increase an individual teacher's knowledge and expertise. It indicates strong areas of science teaching, and which teachers can provide good role models. Observation of other departments and teachers is a powerful professional development tool, allowing the sharing of good practice throughout the school.

How effective is your science curriculum?

It is also necessary to evaluate the quality of the science curriculum from time to time. If pupils enjoy science lessons, work hard and generally record their work accurately and with care it is a reasonable, albeit subjective, indicator of a lively and relevant science curriculum. Schools where this is particularly noticeable have adapted their curriculum to the context of their own school environment. Some schools adopt a commercial scheme of work, and while this often produces thorough teaching to build up well-developed science concepts, it can lack the excitement of teaching and learning science that is found in the best schools.

Most importantly in evaluating the science curriculum, or schemes of work, the head of science needs to check that it stems from the school's mission statement, and links to the main aims of the school science policy. For example, is an intention of providing equality for all pupils reflected in practice? Are the contexts for teaching science of interest to both boys and girls and pupils of all abilities and cultural experiences? Planning at each key stage should also ensure that skills, knowledge and understanding are taught in such a way that key science concepts are developed at the right level and with progression. An evaluation should also check that sufficient time and appropriate timetabling are given to the teaching of science to enable quality teaching and learning.

Where alternative courses are offered to pupils, such as in key stage 4, a self-evaluation should include an evaluation of the range of courses offered and an analysis of the pupils that choose each course. Are there differences in the balance of boys and girls or pupils of different abilities or ethnic origin for each course? An evaluation of pupils' attainment and achievement will indicate whether pupils are following the most appropriate course. Is the guidance given to pupils and the arrangement of options appropriate?

Ensuring the health and safety of pupils

It is the responsibility of employers to ensure that employees and pupils work safely. In most cases the employer is the local authority; in some the school's governing body. In either case, the head of science also has a key role in this respect.

Chapter 14 gives more detail of health and safety responsibilities and sources of advice, such as ASE (2006), CLEAPSS or SSERC. Although the monitoring of health and safety procedures is the responsibility of employers it is desirable for it to be included in any self-evaluation of a science department. A checklist is very helpful (see Borrows, 1995).

Resources for teaching and learning

As part of departmental self-evaluation a review of staffing, accommodation and teaching materials can also identify issues for departmental development.

Have the staff (teaching, technician and other support) the appropriate experience, expertise and training? What staff development needs are identified? How much do the staffing and accommodation limit the courses offered and the schemes of work? There is no limit to the teaching resources, that is apparatus, books and software, that could be thought desirable. The criteria should be whether the resources are appropriate for teaching the scheme of work for each course. Have compromises been made because of the lack of resources? Are there sufficient resources available to provide pupils with first-hand experiences as well as sources of secondary information? (see ASE, 2004; Royal Society, 1997).

Partnership with parents/carers, other schools and the community

Many adults' memories of their own science learning are very different from what goes on in schools today. Parents/carers are very important partners in the education of their children and schools need to evaluate how successful they are in promoting effective and mutually supportive relationships. At its most basic level, this means ensuring that parents/carers get regular information about how well their children are doing in science. To be really helpful in the early years of secondary school, regular information should also outline the main areas of science learning over a set period, including the topic or theme, perhaps through homework diaries or topic summaries. Suggestions of how parents/carers can support their children and the school might include interesting websites.

In order that parents and carers can give informed views, some schools run science evenings so that they can experience the school's approach to teaching science at first hand. This is an 'eye-opener' for many of the adults, who realise not only that science can be interesting and fun but that it requires the learner to develop and use a wide range of skills in different contexts. Parents/carers are introduced to different styles of teaching and learning, all of which promotes a closer partnership based on shared understanding and aims.

The partnership that the school has with other schools and the use it makes of the wider community is a further area for self-evaluation. Are the resources of the local community, visits and visitors used as contexts for developing science ideas and skills? Is there a fruitful partnership with other schools that provides a supportive network of professional development for teachers and other staff? Are scarce resources shared between schools so that all aspects of science can be taught to the required levels?

A school and department's self-evaluation of its effectiveness includes looking beyond itself with a remit to widen the circle of the school community.

References and further reading

ASE (2004) *Laboratory design for teaching and learning* (CD). Hatfield: Association for Science Education.

ASE (2006) *Safeguards in the school laboratory*. 11th edn. Chapters 2 and 3. Hatfield: Association for Science Education.

Borrows, P. (1995) How safe is your science department? A checklist for managers. *School Science Review*, **76**(277), 19–23. Reprinted in ASE (2000) *Safety reprints*. Hatfield: Association for Science Education.

DfES/Ofsted (2005) *A new relationship with schools: improving performance through school self-evaluation*. London: Department for Education and Skills.

Ofsted (Office for Standards in Education) (2001) *Inspecting subjects 11–16 – Science, with guidance on self-evaluation.* London: Ofsted. (Complements *Handbooks for inspecting secondary schools and special schools*, published in 1999.)

Ofsted (Office for Standards in Education) (2005) *Interpreting data training materials* (CD). London: Ofsted.

Royal Society (1997) *Science teaching resources: 11–16 year-olds.* London: The Royal Society.

Websites

DfES Pupil Achievement Tracker: http://www.standards.dfes.gov.uk/performance/pat/

DfES Standards site: http://www.standards.dfes.gov.uk

HMIe (HM Inspectorate of Education, Scotland) *How good is our school?*: http://www.HMIE.gov.uk

NAIGS (2005) *Writing a subject evaluation that works.* Available on the QCA website at: http://www.qca.org.uk/15173.html

Office for Standards in Education (Ofsted): http://www.ofsted.gov.uk/

Qualifications and Curriculum Authority (QCA): http://www.qca.org.uk/

Acknowledgement

Contributions to this chapter on aspects of self-evaluation specific to secondary school science departments were made by Colin DuQueno.

Chapter 13

Teaching science with ICT

Information and Communication Technology (ICT) has come a long way since its introduction into schools over 25 years ago. This

Philip Morris and **John Wardle**

chapter explores the current position and future potential of ICT in science education, with particular reference to the pedagogical argument for its use. It looks at the development of ICT, its importance in modern science and at specific examples of lessons in secondary science that make use of ICT.

Where are we now?

We hear a lot about the rapid development and impact of the digital, information age on all aspects of society: business, entertainment, commerce, education and science. As recognised by the UK Department for Education and Skills, *'digital technology is already changing how we do business and live our lives'* (DfES, 2005). The growth in technology is set to continue: *'we believe Internet usage should continue to grow rapidly (20–30% annually for the next few years) as broadband usage continues to grow and as content providers continue to ramp their creativity and increase user engagement'* (Meeker et al., 2004).

Adoption of technology in the classroom often lags behind the technological development (perhaps no bad thing), but the science education community must be aware of how pupils are growing up with ICT as a central part of their lives and with high expectations of its use in school. There is no doubt that schools and colleges have a responsibility to take this on board. The US are realising the increasing pace of development and its impact on young people: *'to achieve a 25 percent penetration rate in U.S. homes, it took 35 years for the telephone, 26 years for television, 16 years for personal computers, seven years for the Internet, and three years for personal digital assistants (PDAs)'* (Daggett, 2005). Concern about the polarisation of society is an issue, as some people lack access to ICT; as teachers, we have to be careful not to exacerbate this situation. In the context of a changing society, we will be failing our young people if we ignore the trend towards digital technologies, but this should not be the only force driving us. We have to look at the learning gains to be achieved to justify the investment in cost, impact on time, implications for training and social effects resulting from the full adoption of ICT.

In science education many moves to integrate ICT have already taken place. The first UK government initiative in 1981 had the aim of providing 'one computer for every school' (Baker, 1993). The DfES can claim significant success in the provision of hardware in schools, though this is often centrally deployed in secondary schools and not subject based.

The ratio of computers to pupils has halved in the last ten years in secondary schools, from one computer per 4.9 pupils in 2004 to one computer per 10.0 pupils in 1994.

However, providing hardware alone has little impact; effective implementation also needs investment in planning, teaching activities and teacher training. This has been acknowledged to varying degrees and a number of initiatives have taken place over the last two decades to encourage the use of ICT. There is continued government support for BECTa (British Educational Communication Technology agency, see website), which promotes and encourages the use of ICT in schools and colleges. In addition, there have been 'numerous other government-backed programmes, totalling well over one billion pounds' (Wellington, 2003). Several independent organisations have been formed to promote and develop the use of ICT, including professional bodies (e.g. NAACE) and education and industry partnerships (e.g. European Education Partnership) (see websites). With all these initiatives, organisations and funding, it would appear that the picture of the use of ICT in school science ought to be rosy, but is it?

The real position of ICT in science

The use of ICT in science has increased over the last decade but there is concern over the detail of and depth of this use. Ten years ago the National Council for Educational Technology (NCET, now BECTa) reported 66 per cent of science teachers using ICT in their lessons, which sounded encouraging; however, further investigation revealed that only 11 per cent of teachers used ICT for more than three hours per year (Coleman et al., 1993). This seems to be a trend that is still prevalent in the classroom. Table 13.1 shows data from official surveys.

Table 13.1 **Use of ICT in schools** (DfES, 2003a).

	2002			2003		
	Substantial (%)	Some (%)	Little/none (%)	Substantial (%)	Some (%)	Little/none (%)
Science	33	61	6	41	54	4

However, for science teachers *'currently there is a significant gap between what is possible and what happens within most classrooms'* (Denby and Holman, 2002).

It is clear that the use of ICT in science is not as great as it might be. Reasons why this might be include: lack of time; lack of confidence, experience and training; lack of supportive organisational culture within the school; limited access to resources and timetabled use of dedicated ICT suites; unreliability of equipment and lack of adequate technical support (Hennessy and Osborne, 2003). Given these major constraints, science teachers need good reasons to invest the effort required to incorporate ICT into their lessons. So what are they?

Why should you use ICT in science lessons?

We could start from various points:

- **Vision** – a government aim, *'to fully embed ICT within subject teaching at all levels and establish England as a world leader in the use of ICT in subject teaching and learning'* (DfES, 2003b).
- **Entitlement** – the DfES Skills Strategy places ICT as *'a third basic skill alongside literacy and numeracy in our Skills for Life programme'* (DfES, 2003c).
- **Affordability** – as power and speed increase cost comes down, making technology affordable for schools: *'Suddenly, the scenario of every child in every school having a laptop seems a lot closer'* (Freedman, 2005).

But thinking about educational technology means thinking about education not technology. If ICT is to be used then it must prove itself to give true added value to the teaching and learning experience. Chapter 1 lays out arguments for including science in the curriculum. If it is to justify its place in modern science teaching, the use of ICT ought to be able to address all these purposes.

A test for effectiveness?

ICT can be used in many ways in the classroom. A useful way of categorising or indicating its effectiveness is to apply the following three criteria. ICT should:

- **support:** help pupils to achieve tasks;
- **enhance:** add value to tasks;
- **extend:** open up new tasks.

To use ICT effectively we need to have clear objectives, plan appropriate tasks and monitor the pupils' work, which is in essence good teaching. Table 13.2 indicates the range of activities teachers and pupils are involved with in science lessons and shows how ICT could be integrated into this work. It is important to consider how the particular application or software contributes to the learning process, adds value to this process or makes learning more accessible for the pupil. For the teacher, making professional duties easier, enhancing teaching, and developing skills and practice are all criteria to be considered when selecting ICT as a tool.

Table 13.2 **Uses of ICT in science.**

	Process	Activity	Use of ICT
For the pupil	Learn factual content. Understand how scientific ideas develop.	Find information about science. Find out about the ideas and work of scientists.	Searching and retrieving from a database or the Internet. Use simulations and animations to illustrate science processes. Use revision programmes.
	Plan and carry out experiments or investigations and use evidence.	Set up experiments. Collect data. Perform calculations. Draw graphs. Look for patterns in data. Test hypotheses – try out ideas.	Use data-logging systems in practical work. Tabulate results in a spreadsheet, calculate, and graph or chart. Use models to explore the effect of changing variables.
	Communicate and articulate ideas.	Write about experiments. Present ideas to others.	Use word processors to write accounts of experiments. Use the Internet and email to share ideas and build on the experience of others. Use presentation software to explore and demonstrate ideas. Use authoring tools to prepare on-line or interactive reports. Use digital video authoring to present ideas innovatively.
For the teacher	Prepare teaching materials.	Write worksheets. Produce teaching sequences.	Use word processors to prepare materials. Use authoring tools to prepare on-line or interactive resources.
	Update knowledge.	Find out current information about science.	Use the Internet. Keep up to date about the newest science content software.
	Access information about teaching and schools.	Find research, National Curriculum, government strategies, Ofsted findings, etc.	Use the Internet.
	Communicate.	Communicate with teachers, students, parents and scientists.	Use email and conferencing. Use presentation software and hardware (e.g. interactive whiteboard) to demonstrate ideas.
	Organise data.	Collate marks, assessment.	Use spreadsheets and databases.

Activities and benefits

The following sections give examples of how ICT might be applied to particular teaching and learning activities to indicate the benefits that can be gained.

Teaching photosynthesis

The activity outlined in Box 13.1 is adapted from one on the DfES Standards site (see websites). It is one of five 'ICT supporting science' lessons, produced in collaboration with ASE.

Box 13.1

Photosynthesis simulation

ICT used
Simulation software, spreadsheets.

What is this lesson sequence about?
A challenging topic both conceptually and practically, photosynthesis lends itself to an ICT-based approach. Don't lose the 'magic' of the lesson with an over-sterile approach. Use ICT in balance with first-hand practical activities to maximise

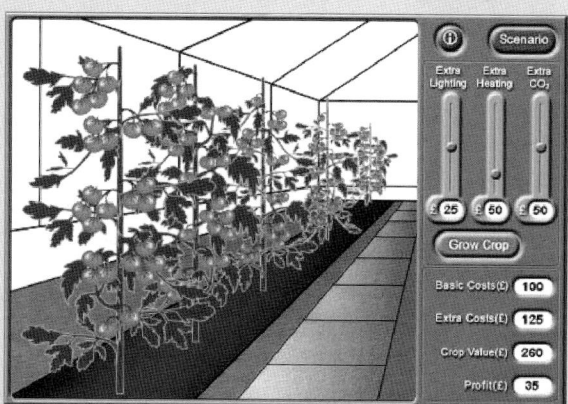

Figure 13.1 **Screen shot from photosynthesis simulation** (Multimedia Science School).

pupil engagement. As most teachers are aware, the real investigation can be difficult to do successfully, particularly at certain times of the year. This simulation/model allows pupils to carry out a reliable experiment, changing variables and measuring the amount of oxygen produced.

Aims
- To help pupils to review knowledge of the part played by carbon dioxide, light, heat and oxygen in the process of photosynthesis.
- To place the topic in an interesting and stimulating context.
  By carrying out a simulated investigation, pupils test their hypotheses of which factors affect the rate of photosynthesis. This is followed by application of the knowledge by using simulation of a commercial tomato-growing operation.

Lesson structure
- Whole–class discussion about factors affecting the rate of photosynthesis of *Elodea canadensis*. Pupils are asked to suggest their hypotheses.
- Working in pairs pupils select a variable to test and are shown the software.
- After preliminary trials and familiarisation, groups carry out more systematic investigations, thinking about the reliability of their experiment. They consider sampling size and experiment duration and appreciate when to repeat sets of measurements. The initial exploratory activity provides a valuable opportunity for pupils to refine their thinking and understanding of the topic.

Subsequent lesson
Pupils are set the task of running a commercial tomato-growing operation using a software simulation (Figure 13.1). Pupil engagement is high in this activity, partly due to the competitive element of maximising profit but mainly through setting the topic in a realistic context. This allows pupils to demonstrate their knowledge through application rather than more traditional recall of information.

Why use ICT here?

The importance of the lesson in Box 13.1, as compared to the normal one carried out in the laboratory, is that pupils will be able to use ICT to see clearly the effect that changing variables, such as light intensity or temperature, has on the production of oxygen, without being misled or confused by the inadequacies of the 'real' apparatus. Simulations or models should not be used instead of real experiments. Pupils should still have opportunities to 'get their hands dirty', carrying out real experiments, but *sometimes* ICT can help cement scientific concepts in pupils' minds, without the encumbrance of difficult-to-handle apparatus or the vagaries of living organisms. The ability to explore the effects of changing variables, repeat measurements and obtain reliable data are all important contributory factors to effective teaching in this situation.

Teaching about the solar system

The activity in Box 13.2 is part of the DfES-funded 'Enhancing subject teaching with ICT' project (see Science Consortium Online CPD website).

Box 13.2

Solar system

ICT used

Presentation software, the Internet, word-processor, desktop-publishing software.

What is the lesson about?

Obvious problems with practical approaches make ICT an ideal choice to bring this topic alive. Setting the lesson around the context of colonisation in the future ensures that information is not just regurgitated by pupils but used selectively and for a purpose.

Figure 13.2 **Slide from the lesson starter presentation.**

Lesson structure

- Starts with an on-screen presentation to the class which suggests that, by 2052, the Earth will be over-populated (Figure 13.2), be plagued by global warming, etc., which gives a context to the proposed colonisation of other planets.

- Working in groups, pupils use various information sources, including the Internet, to research the data about other planets. They are given a list of suggested websites to visit using an electronic worksheet, and a data-sheet to fill in.

- Teacher then leads an active teaching session, establishing a consensus view of the most important criteria for colonisation.

- Finally, groups present their evidence to the class, with information about the utilisation of their planet, using ICT for their presentation where appropriate, in the form of on-screen (e.g. *PowerPoint*), web-publishing or poster display.

Why use ICT here?

Of course, many teachers will have carried out a project like the one in Box 13.2 without using ICT. However, using ICT will give added motivation to the pupils, particularly up-to-date data and images from well-planned and selective use of the Internet.

Many pupils benefit from (and enjoy) the collaborative creation and delivering of presentations. This process of articulating understanding both generates and demonstrates real learning and knowledge acquisition in addition to wider skills, such as communication.

The initial stimulus of the starter activity is an important element of the lesson, capturing the attention and imagination of the pupils, encouraging them into role and setting the context of the lesson on future demands on world resources. The presentation can easily be adapted to meet the needs of different groups of pupils or to update the content as new information emerges.

The use of an electronic worksheet (e.g. Microsoft *Word* document) with embedded hyperlinks to websites acts as an instruction sheet and channels pupils' use of the Internet so that they reach the sites easily, without having to type addresses into a Web browser, and so that they visit sites with reliable and relevant information.

Teaching energy

Box 13.3 describes an investigation of conservation of energy.

Box 13.3

Loop the loop

ICT used

Interactive whiteboard, data-logger sensors and software.

What is the lesson about?

This activity enriched an energy and movement topic following a year-group trip to a theme park, which provided a context to investigate conservation of energy.

Figure 13.3 **Looping the loop**

Lesson structure

- Starts off with a brief video of a white-knuckle ride on the whiteboard, enabling key questions to be asked about the ability to complete a 'loop-the-loop' (Figure 13.3).
- Common answers such as speed, height and the steepness of the loop can then be investigated with a simple loop constructed from curtain track. A light gate clamped just above the track measures the speed of a ball-bearing on the track.
- By entering the diameter of the ball in the software, the speed of the ball can be displayed.
- Pupils can use these data in further calculations, for example estimating how high the ball should travel up the loop using potential and kinetic energy equations.

Why use ICT here?

ICT adds to the investigation in Box 13.3 in many ways, such as: the speed of collecting data enabling repeat measurements; immediacy of display of the results; flexibility of the software enabling calculation of new quantities (kinetic energy, for example). In addition, there is enhanced opportunity for discussion, enabling pupils to make suggestions for improving the investigation, trying out new measurements and developing understanding through real-time interaction, all of which add value to the investigation.

The teacher and ICT: developing professional practice

In our work with initial teacher training students over the last decade, we have seen a dramatic increase in the personal ICT capability of incoming trainees. This capability is rarely, however, translated into classroom use of ICT, and pedagogic input is just as relevant now as it was at the dawn of the ICT age. The Government has addressed this with New Opportunities Fund (NOF) ICT training for subject teachers in all maintained schools in the UK. As ever, sustaining the initiative is often more difficult than initiating it. Being connected with a community of practice will become more and more important for keeping up to date with initiatives, projects, directives and subject knowledge. Teachers can keep informed of Ofsted evidence and current educational research by visiting numerous websites where reports are regularly published.

The Web is also an endless source of teaching materials, from recognised projects to teachers' home-grown websites with their own lesson ideas, worksheets and pupil materials. The principle of sharing ideas and materials across the community is clearly a powerful tool, which should be exploited by the science education community. Quality will be variable but the important aspect of this for teachers is the principle of working together.

Every teacher has his or her own list of favourite sites and it is unlikely that there will ever be one source of material for science teachers, but a list of useful sites is included at the end of this chapter. The development of intelligent Web applications and search engines will make linking between sites more seamless and enhance the experience for the user, but perhaps will never replace word-of-mouth recommendations of resources by fellow teachers!

References

Baker, K. (1993) *The turbulent years: my life in politics*. London: Faber & Faber.

Coleman, M., Hemsley, K., Martin, J. and Wardle, J. (1993) *Evaluation of ICT in science*. Coventry: National Council for Educational Technology.

Daggett, W. R. (2005) *Technology 2008: preparing students for our changing world*. International Center for Leadership in Education. Available on: http://www.daggett.com/pdf/Technology%20White%20Paper.pdf

Denby, D. and Holman, J. (2002) *ICT in support of science education: a practical user's guide*. York: York Publishing Services.

DfES (2003a) *Survey of information and communications technology in schools 2003*. Available on: http://www.dfes.gov.uk/rsgateway/DB/SBU/b000421/bweb05-2003.pdf

DfES (2003b) *Fulfilling the potential, transforming teaching and learning*. Available on: http://www.teachernet.gov.uk/wholeschool/ictis/ict_teaching/

DfES (2003c) Skills Strategy (White Paper) *Realising our potential*. Available on: http://www.dfes.gov.uk/skillsstrategy/_pdfs/whitePaper_PDFID4.pdf

DfES (2005) *Harnessing technology: transforming learning and children's services*. Available on: http://www.dfes.gov.uk/publications/e-strategy/

Freedman, T. (2005) *Managing e-learning and ICT.* Available on: http://www.terry-freedman.org.uk/artman/publish/article_271.shtml

Hennessy, S. and Osborne, J. (2003) *Literature review in science education and the role of ICT: promise, problems and future directions.* Bristol: NESTA Futurelab.

Meeker, M., Pitz, B., Dorr, B. and Srinivasan, R. (2004) *An update from the digital world.* Available on MorganStanley website: http://www.morganstanley.com/institutional/techresearch/pdfs/dw_syndication1004.pdf

Wellington, J. J. (2003) Has ICT in science teaching come of age? *School Science Review,* **84**(309), 39. Available on: http://www.ase.org.uk/htm/journals/ssr/pdf/ssr_2003_june_pg39.pdf

Useful website addresses

Association for Science Education: http://www.ase.org.uk

British Educational Communication Technology agency (BECTa): http://www.becta.org.uk

DfES Standards site: http://www.standards.dfes.gov.uk/keystage3/respub/sc_ict

European Education Partnership: http://www.eep-edu.org/

NAACE: http://www.naace.org.uk

National Grid for Learning: http://vtc.ngfl.gov.uk

Science Consortium Online CPD: http://www.cpd4science.co.uk

TeacherNet, ICT in Schools Division: http://www.teachernet.gov.uk/wholeschool/ictis/

Chapter 14

Health and safety in science education

Teachers are concerned to avoid injury to pupils, colleagues and themselves. They may be anxious that they could get in trouble with the law. Such fears are largely unjustified because science education is very safe. This chapter is not very different from that in the previous edition of the *ASE Guide* because the law does not change very much, and nor do the few accidents that happen in science lessons. It does, however, discuss risk assessment in greater detail and consider ways of recording safety information for daily use and for monitoring the training of staff. Teaching safely is not the same as teaching safety and science teachers can contribute to preparing pupils for the risks outside school.

Peter Borrows

Why be concerned with health and safety?

Science education is very safe. Only two per cent of the accidents to pupils reported to the Health and Safety Executive (HSE) in Great Britain occur in science lessons and less than half of those result in any injury. Some examples of accidents are given here but many more have been published (ASE, 2000). Teachers sometimes use health and safety as an excuse for avoiding practical work when the real reasons are an overcrowded curriculum, limited training, a lack of adequate preparation time, poor resources or insufficient technical support.

There are two types of law in the UK – the criminal law and the civil law. The *Health and Safety at Work Act 1974* (HSW Act) is the main legislation, although it is very general. (It does not apply in Northern Ireland, which has very similar alternative legislation.) The HSW Act requires employees to:

● cooperate with their employer on health and safety matters;

- not interfere with equipment provided for health and safety;
- take reasonable care for their own safety and that of other people.

Under the umbrella of the Act governments have introduced regulations, which are more specific, such as the *Control of Substances Hazardous to Health (COSHH) Regulations* and the *Management of Health and Safety at Work Regulations*. For a serious breach of the Act or its regulations an inspector from the HSE can prosecute an individual or an organisation in the criminal courts. However, in over 30 years since the Act was implemented, only *three* teachers and *three* schools/local education authorities (and *no* technicians) have been successfully prosecuted for a science-related incident and these cases were quite out of the ordinary.

> A teacher had his class making gunpowder. As they were grinding the mixture, it exploded injuring two pupils. The teacher was prosecuted because he failed to exercise his duty of care. No safety precautions were in place – it was self-evidently a stupid thing to do.

If no prosecution takes place, an injured party (or parents on behalf of a child) can sue for damages in the civil courts, attempting to obtain compensation for alleged injuries. Going to court is expensive: it is never worthwhile suing a teacher or technician (or indeed a pupil!) because they are unlikely to be able to afford to pay your legal expenses as well as all the compensation you are hoping for. Complainants sue the employer because the employer will carry insurance. The standard of proof required is much less than in the criminal court. Hence insurance companies usually agree to settle out of court before the trial because that is the cheapest option – but usually this is without admitting liability.

> A sixth-former sued the education authority when he was injured trying to insert a pipette into a safety filler. The teacher was aware that it was important to hold the pipette near to its end and had trained the class accordingly. The judge decided that that the student had suffered a momentary lapse of attention. Damages of £7000 were not payable.

The purpose of the HSW Act is to protect employees, that is teachers, technicians, teaching assistants, cleaners, and so on. If pupils are also protected, that is a bonus. Recent HSE statistics do not allow an easy comparison but in 1991/2 there were 4676 reportable school accidents to pupils (about 0.9 per cent of those in science) and 3289 to school staff. As there are far more pupils than staff it is a matter of some concern that so many involve staff. Teachers must be alert to possible dangers facing technicians preparing or clearing up lessons, or transporting items to or from class. Technicians must warn teachers, and perhaps inform the head of department, if they consider a planned activity unsafe.

Risk assessment

Risk assessment is required by several regulations. In the UK it is the responsibility of the employer to carry out a risk assessment before:

- hazardous chemicals are used or made;

- hazardous microorganisms are used;
- hazardous activities are undertaken.

The employer is the person or body with whom the employee has a contract of employment, variously the local education authority, governing body, proprietor or trust according to the type of school. Although risk assessment is the employer's responsibility, the *task* of assessing the risks may be delegated to employees. However, the *responsibility* cannot be delegated. The employer should check that the employee is carrying out any delegated task competently, in accordance with policy and training. A manager, for instance the head of science, will need to monitor that teachers and technicians are implementing policies on risk assessment and other health and safety matters.

Risk assessment involves identifying hazards, estimating the risk from each hazard and then taking steps ('control measures') to reduce the risk to acceptable proportions.

> A pupil was injured when the bottle he was carrying back to his bench exploded. He had not thought it necessary to wear eye protection as he did not think he had yet started the experiment. If eye protection is necessary, it must be worn by pupils and staff from the time the first person starts until the last person has finished clearing up.

Hazards and risks

A **hazard** is anything with the potential to cause harm. Many chemicals are therefore hazardous, although in the case of solutions the hazard will depend on the concentration. Electricity at high currents is a hazard, as is carrying a tray of equipment through a crowded corridor.

The **risk** from a hazard depends on the:

- likelihood of something going wrong;
- severity of any likely injury;
- number of people affected.

Sodium metal is hazardous (it is CORROSIVE and FLAMMABLE) but the risk from it is small when it is locked in the chemical store. The risk increases when it is taken from the store, through crowded corridors, to the teaching laboratory. How great the risk is depends on who is doing what, with how much of it and adopting what safety precautions. You would not give 11-year-old pupils free use of a bottle of sodium but you might allow post-16 A-level students to use sodium after suitable training. Teaching staff would be allowed to demonstrate the action of sodium on water, but a head of department might expect some hands-on training for inexperienced or non-specialist staff. The hazard in all these cases is the same, but the risk from it (and hence the control measures) varies according to the situation.

Managing risk assessment

Specific guidance for education from the HSC (HSC, 1989) and more general guidance in its *Approved code of practice* (HSE, 2000) encourage employers to adopt nationally available publications as 'model' ('general', 'generic') risk assessments. Those commonly adopted are listed under 'Further reading' at the end of this chapter. It is assumed that this is the approach required by most employers although some do not make their policies clear. If in doubt, science departments are advised to follow the guidance here but to inform the employer that this is what they are doing.

There are two aspects to risk assessment:

- a thinking process;
- subsequent record-keeping.

As far as the thinking process is concerned, science departments should systematically review their courses and the activities that technicians routinely carry out, identifying all significant hazards. If staff are unsure whether there is a recognised hazard, they should be able to find guidance in model risk assessments. These will also identify whether the activity is generally considered acceptable and what control measures, if any, need to be adopted. However, **this is not enough**: the science department then needs to consider whether the model assessment can be used as it stands or whether some adaptation is necessary to meet the special circumstances of the school or particular classes or rooms. For example, the model may suggest a particular activity is suitable for year 9 pupils but the school might decide that its year 9 pupils are insufficiently mature to be trusted. Similarly, the model might suggest an activity is safe if no more than 1 g of a certain substance is used. In such cases, higher-attaining sets might weigh out their own materials but lower-attaining groups might have them pre-weighed by technicians. A teacher will need to know whether there are any pupils in the class with asthma or allergies that need to be taken into account. The presence of pupils with special educational needs may necessitate some modification of the risk assessment. For example, those with visual impairment or motor control difficulties may need to wear face shields rather than safety spectacles. If there are pupils in the class with serious behavioural problems it may be impossible to carry out some activities safely – this is part of the risk assessment.

UK law requires that the 'significant findings' of risk assessment be recorded but does not prescribe any particular way of doing so; nor does it require that the working by which those conclusions were determined be shown. Completion of risk assessment forms is common in industry or higher education, often with numerical values attached to the level of risk. Such forms may have a role in schools when recording risk assessments for handling pesticides by grounds maintenance staff, but they are not well suited to the complex range of activities in school science (Tawney, 1992). Most schools have detailed documents that describe on a week-by-week basis what the teacher is expected to teach. These may be the school's own word-processed scheme of work or a commercially published collection of lesson plans, and are in daily use. **This is the best place to put important safety information.** Neat risk assessment forms tucked away in a filing cabinet will not be read by the busy teacher or technician. An outline of the proposed lesson *will* be read by the busy teacher and the equipment list *will* be consulted by the technician. If the scheme of work has been produced in-house then it is a simple matter to include a health and safety box for each lesson or group of lessons. If it is a published scheme then it is probably easiest to annotate the document, and highlight or underline particular comments. Some published schemes do include health and safety information but **the** school cannot rely on this being correct or compatible with the employer's model risk assessments. Even if correct, it may not be suitable for the conditions in the school. Inspectors from the HSE will be more impressed by a well-thumbed document showing signs of being altered over time than by a pristine risk assessment that nobody ever reads.

> A pupil was badly burned when his shirt was ignited by a candle in an experiment. The HSE initially prosecuted the school, arguing that the risk assessment had been inadequate, but they subsequently withdrew the prosecution when challenged. The school had provided safety rules for pupils and the class had recently done a 'spot the hazard' homework. Even so, it is important not to be complacent about the hazards of *all* naked flames.

Whilst many of the findings of risk assessment will be obvious ones, such as *'Corrosive, wear goggles'* or *'Remind pupils of the hazards of naked flames'*, some may be less obvious. For example, a lesson in which sodium is dropped in water might include the comment *'First-timers need hands-on training'* and the corresponding technicians' notes might say *'Inform the HoD if this is requested by those not on the approved list'*. There is plenty of published guidance about safe performance of this demonstration but staff will only consult it if they are aware of potential problems, flagged up in the scheme of work. When writing comments, it is necessary to consider what the inexperienced teacher needs to know.

Whilst the scheme of work and technician notes will draw attention to curriculum-related health and safety issues it is important to consider risk assessments for routine technician activities. These might cover areas such as:

- avoiding carrying trays of equipment through crowded corridors;
- ways of dealing with heavy fire doors;
- the desirability of not storing items above head height;
- using proper step ladders when reaching items which are at a high level;
- technicians working on their own;
- carrying heavy or bulky equipment up and down stairs.

Much will be common sense, but obliging and over-worked technicians, rushing to prepare one lesson after another, need to be protected from their own enthusiasm. Risks in and around the prep room need to be systematically assessed.

Sometimes a school may wish to carry out an activity for which it cannot find an appropriate model risk assessment. For example, a middle school may not have a fume cupboard but the activity might still be possible on a small scale or by containing the fumes in some way. Similarly, an A-level project may require chemicals or microorganisms not normally met in schools. A visit or activity off the school site will involve hazards not encountered on the premises (see Chapter 11). In all such circumstances a special risk assessment is required and again the employer should have specified how this is to be carried out. In most cases, this is likely to involve consulting CLEAPSS or, in Scotland, SSERC (contacts at end of chapter).

Once a scheme is in place there must be a strict understanding that no deviation can be allowed without going through a further risk assessment procedure. New ideas should be welcomed but first they must be checked against model risk assessments or, if necessary, a special risk assessment obtained.

Learning how to work safely

Teachers and technicians cannot be expected to know everything when they start in a job. There is anecdotal evidence to suggest that a disproportionate number of the serious accidents involve young teachers or new technicians in their first term or two. The *Management of Health and Safety at Work Regulations* require employers to provide adequate health and safety training when somebody is appointed to a job and if their job changes. In practice, much training is likely to be delegated to the science department.

If the department has a good, **up-to-date health and safety policy** this can provide part of the focus. Whether or not required by the employer, it is a useful way of defining training needs since it is a document that gathers together all those decisions made over a period of time about which newcomers need to be informed, for example:

- how risk assessment is dealt with;
- the procedures for various types of emergency;
- policies on locking laboratories and security generally;
- what to do if pupil misbehaviour results in safety problems;
- rules for pupils;
- codes of practice for teachers;
- who does what and when they do it, including the induction of new staff.

Detailed guidance on the content of departmental safety policies can be found in various publications (Vincent and Borrows, 1992; CLEAPSS, 1998) and it also forms a central feature of courses on managing safety run by CLEAPSS, SSERC, ASE INSET Services and others.

> Two teachers, in neighbouring schools, passed hydrogen over hot copper oxide and ignited the excess hydrogen at a jet. In both cases the hydrogen exploded because excess air had not been flushed out. But only one teacher was prosecuted. Although safety screens and eye protection were available, he did not use them and pupils were injured. The other teacher was not prosecuted because there were no injuries. He used the protective equipment provided by his employer.

New members of staff, including experienced staff transferring from other schools, should be made fully aware of the health and safety policy and of the health and safety addenda to schemes of work in daily use, which flag up problems, cross-refer to sources of detailed advice and, where relevant, insist on the need for hands-on training. Heads of department need to monitor that the advice in texts in daily use and the departmental health and safety policy is actually implemented.

> A new teacher was keen to demonstrate some spectacular reactions. The technician drew his attention to warnings on the CLEAPSS *Hazcard* but the teacher went ahead anyway. An explosion occurred and the teacher was off work for more than two months. Teachers and technicians have a duty to follow guidance issued by their employers. They have a duty to warn each other about hazards.

Most newcomers are likely to need some hands-on training. A recent chemistry graduate has probably never made chlorine. Experienced teachers may be asked to teach topics outside their areas of expertise. A technician from an industrial background may be skilled at electronics but ignorant when handling chemicals. Teachers and technicians need to know what they can safely tackle and where they need training. Suitable warnings included in texts in daily use form part of the risk assessment for the activity. Checklists produced by CLEAPSS (2003; 2004) can be used to identify training needs.

Some training will be carried out informally, and some through the medium of departmental meetings. This might include an annual discussion about immediate remedial measures (basic first aid) or training for all staff on a procedure (e.g. sterile technique) to be introduced into the curriculum (see also Chapter 15).

Teaching safety

Teaching safely is not the same as teaching safety. The HSE has expressed concern at the high proportion of accidents happening to young people on work experience or in their first jobs. Teachers have been good at protecting children from the hazards at school but not so good at preparing them for the risks outside school. The attitude may be *'Follow these rules because I say so'*, with not enough teaching about the underlying reasons for those rules and why various control measures are necessary. A quick demonstration with a pig's eye and some concentrated sulfuric acid may be more effective than repeated exhortations to wear eye protection. The National Curriculum for England requires pupils to be taught about hazard, risk and risk assessment (QCA/DfEE, 1999) and there are similar requirements in the national curricula in Wales and Northern Ireland. Applied Science GCSE courses usually have very specific requirements for pupils to carry out risk assessment. The CLEAPSS *Student safety sheets* (CLEAPSS, 2005) may be helpful in this respect. Other ideas for teaching safety have also been published (SATIS, 1997; Borrows, Vincent and Cochrane, 1998).

References

ASE (2000) *Safety reprints*. Hatfield: Association for Science Education. (Updated every few years.)

Borrows, P., Vincent, R. and Cochrane, A. (1998) Teaching safety: using mole calculations to teach aspects of safety in post-16 chemistry. *School Science Review*, **79**(288), 67–70. Reprinted in ASE (2000), pp. h1–h4.

*CLEAPSS (1998) *Model science health and safety policy*. Guide L223. Uxbridge: CLEAPSS.

*CLEAPSS (2003) *Induction and training of science technicians*. Guide L234. Uxbridge: CLEAPSS.

*CLEAPSS (2004) *Health and safety induction and training of science teachers*. Guide L238. Uxbridge: CLEAPSS.

*CLEAPSS (2005) *Student safety sheets*. Uxbridge: CLEAPSS.

HSC (1989) *COSHH: Guidance for schools*. pp. 2–3. London: HMSO.

HSE (2000) *Management of health and safety at work: approved code of practice*. Sudbury: HSE Books.

QCA/DfEE (1999) *Science: the National Curriculum for England*. London: QCA/DfEE.

SATIS (1997) *The world of science*. London: John Murray.

Tawney, D. (1992) Assessment of risk and school science. *School Science Review*, **74**(267), 7–14. Reprinted in ASE (2000), pp. b20 – b27.

Vincent, R. and Borrows, P. (1992) Science department safety policies. *School Science Review*, **73**(264), 9–13. Reprinted in ASE (2000), pp. b6 – b10.

Further reading

Some or all of the following books are usually adopted by education employers as the basis for their model risk assessments:

ASE (2001) *Topics in safety*. 3rd edn. Hatfield: Association for Science Education.

ASE (2006) *Safeguards in the school laboratory*. 11th edn. Hatfield: Association for Science Education.

ASE (2000) *Safety reprints*. Hatfield: Association for Science Education. (Updated every few years as loose-leaf supplements and on ASE's website: www.ase.org.uk.)

*CLEAPSS (2004) *Hazcards*. Uxbridge: CLEAPSS School Science Service.

*CLEAPSS (2004) *Laboratory handbook*. Uxbridge: CLEAPSS School Science Service.

*CLEAPSS (2004) *Recipe cards*. Uxbridge: CLEAPSS School Science Service.

DfEE (1996) *Safety in science education*. London: HMSO. (Available on ASE website: www.ase.org.uk. There is a rolling programme of updating the chapters and these are on the members-only part of the website.)

*SSERC (2002) *Hazardous chemicals*. CD2. Edinburgh: SSERC.

For those carrying out risk assessment for project work, the following gives useful advice:
*SSERC (1991) *Preparing COSHH risk assessments for project work in schools*. Edinburgh: SSERC.

Up-to-date advice on current issues in health and safety will be found in the following journals:
ASE: *School Science Review* (quarterly).

ASE: *Education in Science* (5 times per year).

*CLEAPSS: *CLEAPSS Bulletin* (termly).

*SSERC: *SSERC Bulletin* (termly).

*Most CLEAPSS and SSERC publications, including those listed above, are available only to members but this includes almost all schools and colleges in the UK.

Useful contacts

For schools in England, Wales and Northern Ireland: CLEAPSS School Science Service, Brunel University, Uxbridge, UB8 3PH. Tel: 01895 251496; fax: 01895 814372; website: www.cleapss.org.uk; email: science@cleapss.org.uk

For schools in Scotland: SSERC, St Mary's Building, 23 Holyrood Road, Edinburgh EH8 8AE. Tel: 0131 558 8180; fax: 0131 558 8191; website: www.sserc.org.uk; email: sts@sserc.org.uk

Chapter 15

Support staff in science departments

Traditionally, technicians have been the support staff in science departments. Their role has been, | **Chris Peel** and **Kay Sample**

is, and will be essential in enabling teachers to provide safe and efficient science teaching, and they have often contributed administrative and technical support to other departments. The programme of school workforce reform recognises the value of support staff in fulfilling non-teaching roles and thus enabling teachers to devote themselves to teaching and learning. With workforce remodelling a wider range of support staff are being employed within science departments. This chapter considers separately the role of technicians and that of teaching assistants, concluding with a consideration of whole-department teamwork.

Science technicians

Why science technicians are needed
Science technicians have an essential role to play in current and future science education, providing expertise and skill not otherwise available. They contribute to health and safety and to economy and efficiency in the science department. Practical work is essential in the development of pupils' scientific understanding: it can increase their interest in science and contribute to improved examination results. Technicians enable teachers to teach varied and stimulating practical lessons to all pupils in an efficient and safe environment (House of Commons, 2002; Roberts, 2002).

What science technicians do
Science technicians' roles vary considerably from school to school. In general terms, however, they support the practical aspects of the science curriculum by

preparing, providing, maintaining, organising and managing the resources required for healthy, safe and secure, exciting practical activities to be carried out by staff and pupils. The Royal Society/ASE (2001) *Survey of science technicians in schools and colleges* discovered that most technicians' core activities were similar (Box 15.1). Many of the activities require specialist knowledge, including health and safety, and some demand considerable time.

Many schools expect their technicians to perform some or all of the non-technical tasks listed in Box 15.1; this helps save teachers a considerable amount

---

Box 15.1

The activities of technicians

Activities carried out regularly by most technicians
- making up solutions;
- assembling apparatus;
- delivering equipment to laboratories;
- collecting, checking and returning equipment to stores;
- disposing of waste materials;
- taking care of apparatus;
- carrying out and arranging for maintenance and repair of equipment;
- stocktaking;
- obtaining materials by local purchase;
- placing orders and checking deliveries or invoices.

Activities carried out by many technicians, often
- keeping financial records (usually performed by the most senior technician);
- general laboratory cleaning including sinks;
- caring for plants and/or animals;
- constructing and modifying apparatus;
- trialling practical activities;
- assessing risks for technician activities;
- helping and advising teachers (particularly trainee teachers and NQTs) on health and safety and technique;
- advising pupils;
- carrying out safety checks.

'Non-technical' tasks carried out by many technicians
- photocopying;
- checking textbooks;
- repairing books;
- issuing books and stationery;
- making off-air recordings;
- laminating, collating and binding;
- providing administrative support to other school departments.

of time, which is better devoted to teaching duties. However, schools should consider whether having technicians perform these activities will affect the technical delivery to the department and be detrimental to the health and safety of the technicians and the department as a whole. Within the workforce reform agenda, technicians' responsibilities may be reviewed and such tasks as photocopying allocated to administrative support staff.

Some technicians perform demonstrations in classes and/or help during practical lessons and with pupil project work. They view this as a rewarding part of their job, which they are happy to continue performing. This role has increased over recent years and it is likely that schools will want to develop it further in future. In this case, schools need to consider the number of extra technician hours required to meet the increased workload and the training needs of a classroom role (see 'Science technicians and teaching assistants' below).

How to get the best from science technicians

Teamwork

Technicians are essential members of a science department, who should be encouraged to attend department meetings and to contribute to departmental decisions. They can offer advice on health and safety, laboratory use, timetable issues, alternative procedures, refurbishment, and so on. Technicians can explain the importance of having an agreed policy on the advance notice technicians require to prepare practicals, and the importance of adhering to the agreed procedures. In turn, teachers can explain the importance of their equipment requirements being met accurately and on time.

Line management and supervision

Where, as is common, there is more than one science technician, it is appropriate to have a line-management structure amongst the technicians, with one technician designated as the senior. An efficient system requires a line manager within the department who is familiar with the day-to-day duties and responsibilities, usually a job for the head of science or another senior science teacher. This is not to say that all or most of the technicians' work is directly supervised by a head of science or other teaching staff. It is extremely important that technicians are competent to perform all the activities required, especially with the considerable health and safety aspects of their jobs. The team structure enables the technicians to take responsibility for organising all the practical side, so that the teachers can concentrate on teaching. Responsibilities encourage the technicians to feel more valued members of the science department team. Where new and/or inexperienced technicians are employed it is essential that they are supervised until they are deemed competent. The most senior technician usually achieves this by training and supervising in-house. A small school may be able to seek help from a local large school, possibly with science college status, where the most senior technician may have a community-training role to help local schools. Such a role may be a development in the near future.

Working conditions

Technicians will perform their duties more efficiently and safely if they have good working conditions, with clean prep rooms adequately heated, lit and ventilated for workers and visitors alike. It is becoming increasingly essential for them (like other school staff) to have access to computers in their prep rooms, in order to improve efficiency, access important information and maintain records. While there may be constraints in some existing accommodation, many schools are being refurbished. In refurbishment programmes, consideration should to be given to the prep room and the technicians' working environment, as well as to the laboratories.

Technicians' working hours must be adequate for them to perform the duties required, without the need for working unpaid overtime, and allowing them a reasonable work–life balance. Their actual starting and finishing times are usually arranged to meet the requirements of the department. However, strict times may not allow for busy periods. The Royal Society/ASE survey (2001) discovered that most technicians failed to take contractual breaks on a regular basis. They should be encouraged to take their breaks for reasons of efficiency and health and safety. Imaginative thinking by the departmental team is required to explore and create flexible arrangements and rota systems to meet the needs of the department and of the individuals.

Induction, training and CPD
Induction of all new and particularly inexperienced technicians is essential. An induction programme will enable technicians to become familiar with practices and procedures, but most important it will enable them to become competent in tasks required of them. Schools should appreciate that such a programme could take several months. Even experienced technicians need training and continuing professional development to update and refresh their knowledge and skills. This will not only benefit the technicians, but will also benefit the science department, and therefore the school, by increasing efficiency and motivation and by bringing new skills and knowledge into the departmental team. Not only are recognised training programmes and short courses important, but technicians (and therefore schools) will also greatly benefit from attending conferences and meetings of local and national technician groups. Notable are Association for Science Education Annual Conferences and National Technicians' Conferences where technicians can meet and share good practice, and get new ideas and tips. The national network of Science Learning Centres and other course providers offer a variety of opportunities for technician training (see also Chapters 6 and 14).

Appreciation of the role of science technicians
The skills and expertise of science technicians and their essential role in science education are not always appreciated by those outside the science department, as technicians spend a significant amount of their time in the prep room away from other colleagues. Some technicians and science departments feel that science technicians are less well regarded than other staff and that the school community views them as 'washers-up' or as administrative helpers for the science department seen only occasionally in the staff room or at the photocopier. Heads of science and other science teachers can make colleagues aware of the essential role of technicians so that they are treated as respected members of staff. Technicians should be invited to appropriate whole-staff

117

meetings so as to become informed about and involved in whole-school matters. At staff meetings, they will be able to contribute to debate and decisions; therefore they will be seen as valued members of school staff. They should be invited to social events and welcomed into the staff room during breaks. Technicians themselves should deliberately aim to become part of the whole school, visiting the staff room and participating in whole-school activities.

ASE support and career progression

The Association for Science Education has recommended a four-level career progression structure for science technicians in schools and colleges, linked to National Vocational Qualification (NVQ) levels, which schools and colleges are being urged to implement (ASE, 2004). ASE is also setting up and supporting a National Technicians' Centre (Techcen) as an approved centre for technicians to become involved in National Vocational Qualifications. The ASE Technicians' Committee can help with advice and give support on technician issues. Technicians can gain information and air their views through the ASE magazine *Education in Science*, which has a section entitled 'The Prep Room' dedicated to technicians. In addition to the many regional and local ASE events and meetings that technicians can attend, two major annual events, the National Technicians' Conference (July) and the ASE Annual Conference (January) provide opportunities for professional development in the widest sense. Technicians can discuss issues with other technicians, including the ASE Technicians' Committee, attend workshops, get information, visit the stands of various suppliers in the exhibition, and participate with teachers, advisers and others involved in science education.

Teaching assistants in science

What's in a name?

In the last few years the full potential of teaching assistants, who in the past have been employed mainly to support particular pupils with learning difficulties, has been recognised. The Government, through the local education authorities, is providing quality training which school senior management and individual departments are supporting. Therefore, in turn, classroom teachers are deploying teaching assistants more effectively to support pupils' learning.

The changes in the job title of 'teaching assistants' in school reflect their changing role over recent years. They have been referred to as special needs assistants, non-teaching assistants, learning support assistants and now teaching assistants (TAs). They have a changing part to play in whole-class learning. They are supporting the teacher in ensuring that *all* pupils make progress in their learning in science lessons. It is vital that a head of department or teacher of science takes a careful look at how they use this valuable resource to support their pupils. The responsibility for managing teaching assistants on a day-to-day basis has lain primarily with the head of inclusion or special needs coordinator (SENCo) and marginally with individual class teachers. However, recent moves to support the workforce reform agenda aim to make teaching assistants subject-specific. This increases the responsibility of science departments to consider their effective deployment and support for learning.

Box 15.2

Statements used in lesson judgements by Ofsted inspectors

Description of lesson	Characteristic shown
In lessons judged outstanding	Teaching assistants are well directed, and they reinforce and strongly support learning.
In lessons judged good	Teaching assistants are well deployed and make a significant contribution.
In lessons judged satisfactory	[Not mentioned – but may assume from previous judgements – teaching assistants provide little effective support to learning.]
In lessons judged not adequate	Inadequate use of teaching assistants to support learning.

The 2005 Ofsted framework for inspection recognises the valuable use of TAs to support pupils' learning (Ofsted, 2005). This is shown in the statements in Box 15.2, which are used by Ofsted inspectors as part of their lesson judgements. This is clear evidence that there is a responsibility for science teachers to manage the work of TAs.

Tasks that teaching assistants might carry out

The Key Stage 3 National Strategy document *Framework for teaching science: years 7, 8 and 9* (DfES, 2002, pp. 62–63) stresses the key role of teaching assistants in *'helping some pupils to work as independently as possible in science lessons'*. It lists some of the tasks that they might carry out, as:

- helping pupils to assemble and use equipment safely;
- making sure pupils interpret and follow instructions;
- reminding pupils of previous lessons and links;
- questioning pupils and encouraging their participation;
- evaluating responses, looking for strengths and weaknesses;
- supporting pupils' learning through the use of resources such as word lists, visual aids and models.

Support for teaching assistants in science

In order for teaching assistants to be able to support pupils' learning in science, there is a departmental responsibility to develop their skills and subject knowledge. Although TAs should not take over a teacher's role, many of the skills listed above are those that are developed by teachers. TAs need informal day-to-day training and specific focused training. Sources of support are:

- The DfES, through local education authorities, is providing induction training for teaching assistants in secondary schools, with a specific module for science (DfES, 2004), which includes improving pupils' understanding in science.

- Many local authorities are providing, through the Key Stage 3/Secondary National Strategy, training for teaching assistants in science. This focuses on knowledge and understanding in the Key Ideas and Scientific Enquiry, and on developing a toolkit for supporting science.
- The Key Stage 3 National Strategy document *Framework for teaching science: years 7, 8 and 9* has a section on the use of teaching assistants.

Career development for teaching assistants

The educational background of teaching assistants is very diverse and there are a variety of routes to career development. Science departments need to be aware of these and of the courses their teaching assistants may be following, as there may be implications for supporting the process.

The national accredited training through NVQ levels 2 and 3 is generic classroom training and requires a portfolio of pupil observations. When studying towards the Higher Level Teaching Assistant (HLTA) qualification there is a requirement to have whole-class teaching experience in parts of lessons and to contribute to lesson planning with teachers. This can then lead some HLTAs to follow the Qualified Teacher Status route. In the near future there are expected to be new HLTA courses that are subject-specific, science being one (see website). Each of these courses requires teaching assistants to complete class-based research. The teaching assistants themselves will benefit from class teachers' support in this work, which, in turn, could be of use to the department.

How can science departments support their teaching assistants?

Science departments should aim to:

- provide the TAs with a scheme of work, key words, glossary, and lesson plans;
- provide planning time individually or as a group;
- ensure both teachers and TAs are clear about their roles and responsibilities within each class and within the ethos of the department;
- help the TAs feel part of the team;
- include TAs in departmental meetings and in-service training;
- provide training on the safe use and handling of equipment;
- provide TAs with the knowledge and understanding to be able to identify and correct pupils' misconceptions;

and agree that teachers will:

- ensure pupils know that TAs are part of the science staff;
- ensure TAs are aware of the learning objectives and expectations for the lessons in advance as they may wish to develop resources to support certain pupils;
- ensure TAs are familiar with the equipment and its safe use;
- encourage the TA to be responsible for assessing the learning for their targeted group;
- ensure time for feedback on pupils' learning after lessons;
- provide answer sheets to specific focused questions or work.

A useful and extensive checklist of support needed by teaching assistants in science, paying special attention to health and safety training, has been produced by the ASE Safeguards in Science Committee (2004).

Whole department teamwork

Science technicians and teaching assistants

Science technicians may be required to support pupils in the classroom but their role would be related to their specialist experience, knowledge and skills in health and safety, as well as practical techniques in practical science lessons. This is different from the role of teaching assistants. The temptation to use science technicians as TAs to save money should be resisted. Science departments need to make senior managers appreciate that a TA's role is different from that of technicians helping in classes and they should reinforce their need for the same TA support as non-technical departments. If schools insist on using technicians as TAs then contracts should be renegotiated and schools will need to employ more technicians to perform any neglected technical and health and safety duties, and provide the appropriate TA training to technicians. Technicians will, of course, collaborate with science TAs, for example in advising them on health and safety as they do for trainee teachers and NQTs. In addition to technicians and TAs supporting pupils, science departments should have dedicated support to carry out routine administrative and clerical work. If these tasks are done by the technicians or classroom TAs, time must be allocated accordingly.

Optimising the contribution of support staff

It is essential for a happy, cooperative and successful science department that all staff know their own roles and responsibilities and contribute these to the team. This becomes crucial when new personnel, such as TAs, are added to the existing support structure traditionally provided by technicians. Inclusion in departmental meetings, in-service training and social events has been mentioned above, and fostering respect amongst pupils for all members of the team is vital. In capitalising on the enthusiasm of a new TA or the expertise of a long-established technician, it is important that nobody in the school community regards them as just an extra pair of hands, but rather as a valued part of the team and an integral partner in the pupils' learning experiences.

References and further reading

Technicians

ASE (2004) *A career structure for science technicians in schools and colleges.* Hatfield: Association for Science Education. (A copy of this leaflet has been sent to every secondary school in England. It is also available on CLEAPSS and ASE websites.)

ASE (five times a year) The prep room. In *Education in Science,* ASE members' magazine. Hatfield: Association for Science Education.

CLEAPSS (2002) *Technicians and their jobs.* Guide L228. Uxbridge: CLEAPPS. Available to members from CLEAPSS website: www.cleapss.org.uk/secfr.htm

CLEAPSS (2003) *Induction and training of science technicians.* Guide L234. Uxbridge: CLEAPSS.

House of Commons Select Committee on Science and Technology (2002) *Science education from 14 to 19. Third report of session 2001–02. Volume 1, Report and proceedings of the Committee.* London: The Stationery Office.

Roberts, G. (2002) *SET for success: the supply of people with science, technology, engineering and mathematics skills.* London: HM Treasury. Available on: www.hm-treasury.gov.uk

Royal Society/ASE (2001) *Survey of science technicians in schools and colleges.* London: The Royal Society.

Royal Society/ASE (2002) *Supporting success: science technicians in schools and colleges.* London: The Royal Society.

Teaching assistants

ASE Safeguards in Science Committee (2004) Health and safety training for teaching assistants working in science in secondary schools. *Education in Science*, **208**, 22–23.

DfES (2002) *Framework for teaching science: years 7, 8 and 9.* London: Department for Education and Skills. Available on: http://www.standards.dfes.gov.uk/keystage3/respub/scienceframework/sc_fwkdl/

DfES (2004) *Induction training for teaching assistants in secondary science: Science module.* DfES/0584/2004. London: Department for Education and Skills.

Fox, G. (1998) *Handbook for learning support assistants.* London: David Fulton.

Ofsted (Office for Standards in Education) (2005) *Framework 2005: Inspecting schools.* London: Ofsted.

Websites

Association for Science Education: www.ase.org.uk
CLEAPSS School Science Service: www.cleapss.org.uk
Higher Level Teaching Assistant: www.hlta.gov.uk
Key Stage 3 National Strategy: http://www.standards.dfes.gov.uk/keystage3/respub/scienceframework/science_at_ks3/5_

Section 3 Classroom
level:
Planning and
implementing

Chapter 16   Planning with goals in mind

The key to effective student learning is good lesson planning. This depends on being clear about the learning objectives for the lesson and bearing these in mind through the planning. This chapter discusses lesson planning in the contexts of the notion of curriculum objectives and of the external goals imposed on schools. It exemplifies some of the aspects to be considered in planning lessons and refers to chapters that consider some of them in more detail.

Jenny Versey

Curriculum objectives

> If curriculum planning is a matter of planning the means to specified ends ... the clearer we are about those ends and their nature the more adequate the planning can be. ... We must analyse these ends down to particular achievements we wish pupils to reach. (Hirst, 1974, p. 16)

> The planning of the curriculum, or any part of it, is a logical nonsense until the objectives being aimed at are made clear. (Hirst and Peters, 1970, p. 60)

Nowadays we are very familiar with objectives and targets in every aspect of life, so we may find these 30-year-old comments unremarkable, though their emphasis is as important as ever. The science curriculum has long been planned with broad aims, often as means to ends, social and political, as well as for the benefit of individual pupils (see Chapter 3). By the middle of the twentieth century, interest focused on more specific objectives, for small units of the curriculum and for individuals and groups of pupils. Particularly in the United States, educationists advocated behavioural objectives, that is, every desired outcome should be expressed in 'action' verbs that would provide evidence of what the learner could do at the end of the piece of learning. This movement was criticised by many, especially in the UK (Macdonald-Ross, 1973), as being too atomistic and mechanistic. In 1989, the introduction of the National Curriculum in England and Wales, with its attainment targets expressed as objectives, brought the matter out of academic argument and into everyday reality for all teachers. Later versions of the National Curriculum for Science have pushed the attainment targets to the back of the book, the bulk of it being made up of the programmes of study, which state what *'pupils should be taught'* rather than objectives of what they should learn. The Key Stage 3 Strategy (see Chapter 9) emphasised the importance of having clear objectives for each lesson and sharing these with the pupils.

Schemes of work

A science department will have an overview of what needs to be taught and when. Overall goals are set in this scheme of work, usually influenced by the requirements of a national curriculum, and by the specifications of awarding bodies. These external agents specify all the skills and content that should be taught by law (for the national curriculum) or to enable pupils to gain accreditation by external examinations. There are many potential ways to organise the content to deliver these specifications and schools usually follow advice from a national curriculum authority (e.g. QCA in England) or relevant awarding body. These specify suitable divisions of the content into appropriate units, each unit having an overview of content and skills to be taught; and often with specific learning objectives suggested for individual lessons. There are no rules that say you *only* have to teach what is specified by the national curriculum and awarding bodies, so long as you 'cover' what is required by law. There is considerable freedom to use new contexts and information to help engage pupils' interest in, and develop knowledge of, science. Moreover, in the UK, there are no rules to say how you teach or how you ensure that pupils learn.

Some science departments adopt a published text scheme as a basis for their scheme of work. Many publishers sell a complete course with ready-made lesson plans for teachers to pick up and use, along with pupil texts for each year of the course. Although these can be helpful as a starting point they do not replace your own lesson plans. Textbook ideas should always be questioned: *Is this challenging enough for* **my** *class and* **my** *students?*; *What other strategies and ideas can I use to motivate and engage my class?*

Planning for a successful lesson

The key to effective learning by pupils is good lesson planning. Teachers need to plan their *own* lessons carefully. Every class and every pupil, and mix of pupils, is unique. Every teacher is also unique. New ideas to support pupils' learning emerge from research, from new initiatives, from colleagues and from experience, on which to develop one's own strengths. Too frequently, lesson planning begins *and ends* with what content will be 'delivered' or the next double-page spread in the textbook. This can lead to lack of differentiation and low-level work that is not challenging enough and does not lead to significant progress. A successful lesson is one in which all pupils have been fully engaged in learning and have demonstrably made some progress. A successful lesson depends on planning, however brief, that considers the following questions:

● What new knowledge or skill am I aiming to develop or consolidate – the *learning objective(s)*?

● Which activities will most effectively ensure that *all* learners are engaged, interested and making progress?

- How will I structure my lesson to make the best use of everyone's time and ensure the best learning outcomes for all learners?
- What resources will I need to support these activities?
- How will I know whether the learners have learned what I intended – in other words, how will I assess what they have learned?

Learning objectives and learning outcomes

Over time and by different educators these terms have been applied in various ways. In this chapter we use them as follows:

- The **learning objective** is a statement about what skills and knowledge the teacher wants the students to learn by the end of this lesson.
- The **learning outcome** is what students actually can do or demonstrate as a result of teaching, which they may not have been able to do before.

Learning outcomes may differ from one student to the next according to ability, interest or work rate. There will usually be a minimum outcome that everyone in the class should achieve; but the teacher also needs to consider what the more able students in each group might achieve. These form the *intended* or *expected learning outcomes* for each group (see Box 16.1).

To decide on learning objectives for a lesson, you need to know:

- the appropriate level of challenge for the class. What is the average level at which to target the learning objectives?
- the range of expected outcomes in the class. Will some pupils be able to exceed the general objective? Will some pupils only be able to reach the learning objective with extra support – and what support would be best?

Box 16.1

Sue's lesson objectives

Class: **Year 8**

Topic: **Refraction of light**

Learning objectives:

- To **know** that light changes direction at the boundary between two media.
- To **understand** that light bends towards the normal when entering a more dense medium.
- To **identify the pattern** of behaviour of the light.

(Expected) learning outcomes:

- All **must** measure 3 readings of angles of incidence and refraction and describe a change in direction.
- Most **should** measure 5 readings and describe a pattern of relationship between the angles.
- Some **could** draw a graph; predict next reading; measure angle of rays leaving the block as well as entering.

Judging the level of challenge for the class referred to in Box 16.1, Sue decided not to include graphing or predicting as lesson objectives for the whole class, nor to expect them all to consider light leaving a denser medium. The range of expected learning outcomes helped Sue to differentiate her planning, with an idea of the questions and activities she would use with various individuals and groups to achieve the desired outcomes.

A pitfall of stratified expected learning outcomes is the danger of 'labelling' pupils and the self-fulfilling prophecy. If Sue has a fixed opinion of who is in each of the outcome groups, she may, for example, neglect to extend some average students and not prompt them about predictions.

If the class is set by ability, there will be a narrower range of expected pupil outcomes than in a class of wide mixed-ability range. Nevertheless, it is still useful to know what progress to expect as a minimum and as a maximum from the lesson and set the appropriate level of challenge for the class.

The appropriate level and range of challenge

Teachers may need support in setting learning objectives at an appropriate level and find it useful to check against published documents. The QCA materials *Assessing progress in science* (see website) exemplify different levels for most of the themes and skills in science at key stage 3. For key stage 4, the GCSE specifications give grade criteria. New teachers will probably find learning objectives specified for them in the department's scheme of work or book scheme, but even so they need to consider their specific learning intentions for their particular pupils in their particular lesson.

Depending on the make-up of the group, the teacher may want to vary the expected levels of outcome and the way that he/she presents the content to the pupils. For some pupils with special needs, the teacher may need to set objectives in small steps and intended learning outcomes at low levels. He/she needs to plan very specific support to ensure that the pupils have access to the learning at their own appropriate level.

Knowledge of content and understanding of concepts is only one aspect to be taught. Scientific enquiry skills should underpin science learning. In some lessons the objectives are to develop specific procedures of scientific enquiry. (This is discussed in detail in Chapter 25.) In others, although practical work is undertaken and some skill development may occur incidentally, it is not the main purpose of the lesson to be expressed and assessed as objectives. In the exemplar lesson in Box 16.1, Sue decided to focus on the learning of one procedural skill: identifying and describing patterns in data. She planned that, through the recognition of the pattern, the knowledge and understanding could be achieved. Observation, measurement and tabulation were steps towards this, but learning these skills were not the objectives of the exercise.

Pupils use other skills in science, such as literacy, numeracy, ICT and social skills, the level of which may help or hinder science understanding. Teachers need to consider their objectives in these areas and plan strategies to achieve them. Although incidental improvement in basic skills may be a by-product of any lesson, it is useful to focus on one or two such objectives in certain lessons. This should help in planning supporting strategies such as the use of modelling and demonstrating, dictionaries, computer applications, writing frames and teaching assistant support. By displaying the objectives in areas beyond content knowledge, the teacher makes explicit to the pupils the importance of such aspects to and through science.

Planning a variety of teaching and learning styles

The importance of varying teaching and learning styles is detailed in Chapters 17 and 18. Box 16.2 summarises some points of variety to consider when planning.

Box 16.2

Points to consider about teaching and learning styles

When you want someone to learn something you need to:

- **bombard all the senses**: show visual models and write new words rather than just explaining, include practical science, or other active tasks like card sorts or drama;

- **model** how to do it, whether it is practical or written, so give yourself time for this;

- **plan to challenge** the more able pupils in your lesson with opportunities for higher-order thinking skills;

- **build in choice** for pupils, of presentation formats, of routes to follow, of guided alternatives in investigations;

- **consider a variety of contexts**, cultural, historical, and to suit both boys or girls.

Planning to get feedback on achievement of objectives

The Key Stage 3 / Secondary National Strategy (see Chapter 9) has promoted the idea of sharing learning objectives with pupils. It is quite common to see learning objectives displayed at the beginning of every lesson as a reminder to both the teacher and the pupils of the key goals for that lesson. Many teachers ask their pupils routinely to copy the objectives into their books at the start of each lesson (often used as a calming tactic). The downside of this is that it can become ritualised; the displayed objectives are of little value unless the pupils are made aware of what they mean, and unless they are revisited towards the end of the lesson to check whether they have been achieved. A teacher should always plan how he/she can get feedback from the pupils on what they have learnt, which serves for both summary and assessment (see also Chapter 22). There are three main routes to follow, as given below.

Create questioning opportunities

Create questioning opportunities in your lesson plans, both whole-class and individual. Carefully plan key questions that will be used as assessment opportunities, but, of course, you will also use many impromptu questions. When devising whole-class questioning, consider whether you will get feedback from just one pupil or from all. Don't always take the first 'hands-up' answer or

Box 16.3
A framework for planning

Learning objectives: Consider your overall learning objectives, both for knowledge/understanding and for skill development.

Learning outcomes: Consider what outcomes you will expect to see/assess.
Must: This is what everybody must be able to do or state/write by the end of the lesson.
Should: This is what most pupils should do or state/write unaided; but a few will need extra support.
Could: This is what the more able pupils should be able to do, state or write.

Planning required	Teacher activity	Pupil activity
	*Plan what **you** should be doing.*	*Plan what **the pupils** should be doing – this helps to make lessons more active and less boring than too much teacher talk!*
Settling activity (5 mins) Prepare something quiet for the pupils to do as they enter.	Written question/brainstorm, prepared on board or hand-outs – this gives you time to settle latecomers, do the register, etc. Learning objectives and key words on board.	Pupils working right from the lesson outset – less waste of learning time.
Starter activity (5–10 mins) Your settler may have acted as the starter to review prior knowledge. However, you may want to add a teacher-led starter to prepare pupil thinking for the main part of the lesson.	Starter should be short and sharp activity to: ● review prior knowledge; ● bring prior knowledge to the forefront of thinking; ● brainstorm ideas on something new. *Always* take feedback from this activity.	Pupils should be actively thinking, reviewing prior knowledge, contributing ideas – either to the whole class or in pairs or groups; then to the whole class.
Input (10–15 mins) This is the main introduction to new learning: ● make it visual and interactive; ● focus on new language; ● model how to do it; ● can demonstrations be seen by all? – plan where you will position yourself and the pupils.	Make learning objectives clear to pupils. Ask lots of questions. Ask for pupil ideas. Show models, animations, artefacts, objects, pictures (3D is better than 2D if you can) or real material or living things (even better). Explain well. Check that pupils understand – ask them to tell you back. Demonstrate, model – use pupils.	Pupils should be actively observing, listening, commenting, contributing. Don't expect them just to listen for very long!

Continued opposite

Consolidation (15 mins) Group or individual activities or tasks: • plan visual and hands-on activities – if possible; • choose contexts with inclusion in mind; • allow time for reflection; • set questions or written outcomes.	One or two activities, well timed. Clear outcomes given and explained/modelled. Circulate and check/assess while pupils are working independently. Scan room frequently to check safety and engagement in activity. Use the opportunity to question pupils individually. Give support if required. Keep up the pace by telling the pupils how much time they have.	Pupils should be working independently of the teacher, maybe asking for help if required. They should have something active to do – not copying – practical if appropriate. Group tasks, such as discussions, sorting, organising, analysing, planning – all should be engaged. They should have some written outcome – filling in a table or chart, free writing – so that they get used to writing and thinking after doing. This also helps settle and calm the class after an activity.
	Organising – homework on board.	Tidying up.
Plenary (5–10 mins) Plan short activities, and plan questions to ask – vary the type daily.	Check that pupils have learned what was intended and reinforce key learning points. Ask prepared questions. Consider interesting and 'fun' activities – quizzes, games. Look forward to next lesson/ homework task.	Pupils should be encouraged to contribute and feed back on what they have done and learned in this lesson.

Risk assessment: Always do a risk assessment.

Resources: Consider what resources are needed to support your plan, both general, such as equipment, worksheets and OHT transparencies, and specific for differentiation, such as writing frames, visual material, ICT, etc.

Lesson evaluation: Always evaluate your lesson and keep your lesson plan with suggested improvements if necessary. This will save time next time you teach this. If it went well, contribute to departmental lesson plan ideas.

you will not know whether the whole class knew the same answer. Create opportunity for whole-class feedback by using:

• small whiteboards, for pupils to write on and hold up;
• coloured cards for pupils to hold up (e.g. 'traffic lights' or true/false) in response to questions with a choice of answers;
• quick-fire sequential questioning around the room (e.g. parts of digestive system and functions) – useful as a dismissal procedure too;
• open rather than closed questions, where you can take several correct answers;
• challenging questions for your more able pupils to check that they have learnt the more challenging learning objective.

(See also Chapter 21.)

Create writing opportunities

Plan carefully to focus the writing on the learning objectives, so that when marking the work you will know who has learned what was intended and who still needs further support. Written feedback can be in the form of tables, graphs, diagrams, annotations, flow charts, and so on, or it can be reporting, explaining, arguing a case from evidence, concluding, analysing, or a creative piece. By varying the expected written feedback you support many preferred writing styles. Weaker writers can be supported with writing frames. Pupils' own writing (not copying) both helps them and you to improve; if they can't explain something in their own words then you may need to help them further.

Create demonstration opportunities

These can include pupils carrying out drama/role play, practical demonstrations, *PowerPoint* presentations, or poster displays. Too much of this can be time consuming and not always helpful for the whole class (for example, getting poor quality oral feedback from 10 groups of pupils). However, for those pupils who find writing difficult, other forms of demonstrating what they know can be valuable.

Putting all these ideas together in a lesson plan

Breaking the lesson into several episodes generally makes it more interesting and productive. Box 16.3 shows a template for lesson planning that has been found to be useful at any level of learning. The timings are variable and sometimes one episode, such as a practical activity with minimum introduction, will be planned to take the whole lesson.

References

Hirst, P. H. (1974) Curriculum objectives. In *Knowledge and the curriculum*. London: Routledge and Kegan Paul.

Hirst, P. H. and Peters, R. S. (1970) *The logic of education*. London: Routledge and Kegan Paul.

Macdonald-Ross, M. (1973) Behavioural objectives: a critical review. Abridged in *Curriculum design*, ed. Golby, M., Greenwald, J. and West, R. (1975) pp. 355–386. Buckingham: Open University Press.

Website

QCA *Assessing progress in science* multimedia toolkits: http://www.qca.org.uk/13116.html

Chapter 17 Access and engagement for all

Any classroom contains pupils of widely differing interests, experience, ability and motivation for learning, presenting a

Brenda Keogh and
Stuart Naylor

considerable challenge to their teachers who have to maximise opportunities for each one to learn. This chapter sets out the principles for meeting this challenge in the science classroom. It begins with the description of a lesson where these learning opportunities are indeed present and then discusses six aspects of teaching that are significant in providing engagement for all in learning.

Engaging all pupils

In Box 17.1 there is a glimpse of a classroom in which the teacher has created learning opportunities for all the pupils despite their individual differences in development and experience. How has the teacher managed to maximise access and engagement in this way? What factors have been taken into account in planning and teaching the lesson? Some of these factors relate to the nature of the activities provided for pupils, but how they are presented to pupils makes a big difference to access and engagement. For example, in the activity using true/false statements the teacher was able to:

- create an engaging stimulus that captured their attention;
- get pupils thinking and talking;
- provide problems to be solved;
- help pupils to set their own learning agenda;
- ensure there was a clear sense of purpose to follow-up activities.

The range of activities that followed also helped to provide:

- further opportunities for discussion and argument;

Box 17.1

A glimpse into a productive classroom

Imagine the situation. You walk into a science lesson. There is an intangible but noticeable buzz as pupils work. As you look around all the pupils seem to be productively occupied. They are engaged in activities that maintain their concentration. They are talking animatedly. You can tell from the expressions on their faces that there is a lot of thinking going on.

You find yourself wondering how the teacher achieved this. You talk to some of the pupils and find out that the teacher began the lesson with a set of true/false statements, which they discussed in small groups. After a few minutes the teacher gathered their ideas together and identified areas where they couldn't agree or were uncertain. This was followed by thinking and discussion about how to resolve these areas of uncertainty. Pupils used a range of resources to explore their ideas, including models, books, CD-ROMs, Internet access and structured worksheets. Towards the end of the lesson they reported back on what they had found out, with a range of types of evidence gained from the different sources. The teacher asked questions and contributed ideas to clarify, challenge and support their understanding. Finally they summarised their learning in pairs.

- questions to promote thinking and reasoning;
- opportunities for active involvement of pupils – minds on, not just hands on;
- a range of ways of accessing ideas and information.

Underpinning the lesson was the teacher's awareness of more complex aspects of teaching and learning that influence pupils' access and engagement. Some of the most important aspects include:

- recognising the importance of pupils' feelings;
- taking pupils' ideas into account;
- using a range of teaching and learning styles;
- using a range of differentiation strategies;
- using language to promote access and engagement;
- making good use of assessment.

In the following sections each of these aspects is considered further.

Recognising the importance of pupils' feelings

This may seem like an odd place to begin to describe factors that influence access and engagement. But learning isn't just an academic, cognitive process. Learners also have emotional and social needs (Hodson, 1998), and if those needs are not met then engagement and learning will suffer.

Pupils' feelings count. How pupils feel about themselves, the activity they are engaged in, their teachers and their schools, makes a difference to how they engage in learning (Keogh and Naylor, 2004). As adults we realise how close the connection is between how people respond to our ideas and how we feel about ourselves. Pupils are no different. If we want them to engage fully with learning activities and to put real effort into their thinking, then we need to provide the kind of learning environment in which they feel comfortable doing that.

That means doing all that we can to provide a supportive classroom climate. We need to respect pupils as individuals, to respect their ideas, to suspend judgement when they offer their ideas and to maximise opportunities to succeed. Pupils who are willing partners in learning are more effective learners. Motivated pupils are more willing to share the responsibility for their learning with the teacher, showing commitment to their learning, working at overcoming problems, asking for advice when necessary and keeping the teacher informed about their progress where possible. This sharing of responsibility helps to ensure that the demands of an activity are reasonably well matched to their capabilities and that activities are appropriate and accessible.

Taking pupils' ideas into account

This can be easier to say than to carry out in practice. Teachers often suggest several reasons why it can be difficult, such as the need to plan lessons in advance, the time it takes to find out pupils' ideas and the practical difficulties of responding to individuals at the same time as teaching the rest of the class. However, recognising and valuing their ideas is an important part of engaging pupils. Starting lessons by getting pupils to share their ideas in a structured way, with the teacher and with each other, helps them to clarify what they think. This provides a focus for discussion and argument and makes follow-up activities more purposeful and engaging.

Of course, taking pupils' ideas into account can't mean planning a different investigation or activity for every pupil. In most circumstances this isn't possible. However, it is often possible to start with some structured activity in which pupils clarify what they understand and where they are uncertain so that the purpose of an enquiry or investigation is related to testing out their ideas. In this way, pupils can be working on the same topic, carrying out similar investigations, but with different purposes in mind; for example either a qualitative or more quantitative answer to a question. Learning becomes personalised as pupils build on their individual starting points, and this helps to ensure access at the most suitable level. This is precisely what the teacher did through the use of true/false statements in the lesson described in Box 17.1.

There are many other strategies, such as card sorts and predict–observe–explain, that are ideal for helping pupils to explore their ideas in this way. When used as the focus for discussion they can make eliciting the pupils' ideas a natural part of the learning process. More examples can be found in White and Gunstone (1992) and in Naylor, Keogh and Goldsworthy (2004). It is also discussed in Chapter 19. These kinds of strategies can all be used to present alternative viewpoints, to give pupils challenges and to link the sharing of ideas with productive learning opportunities. Teachers who use these kinds of approaches are quick to identify how effectively they get pupils motivated and engaged in the learning process, so that sharing ideas creates a purpose for follow-up activities that help to develop their ideas further.

Using a range of teaching and learning styles

It is now commonly accepted that people can have different preferred learning styles. Some of us may learn most effectively through text, others through discussion, others through hands-on activity, and so on. Clearly this is relevant to access and engagement, since some pupils will respond better to certain styles of teaching than others.

As discussed in detail in Chapter 18, we need to be very cautious in how we interpret this information. Making simplistic judgements about a pupil's learning style will not enhance either access or engagement. The issue of whether to *reinforce* pupils' preferred learning styles or *extend* their possible learning styles is crucial. Edward de Bono provided a different perspective in his book *Six thinking hats* (de Bono, 1985). In this he recognises six different styles of thinking, each of them valuable at different times and for different reasons. Similarly, a good way forward in the classroom is to recognise and use a broad range of learning styles that will be helpful to all pupils (as in the lesson in Box 17.1) and not continually disadvantage any. This can apply to how activities are presented, how they are recorded and how much independence pupils have during the activity. Offering pupils some choice of learning styles where possible increases the opportunity for personal preferences to be taken into account.

Using a range of differentiation strategies

There was a time when differentiation in science teaching and learning seemed to mean that teachers should provide different activities for pupils of different 'abilities'. Teaching often became organised around a series of graded worksheets for pupils to follow. As well as presenting severe practical difficulties, this approach did not necessarily lead to better engagement by pupils. Learning sometimes became fragmented as pupils did everything on their own, and 'death by a thousand worksheets' became a common expression. Another consequence was that pupils with less well-developed linguistic skills were often given tasks that were scientifically undemanding.

There are now many useful outlines of a wider range of strategies that can be used to promote better differentiation in science education. These include, for example:

- varying the level of scientific procedural skill required, while the scientific conceptual demand remains the same;
- varying the level of linguistic or mathematical demand in an activity and providing different levels of support in these respects;
- using a wide variety of resources to support learning, including information technology;
- using the same set of activities but varying the pace or sequence of learning;
- offering different types and amounts of support for learning, including small-group tutoring, peer support, careful monitoring, additional guidance and additional challenges;
- expecting different outcomes from pupils and responding in different ways to these outcomes, including careful use of productive questions;
- providing a degree of pupil choice where possible to enable them to develop their differing interests and aptitudes.

Further details of these and other strategies can be found in Keogh and Naylor (2002) and McNamara and Moreton (1997).

Offering variety in the approaches used for differentiation is realistic for teachers and engaging for pupils. Actively involving pupils in the learning process is a key principle for maximising engagement. This can include building on their ideas and giving some choice in how an activity is carried out, how it is recorded or presented and what resources are used. If pupils have a useful part to play in ensuring differentiation then they will find lessons more accessible and engaging than if they view it as a process done to them by teachers.

Using language to promote access and engagement

There are plenty of well-documented challenges concerning the language of science, such as the specialist vocabulary and the formal structure of scientific reports. However, good use of language can really open doors for access and engagement.

Variety in the language used in the classroom can make lessons more interesting and therefore more engaging. Using a multisensory approach connects with different pupils' preferred learning styles and makes science more accessible. Wellington and Osborne (2001) provide very useful guidance about all aspects of language use in science lessons.

Talk

Providing opportunities for talk is crucial, especially talk involving some kind of scientific argument. Talk should not be just between teachers and pupils, important as this is, but also amongst pupils themselves. The lesson described in Box 17.1 contains plenty of opportunities for talk amongst pupils. Pupil–pupil talk not only clarifies thinking, promotes understanding and helps them to learn to reason; it also makes a massive difference to their engagement. There are few stimuli more effective at the beginning of a lesson than getting pupils engaged in an argument about that topic. Unfortunately it is all too easy for teachers to dominate classroom talk. Giving pupils information, asking lots of recall questions, being judgemental about pupils' answers, being anxious about talking getting out of control: all of these tend to lead to teachers filling the spaces and leaving little opportunity for pupil talk. While confident pupils are likely to create their own spaces for talk, less confident pupils can easily be excluded from classroom conversation (see Chapters 20, 25, 27).

Questions

Talk also involves questions. Questions from the teacher may be closed, low-level and unproductive, or more open, more exploratory and more productive. Which type of question do you find more engaging as an adult? Which type of question do you think pupils will find more engaging? Questions from pupils can be a superb stimulus for learning. This is especially evident with young children, who soon begin to recognise the value of asking questions. It is possible to create a climate of enquiry in the classroom in which pupils' questions are encouraged and valued (see Chapter 21). It is also possible to discourage their questions (*'they ask too many questions, they ask trivial questions, I may not know the answers, it takes too long, ...'*), and it is noticeable how quickly they can get out of the habit of asking questions as they go through school.

Writing

Writing in science lessons can be low-level, routine and time-consuming, so it isn't surprising that so many pupils don't like doing it. Low-attaining pupils are often slow writers and they can easily become bogged down in writing, leaving little time for anything else. Writing can be made more active and engaging by using a wider variety of writing styles, such as news reports, diary entries, information leaflets or sets of instructions (see Chapter 27). These provide an obvious purpose for writing, but it is important to avoid writing dominating the lesson.

Making good use of assessment

There is no conflict between teaching that is engaging and high levels of achievement by pupils. Quite the opposite, since engagement and motivation are necessary for effective learning and high levels of achievement. Even dull and uninspiring formal testing doesn't require dull and uninspiring teaching as preparation for the tests.

Assessment also influences how we feel about ourselves, by giving us feedback about how well we are doing, and this can make a big difference to engagement and learning. Harlen (2003) summarises a wealth of evidence that highlights the impact of assessment on self-esteem, motivation and learning. Of course this can be a positive or a negative difference, and one of the challenges for teachers is to try to use assessment in ways that enhance rather than damage self-esteem.

The term 'active assessment' (Naylor, Keogh and Goldsworthy, 2004) refers to activities that begin the learning process at the same time as providing valuable assessment information. Generally these will be used as collaborative activities that promote discussion and argument. The true/false statements in the lesson described in Box 17.1 are a good example of active assessment. Pupils do not usually view these strategies as assessment, with all the negative connotations that assessment can have for them, but they do provide valuable assessment information. In this way, through a combination of self-, peer- and teacher-assessment, the learning needs of pupils can become more apparent but without the damage to self-esteem sometimes caused by more formal assessment procedures.

More extensive detail about the links between assessment and learning is provided in Chapters 22 and 23.

Conclusion

Two themes that run through this chapter are collaboration and personalisation. Collaborative activities give pupils confidence and security; they promote thinking and reasoning; they encourage talk and argument; they enable self- and peer-assessment to occur. Paradoxically, they can also help to personalise learning. As pupils become more involved in the activity they begin to make judgements about their own ideas in relation to some of the alternative possibilities. As they recognise the boundaries of their own understanding they begin to create their own learning agenda and see the purpose of follow-up activities. For most pupils most of the time collaborative learning is accessible and engaging; equally, personalised learning is accessible and engaging.

Other important themes in this chapter are variety, creativity and pupil choice. They are evident in the teacher's choice of elicitation strategies, teaching and learning styles, the approaches used for differentiation, the language register used, and so on. These themes overlap and interact, enabling teachers to develop a coherent teaching style designed to engage and motivate pupils. Of course there is never any guarantee that pupils will be engaged, but there is every point in trying to achieve this. As Woolnough puts it:

> If students are motivated, and if they are given the freedom and opportunity, they will find ways of learning. If they are not, they will not bother.
> (Woolnough, 1994, p. 111)

References

de Bono, E. (1985) *Six thinking hats*. London: Penguin.

Harlen, W. (2003) How high stakes testing impacts on motivation for learning. *Science Teacher Education*, **37**, 2–5.

Hodson, D. (1998) *Teaching and learning science*. Buckingham: Open University Press.

Keogh, B. and Naylor, S. (2002) Dealing with differentiation. In *Aspects of teaching secondary science*, ed. Amos, S. and Boohan, R. pp. 269–278. London: Open University Press.

Keogh, B. and Naylor, S. (2004) Children's ideas, children's feelings. *Primary Science Review*, **82**, 18–20.

McNamara, S. and Moreton, G. (1997) *Understanding differentiation*. London: David Fulton.

Naylor, S., Keogh, B. and Goldsworthy, A. (2004) *Active assessment: thinking, learning and assessment in science*. Sandbach, Cheshire: Millgate House Publishers.

Wellington, J. and Osborne, J. (2001) *Language and literacy in science education*. Buckingham: Open University Press.

White, R. and Gunstone, R. (1992) *Probing understanding*. London: Falmer Press.

Woolnough, B. (1994) *Effective science teaching*. Buckingham: Open University Press.

Chapter 18

From learning styles to learning strategies

The first part of this chapter challenges the terminology of learning styles. Learning may be better modelled in terms of learning strategies, which interact with cognitive styles. It outlines

Paul Hamer,
Jasmin Chapman and
Barbara Allmark

how, using a specific model to frame learning, judiciously deployed strategies can inform our approach to differentiation and assessment in science. We promote progression in dialogue with pupils about their learning, and strive to make them more skilful and independent learners.

Style versus strategy

Paradoxically, authors who have been exploring the utility of learning styles in their classrooms over the last 15 years are opening this chapter on learning styles by challenging that terminology! However, there is good reason to do so, and to advocate deliberation when reading about style. Riding and Rayner (1998) make the point that 'Style probably has a physiological basis and is fairly fixed for the individual' and that learning strategies describe the approaches used by learners. They argue that strategies can be taught and developed in order to provide students with more ways to access the intended learning. Our second reason to question the terminology is that much of the literature uses style as a label for things that are malleable/adaptive and therefore more appropriately referred to as strategy. Our third reason is that thinking in terms of strategy rather than style helps to avoid the pitfall of labelling learners with a fixed style profile, which can result in a monotonous and/or inappropriate learning diet and constrain their development.

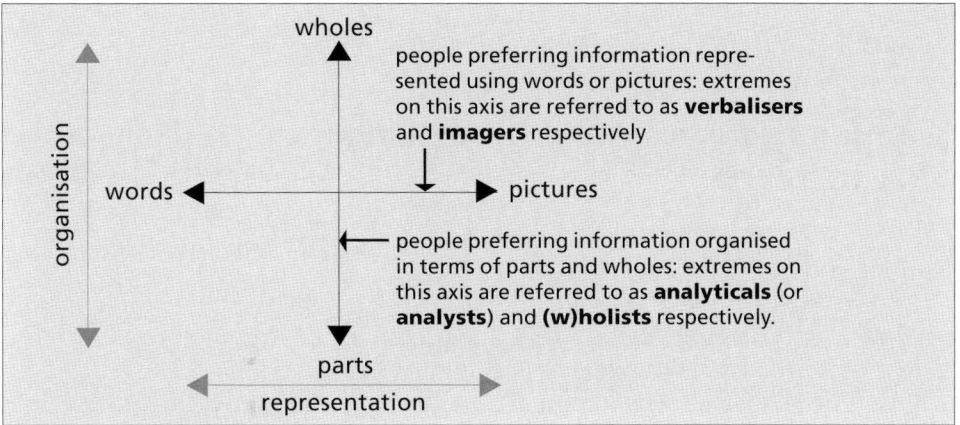

Figure 18.1 **Cognitive styles.**

Cognitive styles

Riding and Rayner suggest that people are different, in terms of learning and thinking, in two fundamental ways summarised on the axes in Figure 18.1. Some individuals will prefer working with words and wholes (big ideas), while others will prefer dealing with words and parts. Similarly, those who prefer pictures can be either holists or analysts. These differences are what Riding and Rayner call cognitive style. They contend that a 'personal learning style' develops over time through interaction between your cognitive style and an increasing range of learning strategies.

Our argument, therefore, is that we should work to equip learners with a suite of strategies and encourage them to reflect on the personal utility of each strategy, rather than concerning ourselves with developing their learning style directly. It is important to distinguish between strategies for taking in new information and those for processing and organising that information. The approaches used are described in the section on learning strategies below.

Provision to accommodate learner differences through resourcing to match cognitive style could be viewed as a minimum (see Box 18.1). Our concern is that this minimum fails to provide for learners who, experience tells us, need

---

Box 18.1

Resourcing to match cognitive style

For teaching the particle model to year 7:

- **verbalisers** need interaction with key words and gain understanding from teacher description and text sources;
- **imagers** need to see particle diagrams and gain understanding from animations and models; iconising key words is very helpful;
- **holists** need the big picture at the start of the teaching sequence, via a mind map or poster, and find it helpful to condense the entire unit in a single summary;
- **analysts** do not need the big picture at the start and are not affected by its provision to holists; they develop their understanding progressively through the teaching sequence and find it helpful to summarise each key idea in the unit as it is covered.

auditory, kinaesthetic and tactile inputs, and that it might restrict the range of formats we can offer to learners for communicating their ideas and summarising their learning.

Learning strategies and differentiation

When first considering which strategies to focus on (in 1989), our primary concerns were to differentiate effectively without pre-judging pupils and to develop an approach that genuinely facilitated the development of independent learning (Chapman, Hamer and Sears, 2000).

The six-stage model of learning (Rose and Goll, 1992), outlined in Box 18.2, seemed to offer a practical solution for a number of reasons: it paralleled a number of more formal models of learning (Chapman, 1998); it embedded the *distinction between perception and processing* within a model of learning that we felt able to share with our pupils; and it allowed us to actively integrate motivation strategies, revision and formative assessment. It also included mechanisms for getting learners to think about their own learning and to remember the model, as its number of steps fit within 'Miller's Magic 7' (Miller, 1956).

Outcomes that encouraged us to continue developing the approach are:

- we now had a shared lexicon of learning as the basis for dialogue with our pupils;
- learners commented that they really appreciated being treated as individuals and having the interesting opportunity to be creative in summarising their science;
- our planning became easier because we were more readily able to see how to integrate all the good practice being advocated;
- using accelerated learning techniques such as cognitive maps (Hamer *et al.*, 1998), led to a marked increase in genuine pupil discussion of the science;
- the approach more comfortably allowed for the diversity in every class and provided equitable alternatives for any pupils with special needs;
- pupils who became expert in a given learning strategy coached others;
- gifted pupils rapidly moved towards significant independence; for example Nancy, who, early in the spring term of year 7, said '*I'm going to start summarising each different unit in a different format – this will help my revision, as I will remember the format that each bit of science is in*'.

Most of the outcomes nurture pupils' intrinsic motivation, for example by:

- recognising their individuality and responding to it;
- giving them choice, ownership and responsibility, and thus self-esteem;
- rewarding readiness to learn;
- giving up copying, combined with assessment of prior learning that identifies parts of units that need to be reviewed, not taught, so that much more time is available for skills development.

In engaging with learners who have been attempting these learning strategies, we have developed and published a range of classroom resources intended to support their skills acquisition and to facilitate development of practice for

Box 18.2

A six-stage model of learning

Stage	Name	Comprising learning strategies	Comment (✓ = formative assessment opportunity)
1	Right frame of mind	Establishing prior knowledge, connecting the learning, giving the big picture and setting targets; getting learners relaxed, confident, motivated and unstressed.	✓ Minimum = 'meet and greet' as pupils arrive.
2	Getting the facts	Multisensory input to accommodate learners' preferred perception modality with more dependent learners; more independent learners choose sources of information and acquisition steps.	Visual, auditory, kinaesthetic, tactile (VAKT) plus olfactory (smell), gustatory (taste) (out of the lab!) when appropriate; some authorities extend VAK to VARK by including reading and writing (R); ✓ – with independent learners or when coaching towards independence.
3	Exploration and summarising	Individual/pair/small-group activities; summarising differentiated by preferred processing mode (Gardner's multiple intelligences); checking and correcting; making notes in chosen form – meaningful reorganisation of information.	✓ Stage 3 products are stage 4 tools; making notes (active learning), not taking notes (passive learning).
4	Memorising	Review, using notes (= aide-memoire / revision portfolio) to transfer learning from short-term to long-term memory.	A review cycle (explained below) is used to prevent forgetting; drafting and redrafting on cycle; ✓ – by questioning at review points.
5	Show you know	Opportunities for learners to demonstrate new knowledge and understanding; further reflection.	✓
6	Reflection	Learners reflect, and discuss with peers and teacher, 'What went well?' 'What could have gone better?' – in terms of approaches to learning; metacognition; diagnostic self-assessment; setting own targets for skills and strategies.	Evaluation of learning strategies and skills. ✓

their teachers. These include *Byte packs* (Hamer, 2005), *Differentiated concept maps*, *Big idea maps* and *Continuity maps* (Chapman, 2005).

Our approach to learning strategies and differentiation is not without its critics. Video evidence of concerns expressed by year 10 pupils introduced to the approach is available. Some critics even claim that there is *'an utter failure [in the research] to find that assessing children's learning styles and matching to instructional methods has any effect on their learning'* (Stahl, 1999). We cannot agree that this invalidates the approach: the pupils we have seen progress, whether they have made small steps or giant, speak more clearly to us than research at odds with it.

Teaching strategies – to promote deeper learning and encourage independent learners

The training ground: stage 3

In using the six-stage model as the basis for developing strategies to provide students with greater independence, we always institute a 'no copying' rule and initially focus on stage 3. Our rationale is:

- when beginning the process, learners are insufficiently skilled at using their time in getting the information for themselves – by our coverage which determines the input during stage 2, we set the boundaries of what needs to be summarised at stage 3;
- the resource demand is less when one focuses on learner output (to encourage active learning) than if one focused on diversifying information sources.

Experience has led us to be flexible in the use of the model. We now refer to the stages as elements of learning and consider which elements are applicable to a given lesson, or to specific learners within that lesson. These might now appear in a lesson sequence as shown in Box 18.3.

Identifying pupils' 'styles': modalities and intelligences

It is worth profiling how your pupils perceive and process information most effectively as a starting point for dialogue. The best approach is through observation of choices made and activities enjoyed and/or eliciting better than usual performance. Questionnaires are less useful. Questions such as:

- How do you (currently) approach learning (in this context)?
- What approach(es) do you enjoy most?
- Which approaches are most helpful to you?

and specific derivitives, are all more useful questions to ask of learners than *'What is your learning style?'* They are also essential to a teacher who is trying to sustain and improve learner motivation, and far more useful than assessment of attainment alone.

In stage 3 episodes, where the focus is on producing a summary of the learning, we talk to pupils about processing the information in ways that draw on Gardner's notions of multiple intelligences: linguistic, mathematical–logical, body–physical, musical, visual–spatial, naturalist, interpersonal and intrapersonal. In addition to using our own resources, we provide learners with a menu to work from in stage 3 summarising episodes; see for example

Box 18.3

Year 7: Why do things float?

(1) (2) (3) (4) (5) (6) = activity matched to element from six-stage model

Phase	Lesson A	Lesson B	Lesson C
Starter	Review placemat of work on floating (unit 6E), focusing on meanings of upthrust and weight; teacher questions pupils after they have had a few minutes to look at the placemat **(1)**.	KWL* review of previous lesson **(1)**, **(4)**. Pupils asked to predict which materials will float/sink – and to hypothesise if they feel they can offer an idea to explain their predictions **(3)**.	Pupils test whether selected blocks from previous lesson float in other liquids (oil, syrup, glycerol, washing up liquid and salt water) **(3)**.
Main	**(a)** Teacher introduces density and displacement of water to measure volume **(2)**. **(b)** Guided discussion of how to investigate whether density determines whether things float or sink **(2–3)**. K&T modalities catered for: **Tactile:** Materials for testing provided to handle. **Kinaesthetic:** Move to sinks and try out materials in water during discussion.	Pupils determine density of 3–5 objects (all regular blocks) and whether these float or sink; class data shared via projected *Excel* sheet **(3)**. Fast finishers given access to book box to research floating and sinking **(3)**.	**(a)** Q & A based round cognitive conflict from starter; pupils encouraged to offer all ideas; any consensus? **(3)**. **(b)** Density figures for liquids provided – what do we think now? **(3)** **(c)** Pupils reminded of meaning of fluid (from particles work) and shown He and CO_2 filled balloons plus simulation of particle packing in high and low density solids **(2)**. **(d)** Can we derive a general statement (to go with a provided force arrow diagram) about upthrust and floating in fluids? **(3)**
Plenary	Pupils summarise what they have learnt / note steps for investigation **(3)**. Some reflection on learning **(6)**; randomly selected pupils asked to share with class **(5)**.	Q and A based on data, pupil comments during practical, findings of fast finishers **(3)**. Agreed summary statement recorded in pupil books **(3)**.	Pupils summarise what they have learnt **(3)**, some reflection on learning **(6)**; randomly selected pupils asked to share with class at end of lesson **(5)**. All are reminded to carry out same day and next day review **(4)**.

K&T: Can you see other instances where extra provision could be made to assist access to these modalities?

*KWL = Know, Want to know, Learnt.

Box 18.4

Menu for summarising (using Ellen Arnold's (1999) pupil-friendly descriptions of the intelligences)

If you want your summary of animal cells to be	Do one of the following:	
Word-smart	Write your own glossary of key words, using the list provided, or produce a mnemonic.	Prepare a presentation about animal cells for year 6 induction day or do the provided DART.
Number-smart	Make a concept map, using the key words provided.	Write a key points list.
Body-smart	Make a display using models.	Make a set of flash cards.
Music-smart	Write new words for a favourite tune.	Make up a jingle or rap.
Picture-smart	Make a mind map or poster.	Colour code the provided summary text.
Nature-smart	Group and annotate the provided photomicrographs.	Make a classification tree for animal cells and the cell parts or complete the provided parts-wholes template map.
People-smart	Work with up to 3 other people and share ideas.	
Self-smart	Work on your own and include an explanation of why you have summarised the work the way you have.	

the menu in Box 18.4 for summarising work on animal cells in year 7.

Many learners find this kind of work very demanding when first asked to do it – hence our modelling and scaffolding in our classroom resources. This is unsurprising: creating a unique summary should involve some evaluation along the way and may, if new source materials are referenced, involve analysis of that source – all higher order cognitive processes (as defined in the 2001 revision of *Bloom's taxonomy* – Anderson and Krathwohl, 2001). This challenge to learners is shown to be worthwhile, however, when one considers the benefits previously described. Examples of pupil summaries are given in our *Non-judgemental differentiation* video (Sears *et al.*, 2001); for other examples see the Learners' Co-operative website. One strategy used with learners having problems deciding how to summarise a given chunk of science is to discuss with them how they best remember things – in Bruner's terms, whether they remember enactively, iconically or symbolically. This generally helps them get started.

The marked increase in genuine pupil discussion of the science is accompanied by a similar increase in dialogue about learning strategies. Getting pupils to work together by encouraging them to make use of their interpersonal intelligence is reinforced by encouraging them to use their intrapersonal intelligence in reflecting on approaches used. This accounts for much of the progress made. If, in your classroom, a given individual has tended to prefer a particular method of summarising, one way of providing challenge to that learner is by encouraging him/her to step outside their 'comfort zone' and to try a different style of summary. However, the option to work inside the comfort zone can be less stressful.

Getting the facts: stage 2

One of the reasons we need to avoid labelling learners with a fixed style profile is that an individual's preferred input is not set in a particular modality. It is affected by context, working partners and mood. So, a typical class on a given day needs a mix of presentation styles, but they might not be those you would predict. Providing new information to match as many perception modes as possible is also necessary because any learner not in tune with a single chosen mode is at risk of 'tuning out' or even of being unable to 'tune in.' A typical pupil has equal facility in visual (V), auditory (A) and kinaesthetic–tactile (K–T) perception modes, and is able to access information in any of these three modes, whatever their current preference. However, some pupils are disadvantaged by being given information solely matching a mode in which they are dysfunctional. As many as 10 per cent of pupils may only be able to access information via a single mode – the 'V-noughts', 'A-noughts' and 'K-noughts'. K0s are very common amongst youngsters who fail in or drop out of traditional teaching environments.

Whilst we initially concentrate on stage 3 episodes as our training ground, we also look for teaching strategies to reduce dependence on the teacher for information. Progression in this area depends on the facility shown by the class in stage 3 work; increasing independence is usually phased in as appropriate to individuals / small groups. One strategy used is Reciprocal Teaching: '*an instructional activity that takes place in the form of a dialogue between teachers and students regarding segments of text. The dialogue is structured by the use of four comprehension strategies: summarising, question generating, clarifying, and predicting. The teacher and students take turns assuming the role of teacher in leading this dialogue.*' (Palinscar and Brown, 1984). This activity is 'multimodal', and is a powerful DART (directed activity related to text), combining aspects of think–talk–write (see *10 steps to better writing in science* – DfES, 2005a). Combined with a snowball approach where pairs consist of a verbaliser, who has the text, and an imager, who has a diagram with key words and questions, this can also be used to develop peer assessment. The *Leading in learning* materials of the Key Stage 3 National Strategy (DfES, 2005b) give us, in the suite of strategies for developing thinking skills, more multimodal activities (e.g. advance organisers, collective memory, reading images) that can used in a similar way to, or integrated with, the reciprocal teaching approach.

Memorising: stage 4

The main teaching strategy we have deployed for the fourth element of learning, memorising, is the use of a review cycle. Learners are taught this cycle and encouraged to use it independently. Its purpose is to move learning from short-term to long-term memory and to prevent forgetting. The cycle, for a given chunk of learning, is: same day, next day, one week, one month, three months, six months, one year and annually – with varying (re)drafting/review activities at each point according to individual need and targets. This independent work can be the basis of a homework programme; the cycle can also be a means of ensuring that ideas are reviewed – perhaps via a settler activity preceding the lesson starter – on specific dates.

Completing the stages

Learning elements 1, 5 and 6 are more frequent and diffuse than shown in Box 18.3. Dialogue with individuals throughout a teaching sequence gives plentiful opportunity to appraise understanding and/or the approach being used, encourage reflection and offer praise with 'next steps' feedback as appropriate. In giving feedback we have long adopted the one-minute manager (Blanchard and Johnson, 1983) principles of starting with the positives and ending with reaffirmation when giving constructive criticism. We also encourage pupils to see mistakes as useful – *'they tell you what you need to learn'* – and refer to common mistakes people make, such as failure to read and interpret explicit instructions, to appreciate the need for precision and accuracy and to recognise and define the problem (see Blagg, 1988).

Some teaching strategies, such as active and appropriate questioning, can, of course, occur at any point in the six-stage model. Student motivation impacts on teaching and learning strategies and is important to consider; however, space does not permit further discussion (see Biggs and Moore, 1993; Covington, 1998).

We feel that the approach described above should be department-wide, if not school-wide: we have seen the effect on learners who have gone from a situation where they thrived on this approach one year and were constrained by a more traditional approach in the following year. Our suggested progression for dialogue about learning is: consideration of words–pictures and parts–wholes in key stage 1; VAK and multiple intelligences in key stages 2 and 3; and exposure to other ideas about learning once pupils are securely independent.

References

Anderson, L. W. and Krathwohl, D. R. (2001) *A taxonomy for learning, teaching and assessing – a revision of Bloom's taxonomy of educational objectives*. London: Longman.

Arnold, E. (1999) *The MI strategy bank*. Tucson, Arizona: Zephyr Press.

Biggs, J. B. and Moore, P. J. (1993) *Process of learning*. 3rd edn. Englewood Cliffs, NJ: Prentice Hall.

Blagg, N. (1988) *Somerset thinking skills course handbook*. Oxford: Blackwell.

Blanchard, K. and Johnson, S. (1983) *The one minute manager*. London: Collins-Fontana.

Chapman, J. ed. (1998) *The Learners' Co-operative differentiation manual*. 2nd edn. Plymouth: The Learners' Co-operative.

Chapman, J., Hamer, P. and Sears, J. (2000) Non-judgemental differentiation; teaching and learning styles for the future. In *Issues in science teaching*, ed. Sears, J. and Sorensen, P. London: Routledge.

Chapman, J. ed. (2005) *Differentiated concept maps for KS3 science*. Plymouth: The Learners' Co-operative.

Chapman, J. ed. (2005) *Big idea maps for KS1–4 science*. Plymouth: The Learners' Co-operative.

Chapman, J. ed. (2005) *Continuity maps for KS1–4 science*. Plymouth: The Learners' Co-operative.

Covington, M. V. (1998) *The will to learn, a guide for motivating young people*. Cambridge: Cambridge University Press.

DfES (2005a) *10 Steps to better writing in science*. DfES 0179-2005. London: Department for Education and Skills.

DfES (2005b) *Leading in learning: developing thinking skills at key stage 3*. DfES 0034-2005 G. London: Department for Education and Skills.

Hamer, P., Chapman, J., Allmark, B. and Jackson, J. (1998) Mapping concepts in science. In *ASE guide to secondary science education*, ed. Ratcliffe, M. pp. 74–83. Hatfield: Association for Science Education.

Hamer, P. ed. (2005) *Byte packs for Y7: Units 7a, Cells; 7g, Particles; and 7i, Energy resources*. 2nd edns. Plymouth: The Learners' Co-operative.

Miller, G. (1956) The magical number seven, plus or minus two. *Psychological Review*, **63**, 81–97.

Palincsar, A. S. and Brown, A. (1984) Reciprocal teaching of comprehension – fostering and comprehension monitoring activities. *Cognition and Instruction*, **1** (2), 117–175.

Riding, R. and Rayner, S. (1998) *Cognitive styles and learning strategies: understanding style differences in learning and behaviour*. London: David Fulton.

Rose, C. and Goll, L. (1992) *Accelerate your learning*. Accelerated Learning Systems.

Sears, J., Chapman, J., Hamer, P. and Cozens, P. (2001) *Non-judgemental differentiation* (video and handbook). Hatfield: Association for Science Education.

Stahl, S. (1999) Different strokes for different folks. In *American Educator*, **23** (3), 27–31.

Further reading

Readers in England are likely to be familiar with the following two items. These self-study materials reprise, distil and reinforce the key messages from the National Strategy training. We hope that links between these materials and this chapter will be clear to the reader:

National Strategy 'Ped Pack':
DfES (2004) *Pedagogy and practice: teaching and learning in secondary schools*. (20 cross-curricular self-study units). DfES 0423-2004 G. London: Department for Education and Skills.

'Science Ped Pack':
DfES (2004) *Strengthening teaching and learning in science through using different pedagogies* (5 science-specific self-study units). DfES 0703-2004 G. London: Department for Education and Skills.

Websites

Learners' Co-operative: http://www.learnersco-opltd.co.uk

A selection of online diagnostic tools:

VAKT(R):
Plymouthnwlink.com/~donclark/hrd/vak.html
http://www2.umist.ac.uk/staff/talsc/TaLSC/VARK/questionnaire.htm
http://www.vark-learn.com/documents/younger.pdf
Multiple intelligences:
http://www2.bgfl.org/bgfl2/custom/resources_ftp/client_ftp/ks1/ict/mulitple_int/index.htm
http://www.ldrc.ca/projects/miinventory/miinventory.php
http://homepage.tinet.ie/~seaghan/play/mi.htm

Chapter 19

Learning scientific concepts: teaching for understanding

Science teachers have a fundamental role in communicating the content of science to their pupils. This chapter will focus on teaching and learning scientific concepts in secondary science in such a way that pupils understand it. There is a significant body of research from around the world on teaching and learning secondary science which is drawn upon as evidence in the chapter.

John Leach

Content matters

According to the philosopher Rom Harré (1986), the major achievement of the scientific enterprise is that it has produced a body of knowledge that is remarkably reliable at predicting and explaining the behaviour of the material world. This body of knowledge does not take the form of a list of isolated facts. Rather, it is organised around networks of concepts, theories and models that have been agreed by experts as providing the best possible explanations for the available evidence. Although science is more than a body of knowledge, it is certainly the case that the *content* of science is a valuable cultural product. Perhaps the *central* role of science teachers is the passing of this cultural knowledge down through the generations; although there is more to science than content alone, it is hard to imagine a science education that is of value to pupils that does not include significant scientific content.

Progression in knowledge and understanding: what does it look like?

Imagine the scene: a physics teacher has just finished a teaching unit with his class about forces. Overall, he is happy with his pupils' answers to the simple calculations presented in the end-of-unit test. When going through one question on the test, about the motion of a trolley, the teacher asks the class to imagine that there is no air – to remove the complicating factor of air resistance. To his amazement, several pupils say *'The trolley will float away!'*, *'How can gravity work without air?'*, *'There is no air in space, and objects just float around'* ...

This is how Jim Minstrell, a physics teacher and educational researcher from Seattle, describes the event that prompted him to start researching his pupils' learning in physics. His pupils had already learnt a lot about force and motion from his teaching – after all, they were able to answer simple quantitative problems about motion. However, Minstrell wanted his pupils to make further progress in their understanding. In his own words, *'What good is having my students know the quantitative relation or equation for gravitational force if they lack a qualitative understanding of force and the concepts related to the nature of gravity and its effects?'* (Minstrell and Kraus, 2005, p. 476). I agree with Minstrell's position: for me, scientific understanding involves knowing some of the concepts and theories of science and how to use them. Unfortunately, it is much easier to test pupils' knowledge of facts and simple algorithms than to test their conceptual understanding, and this can lead to the teaching of facts in isolation.

There is now overwhelming evidence that when pupils arrive at their science lessons they already have ways of explaining the natural world. For example, electricity *'gets used up'* in a torch as the batteries run down, vacuums *'suck'*, gases *'make things lighter'*, matter *'burns away'*, and so on. It isn't hard to see where these ideas come from: they explain what we see happening in the world, and are reflected in everyday ways of talking. By contrast, the accepted scientific explanations for many phenomena run counter to our perceptions of the world and everyday ways of talking. Who would believe that wood is made from gas and water, or that a piano could move in a direction for ever following the application of a force, or that you should really shut the door to keep the heat in rather than the cold out?

If pupils are to understand and be able to use scientific concepts, they need to recognise how the concepts work, how they differ from everyday ways of knowing, and why the concepts are useful and powerful. This presents a real challenge for science teachers in some areas, because pupils' everyday ideas are strongly held, and a profound influence on what they learn during science lessons. In Jim Minstrell's physics class, for example, although the pupils had learnt to answer problems about force, they still had not moved beyond their strongly held, everyday view of how gravity works.

A large volume of research has been conducted around the world on pupils' everyday ideas in various science topics and how these appear to influence what pupils learn from science lessons. Box 19.1 gives a snapshot of some key areas in secondary science.

It is not the case, however, that all areas of science are counter-intuitive for pupils because of their everyday knowledge. The youngest children, for example, already have a sense of how to make a race 'fair', and there is no evidence that

Box 19. 1

Some examples of secondary pupils' everyday thinking
Air
Air is weightless or has negative weight.
Vacuums *'suck'*.
Heat
Heat is a kind of substance.
The temperature of an object depends on the kind of stuff it is made of (e.g. metals are cold, plastics are warm).
Heat and temperature are not differentiated.
Energy
Energy is primarily associated with (human) action/motion.
Energy gets used up.
Matter
Matter can appear and disappear in change processes; matter is thought to disappear in burning.
Particles
Macroscopic properties are given to microscopic particles (they can *melt, expand, be blue*, etc.).
The space between particles is not empty (for example, the space between 'air particles' is thought to be filled with *air* ...).
Plant nutrition
Plants ingest their food from the environment in the same way as animals do.
Plants take in food through their roots.
Food for plants includes anything that they take in (air, fertilisers, sunlight ...).

they struggle with the idea of a 'fair test' (so long as they understand the concepts that are being used). Similarly, pupils have an intuitive sense of what *speed* is, what *muscles* do, and so on. Although pupils may take some time to develop an acceptable notion of *chemical change*, once they have done so it appears quite easy for them to extend their knowledge of different types of reactions and it is therefore not difficult for them to understand what is going on in new situations such as thermal decomposition.

In some areas of the curriculum, all the evidence suggests that pupils know rather little prior to teaching, and everyday knowledge does not exert a particularly profound influence. The functioning of volcanoes is an example of such a case: pupils' difficulties come from issues such as the size and scale of volcanoes rather than any deeply held everyday knowledge that is counter to scientific explanations.

Using insights about pupils' thinking to support their learning

Given that pupils live in the same world, and share many aspects of culture, it is not at all surprising that they also share many aspects of everyday knowledge about the material world. There are several publications designed for teachers that present pupils' likely everyday knowledge in a variety of topic areas (e.g. Driver *et al.*, 1994). Many experienced teachers will be familiar with this and able to predict their pupils' likely starting points. However, many teachers may wish to get more direct information about their own pupils' thinking. There are several sources of good diagnostic assessment questions available, some of which are listed in Box 19.2, and teachers may wish to get their classes to complete such questions *before* teaching. This process is time-consuming, and it is unlikely that teachers (or pupils!) would welcome the introduction of regular *before*-topic tests as well as end-of-topic tests. However, in some key topic areas, teachers may find it useful to get pupils discussing their own responses to diagnostic questions as an introduction to a new topic.

Box 19.2
Some sources of questions for assessing pupils' thinking prior to teaching

As part of the *Evidence-based practice in science education* research network (see website), Robin Millar and Vicky Hames worked with a group of teachers to develop sets of diagnostic questions on electric circuits, force and motion, and matter and chemical change. You can download these materials at:

http://www.york.ac.uk/depts/educ/projs/DiagQuestionsIntro_Dec02.htm

Stuart Naylor and Brenda Keogh have published *Concept Cartoons* on a variety of topic areas. Although many were designed with primary pupils in mind, many of the core ideas also feature in the secondary science curriculum. Further information is available at:

http://www.conceptcartoons.com/index_flash.html

Phil Scott and I have referred to differences between pupils' everyday knowledge about a topic and the scientific view to be taught, as *learning demands* (Leach and Scott, 1995). Thinking back to Jim Minstrell's physics class, by the end of the teaching the pupils were able to solve quantitative problems: there were no major learning demands in this area. However, one learning demand that remained, and became evident at the *end* of the teaching, involved coming to appreciate that gravity is a force that acts at a distance and does not require a 'medium of transmission' (i.e. the air).

There is no algorithm for using insights about learning demands to inform the design of teaching. As always, it is the job of creative science teachers to think through how insights about pupils' everyday knowledge might influence teaching. In some cases, it will not be necessary for teachers to change the scheme of work that is being used for a topic. However, they will probably have very different *conversations* with the class about some activities once they know more about pupils' everyday thinking. An example of this can be found in Box 19.3.

In other cases, teachers may decide that their scheme of work does not provide particularly good opportunities to address the learning demands of the topic. They may introduce new activities to the scheme of work to provide a

Box 19.3

Knowing about learning demands influences how teachers use standard activities

A year 10 class is working on a sheet about photosynthesis, after the content has been explained in a whole-class session. Their teacher, Laura, is moving around the room, monitoring the pupils' progress. She approaches a group of three girls:

Laura: *Right, have you started then?*

Sophie: *We have put that the plants take in nutrients through their roots.*

Laura: *Right, what makes you think they need nutrients; where have you come across the idea that plants take in nutrients through their roots?*

The obvious conclusion from Sophie's answer is that the girls are progressing well and that they understand the worksheet. However, Laura is aware that many pupils of this age are likely to think that plants ingest 'food', rather than synthesising it – and that even when such pupils have learnt about photosynthesis, many still think that plants ingest some of their 'food' through the roots. Laura therefore pushes Sophie a little, to see if she has really grasped the key idea that plants synthesise biomass and the substrates of respiration, rather than ingesting them. Here is Sophie's response to Laura's question:

Sophie: *Miss, I don't understand why the nutrients aren't involved in photosynthesis.*

Laura then reviews once again the difference between the products of photosynthesis and the matter (i.e. inorganic mineral nutrients) ingested through plants' roots, helping the pupils to make this subtle but central distinction:

Laura: *This is not saying that they don't affect plants, it is just saying that they're not involved in photosynthesis. So can you see why ... they talk about* **nutrients** *here, rather than* **food***, because it is a very funny point.*

This piece of teaching does not include novel activities that have been designed as a result of research-based insights on learning. Rather, it involves a teacher in pursuing a line of questioning with her pupils because she is aware of some of the key learning demands in the area of photosynthesis.

vehicle through which everyday knowledge can be made explicit and scientific knowledge can be introduced. An example of this is presented in Box 19.4.

Clive Sutton (1996) suggested that it is a mistake to think about the job of science teachers as involving *proving* things to pupils through the use of evidence. If you are sceptical of this view, ask yourself how many of the practical activities that you conduct in your teaching actually prove anything. Rather, the purpose of such activities is to provide science teachers with opportunities to *persuade* pupils of the power of scientific explanations of phenomena, when compared to the alternatives. This is the exact opposite of 'discovery learning'. Rather than providing pupils with opportunities to explore the world and build scientific knowledge for themselves, the teacher introduces the concepts and theories of science to pupils, modelling how to use these concepts and theories

Box 19.4

The BIG Circuit question

A bulb is set up at one end of a room. Long wires are stretched around the walls to the other end of the room, and one of the wires is connected to a power supply. When the other wire is connected to the power supply, what will happen?

There is clear research evidence that most people who are not educated in physics – including school pupils – tend to answer assuming a 'source–consumer model': electricity leaves the battery (the source) and travels to the bulb, where some is used up in lighting the bulb (the consumer). The remaining unused electricity returns to the battery. You might therefore expect a short delay between connecting the battery and seeing the bulb light. (Some fairly advanced physics students answer in this way, too!)

However, when a circuit like this one is connected, the bulb lights instantaneously. The physics explanation is not based on a simple source–consumer model. One teaching goal was therefore to get pupils to recognise that some of their assumptions about the behaviour of electric circuits were not correct, creating the need for a new explanation. The first lesson of the electricity teaching sequence begins with an activity called *The BIG Circuit*. The teacher prepares a circuit with a bulb at one end of the room and a battery at the other end, with wires stretched right the way around. When asked to predict what will happen when the circuit is connected, many pupils expect a significant time delay before the bulb lights, due to the length of wire involved. This allows the teacher to create amongst pupils the need for a model to explain the instantaneous lighting of the bulb.

and supporting pupils in their attempts to try using scientific explanations for the first time. In this perspective, good science lessons have to be both pupil- and teacher-centred.

Postscript: it works!

In a recent project in the *Evidence-based practice in science education* research network, a group of science education researchers and science teachers worked in collaboration to design three short teaching sequences for use with key stage 3 and 4 pupils. The teaching sequences were designed to address known learning demands in particular topic areas. The teachers then implemented the teaching sequences with classes that they were already teaching in their own schools. We compared the pupils' attainment after teaching with that of similar pupils in the school who had followed the school's normal approach to teaching. We also asked teachers not involved in the design of the teaching sequences to teach them, and made similar comparisons between the attainment of pupils who had followed the designed teaching and similar pupils who had followed the school's usual approach. Interested readers can find out more about this work (see websites), but the headline finding is that the attainment scores of pupils who had followed the designed teaching were better than those of their peers who had followed the school's usual teaching approach. This applied in all 15 cases where it is valid to make a comparison. Although the designed teaching sequences were better than the school's usual practice in promoting conceptual understanding amongst pupils, there is certainly no reason to assume that they represent the only way of addressing the learning demands in each topic area.

This evidence suggests that some approaches to teaching particular ideas in science achieve better levels of conceptual understanding than others. The implication is that we can now design the more effective schemes more explicitly to address learning demands, by using research evidence about pupils' learning, teachers' professional expertise and evidence from the systematic evaluation of teaching. Collaborative curriculum development involving teachers and researchers working in partnership appears to be a fruitful approach for improving pupils' conceptual understanding through science teaching.

References

Driver, R., Squires, A., Rushworth, P. and Wood-Robinson, V. (1994) *Making sense of secondary science: research into children's ideas*. London: Routledge.

Harré, R. (1986) *Varieties of realism*. Oxford: Blackwell.

Leach, J. and Scott, P. (1995) The demands of learning science concepts: issues of theory and practice. *School Science Review*, **76**(277), 47–51.

Minstrell, J. and Kraus, P. (2005) Guided inquiry in the science classroom. In *How students learn: science in the classroom*, ed. Donovan, M. S. and Bransford, J. D. Washington, DC: National Research Council.

Sutton, C. (1996) The scientific model as a form of speech. In *Science education research in Europe: current issues and themes*, ed. Welford, A. G., Osborne, J. and Scott, P. H. London: RoutledgeFalmer.

Websites

Evidence-based practice in science education network: http://www.york.ac.uk/depts/educ/projs/EPSE (The project was funded by the Economic and Social Research Council's Teaching and Learning Research Programme. By following links to Project 2, you can find the teaching materials used in the project.)

A short summary of the project on designing and evaluating science teaching can be found in a Research Briefing, at: http://www.tlrp.org/pub/research/no2.pdf

Chapter 20

Talk in science classrooms

Effective teacher–pupil and pupil–pupil interactions are central to supporting children in making **Phil Scott** and **Hilary Asoko**

personal sense of science. We can think about the activities of science lessons in terms of stimulating different kinds of talk as the scientific story develops, rather than simply in terms of 'what pupils will be doing'. In this chapter we focus on the different kinds of teacher–pupil interactions that occur in science classrooms and consider how these interactions relate to specific teaching purposes.

A shocking observation

Earlier this year a trainee science teacher (PGCE student), at the start of his school placement, participated in an activity that involved 'tracking' a year 7 pupil from lesson to lesson during one school day. The trainee was shocked by one key observation in the exercise: *the pupil did not utter one word in any lesson throughout the day*. Although clearly a sociable and popular boy (as witnessed in the playground), he remained silent in lessons.

Why is talk important?

In any classroom, talk is clearly important to the teacher as a way of communicating expectations, giving instructions, explaining ideas, monitoring understanding and controlling activity. It is also central to the process of *learning*. Talk provides children with the means to express and to work on ideas, to explore their implications and to share, compare and consolidate understandings. It is common experience that if we want to 'get our heads around' a difficult idea then it is helpful to talk it through with others. Talking is intimately connected to meaning-making and, indeed, this is why the observation of the year 7 pupil is troubling: if he was not talking in class to what extent was he able to work on developing his understandings?

Science lessons provide plenty of opportunities for talk. There are phenomena to discuss, ideas to explore, practical activities to carry out, results to report and evidence to interpret. Through these activities children can learn how to talk and think about natural phenomena in a scientific, as opposed to an everyday (or common-sense) way. This means using the ideas, explanations and approaches of the scientific community and it is important to recognise that these ideas and explanations are not there to be 'discovered' from hands-on activities. Rather, they must be introduced by the teacher and talked into existence (Ogborn *et al.*, 1996) with, and by, the pupils. In some science topic areas there may be big differences between everyday and scientific accounts of phenomena and this can lead to big teaching and learning challenges (Leach and Scott, 2002) – see Chapter 19. For example, if we take the phenomenon of a ball falling, there is a considerable difference between an 'everyday' explanation, such as *'it falls because it's heavy and you let go of it'*, and the scientific view that is based on action at a distance, *'the ball falls because of the pull of the Earth'*.

Teacher–pupil interactions in science classrooms

In a recent PGCE class a trainee (a different one) commented that she was *'really looking forward'* to her tutor visiting her lessons in school. Given that this kind of enthusiasm for a tutor visit is somewhat unusual, we were keen to find out why. This student's answer was something along the lines of, *'Oh, my classes are really interactive, just like you told us ... lots of questions and answers'*. However, when the day of the visit came, the lesson proved to be disappointing. There was certainly lots of interaction, *but* the trainee was not really listening to and taking account of the pupils' ideas. This is a critical point, which we shall now consider in more detail.

Interactive and non-interactive dimension: who is speaking?

Interactive teaching allows for the verbal participation of teacher and pupils and *non-interactive* involves only the teacher, excluding the participation of the pupils. Thus in interactive teaching the teacher might typically engage the pupils in a series of questions and answers, whilst in non-interactive teaching the teacher is presenting ideas in a 'lecturing' style. These ideas offer one dimension for characterising science teaching: the interactive/non-interactive dimension.

Dialogic and authoritative dimension: whose ideas are being discussed?

What then do we mean by 'taking account of pupils' ideas'? The idea here is that the teacher asks pupils for their points of view and explicitly takes account of them by, for example: asking for further details (*'Oh, that's interesting, what do you mean by ...?'*); or writing it down for further consideration (*'Let's just put that down on the board, so that we don't forget it'*); or asking other pupils whether they agree with it or not (*'Do you go along with what Anita has just said?'*). In a nutshell, the teacher makes room in the classroom talk for a whole range of ideas and this kind of talk is *dialogic*. In dialogic talk there is always the attempt to acknowledge the views of others, and through dialogic discourse the teacher attends to the pupils' points of view as well as to the school science view.

Of course, classroom talk is not always dialogic in form. There are occasions when the teacher does not explore pupils' ideas and take account of them as he/she develops the lesson. The teacher keeps the focus on the science point of view and if pupils raise questions or ideas that do not contribute to the development of the school science story they are likely to be reshaped or ignored by the teacher. This is *authoritative* talk. We therefore have a second dimension for thinking about teacher talk: the authoritative–dialogic dimension.

The communicative approach

Any episode of classroom talk can be identified as being either *interactive* or *non-interactive* on the one hand, and *dialogic* or *authoritative* on the other, generating four broad classes of *communicative approach* (Mortimer and Scott, 2003) as illustrated in Figure 20.1.

	Interactive	**Non-interactive**
Authoritative	*interactive/ authoritative*	*non-interactive/ dialogic*
Dialogic	*interactive/ dialogic*	*non-interactive/ authoritative*

Figure 20.1 **Four classes of communicative approach.**

What might each of these classes of communicative approach look like in the classroom? We start with the two *interactive* approaches.

Interactive/authoritative communicative approach

The episode shown in Box 20.1 is taken from a year 8 science class (12/13 year-olds) in a comprehensive school in a large city in the North of England. In the previous lesson the class had started some work on the theme of energy, carrying out a practical activity with electric bells.

You will probably recognise this kind of question-and-answer routine, where the teacher is searching for a single answer. Here the teacher wants to focus on the fact that the bell had heated up, but the pupils offer other responses: *'vibration'*, *'loud'*, *'sparks'*, which the teacher ignores as he homes in on the notion of *'heat'*. In this way, the teacher adopts an *interactive/authoritative* communicative approach. The talk is interactive in the sense of there being lots of questions and answers and is authoritative as the teacher focuses on just one acceptable answer.

Interactive/authoritative talk is the most common form of communicative approach in science classrooms, not only in the UK but around the world. Some observers estimate that it accounts for as much as 90 per cent of the talk in science classrooms: in other words, the teacher spends most of the time asking

Box 20.1
Electric bell

At the start of the lesson the teacher invites the pupils to think back:

Teacher: *Do you remember the electric bell?*

Pupils: *Yes! [in chorus]*

Teacher: *OK! Did any of you notice, did any of you actually hold on to the bell after it had ... been working? What did you notice?*

Suzanne: *Vibration.*

Teacher: *Well, the arm vibrated, yes. Sound. What else did you notice?*

Tom: *It was loud.*

Teacher: *That's not quite what I'm getting at. Remember the bell. There's the bell [holding up a bell in front of the class]. You did the experiment. If you held on to this bit here where the wires were [indicating], did you notice anything there?*

Jason: *There were sparks there.*

Teacher: *Heat, did you notice some heat?*

Jason: *There were sparks from there.*

Teacher: *There were?*

Jason: *Sparks.*

Teacher: *There were some sparks, yes. Let's just ignore the sparks a minute ... some heat. There was a little bit of heat there with that one.*

streams of questions and the pupils are required almost to 'guess what the teacher is thinking'.

This form of classroom talk is identifiable in a second way. Look back at the transcript. The teacher starts by asking a *question*: '*Do you remember the electric bell?*' The pupils *respond* '*Yes*'. The teacher then makes an *evaluation*: '*OK*', before moving on to ask another *question*: '*Did any of you notice, did any of you actually hold on to the bell after it had ... been working? What did you notice?*' Suzanne *responds* with '*vibration*' and the teacher *evaluates*, '*Well, the arm vibrated, yes. Sound.*' and moves on to ask the next question.

In this way we can see a clear *pattern of discourse*, whereby:

- teacher asks a question: INITIATION [I]
- pupil responds: RESPONSE [R]
- teacher evaluates: EVALUATION [E]

This 3-step pattern, I–R–E, is the ubiquitous 'dance-step' (1–2–3, 1–2–3, 1–2–3 ...) of science lessons. Once you become aware of it you can't fail to notice how common it is.

Interactive/dialogic communicative approach

Of course, there is an alternative to the authoritative form of interactive talk set out above. This is where the teacher sets up interactions that are dialogic in approach. In the episode in Box 20.2, a year 7 science class (11/12 year-olds)

Box 20.2

Solids

The teacher asks the class whether *'solids are hard'*, an idea that has been suggested by one of the pupils:

Teacher: *Solids are hard?*

Pupils: *No, no. Soft! [together]*

Teacher: *Well, if you say 'no', put your hand up and tell me, give me an example, which would prove an exception to that ... [the idea that solids are hard].*

Suzanne: *Powder's a solid, but you can crush it.*

Teacher: *Powder's?*

Suzanne: *... a solid but you can still crush it.*

Teacher: *Powders aren't particularly hard, yes, if you're talking about hard to the touch. Paul? [who has his hand up]*

Paul: *It's ... 'cos...it's [the powder] got a gas in between, so it's hard.*

Teacher: *So you think that all solids are hard?*

Paul: *Yeah.*

Teacher: *Other people are desperate to say that all solids aren't hard. Martin?*

Martin: *Er ... fabric's soft.*

Pupils: *Yeah ... yeah ... [lots of muttering]*

Teacher: *Wait. Just a minute. If you're saying things, can you say it to the front, so that we can all share these ideas.*

is considering the characteristic properties of solids, liquids and gases.

The nature of these interactions is quite different from the electric bell episode. Here the teacher is seeking the views of the pupils and excellent examples of solids that are *not* hard are forthcoming from the class (powders, fabrics). Rather than evaluate the pupils' responses the teacher acts to *prompt* pupils to make further contributions (*'Well, if you say 'no', put your hand up and tell me, give me an example, which would prove an exception to that ...'*) and to elaborate upon their ideas (*'So you think that all solids are hard?'*). In this way, the teacher adopts an *interactive/dialogic* communicative approach in which a whole range of pupil ideas are explored (this episode actually continued for 10 or so minutes in this way).

The distinctive **pattern of discourse** in this case involves chains of interaction rather than the I–R–E pattern of the authoritative talk. Thus the teacher starts by asking a **question**, *'Solids are hard?'*, and the pupils **respond**, *'No, no. Soft!'* Now the teacher **prompts** further contributions on this question, *'Well, if you say "no", put your hand up and tell me, give me an example, which would prove an exception to that ...'*. Suzanne **responds**, *'Powder's a solid, but you can crush it'*, and the teacher **prompts** her to say a little more, *'Powder's?'* In this way we see a pattern emerging in the discourse:

- teacher asks a question: INITIATION [I]
- pupil responds: RESPONSE [R]

- teacher prompts: PROMPT   [P]
- pupil responds: RESPONSE   [R]
- teacher prompts: PROMPT   [P]

So a chain of interaction, I–R–P–R–P–R–P–, is set up and the skill of the teacher lies in sustaining the development of the interaction, encouraging responses from a range of pupils. An alternative version of this interactive/dialogic approach emerges when a number of pupils answer the same question from the teacher, generating an $I–Rs_1–Rs_2–Rs_3–$ form, where Rs_n indicates a response from a particular pupil. Here, the response from pupil 3, for example, might not necessarily address the initial question posed by the teacher; it might be a comment on a previous pupil's response.

The key feature of the interactive/dialogic approach is that the teacher makes room for and explores pupils' ideas. If you want to find out what pupils' are thinking you need to engage them in this kind of teacher–pupil talk.

Non-interactive approaches

What of the non-interactive communicative approaches? By this stage it is probably clear that a *non-interactive/authoritative* communicative approach involves the presentation of a single point of view, which is likely to be the school science story. For example, the teacher might outline the idea that electric current is conserved in simple circuits or offer an account of what is involved in photosynthesis. There is no room here for pupils' ideas, the focus is on the science.

At first glance, the very notion of a *non-interactive/dialogic* communicative approach might seem like a contradiction in terms. How can the teacher act in such a way that they are presenting (non-interactive) and yet attending to the pupils' points of view as well as to the school science view? The idea is that the teacher presents a range of ideas, usually in the context of a review of ideas that have been offered by pupils, as seen in Box 20.3, often before moving on to the next phase of the lesson.

Box 20.3

Review

Teacher: *Ok! Well that's been very useful. On the one hand, Paul has been arguing that all solids must be hard, but Suzanne seems to have a different point of view when she talks about powders and that was a bit like Martin's ideas on fabrics. So, where do we go from here? What would be a clear way of thinking through this question?*

Matching communicative approach to teaching purposes

In the previous sections we have set out and exemplified four distinct communicative approaches that might be used in the classroom. Is one communicative approach intrinsically better than another? For example, is it the case that interactive/authoritative teaching is somehow *bad*, whilst interactive/dialogic teaching is *good*? Is non-interactive teaching bad, simply because it is the teacher who is doing all the talking? These are important and absolutely fundamental questions. The answer to them is that effective teaching involves all these approaches. It depends on what you are trying to do! If you think about the purpose of a teaching episode you can employ the appropriate communicative approach, as summarised in Box 20.4.

Box 20.4
Matching approach to purpose

Teaching purpose: To explore pupils' ideas.
    Communicative approach: Interactive/ dialogic.
    Pattern of interaction: I–R–P–R–P–R–P ...

Teaching purpose: To introduce a key scientific concept or develop a clear line of argument.
    Communicative approach: Non-interactive/authoritative or interactive/authoritative.
    Pattern of interaction: Presentational and/or I–R–E.

Teaching purpose: To review/summarise a range of points of view.
    Communicative approach: Non-interactive/dialogic.

The 'rhythm' of the classroom talk

The point was made earlier, that by far the most common form of classroom talk is the *interactive/authoritative* approach. What we are suggesting here is that in any teaching sequence it makes sense to adopt a range of approaches matched to teaching purposes in the ways outlined above. Expert teachers demonstrate a 'rhythm' in their teaching, whereby now they open-up matters for discussion (*interactive/dialogic*), now they work on the science point of view (*interactive/authoritative*), now they summarise the science view (*non-interactive/ authoritative*) and link it to children's thinking (*non-interactive/dialogic*). There is no special order in which they go about these transitions but there is a strong sense of *rhythm* as ideas are opened up for discussion and then closed down.

This idea of opening-up and closing-down discussions is directly linked to the very nature of scientific knowledge. Science itself is an *authoritative* body of knowledge that has been developed within the scientific community, and it is the responsibility of the science teacher to introduce their pupils to the concepts, conventions and ways of working of science. Science lessons cannot revolve entirely around free-for-all discussions: there must be authoritative interventions by the teacher. The constant teaching challenge for the science teacher is how to handle this tension between promoting authoritative and dialogic approaches.

Pupil–pupil talk

In a whole-class setting, the opportunities for individuals to talk are inevitably limited. Working in groups or pairs provides opportunities for more pupils to participate and to explore and develop their understanding but, without the support of the teacher, children may lack the skills to talk productively. Teachers, therefore, have a responsibility to *model*, in their interactions with pupils, the kinds of interactive/dialogic talk that they are aiming for in group work: offering ideas, listening to others, asking for clarification, making links to others' ideas and so on. In addition, the skills needed for such talk can be taught (Dawes, 2004), to allow pupils to develop their ability to talk and think things through both together and alone.

The importance of pupil talk is also discussed in Chapters 17 and 27 and others.

References

Dawes, L. (2004) Talk and learning in classroom science. *International Journal of Science Education*, **26**(6), 677–695.

Leach, J. and Scott, P. (2002) Designing and evaluating science teaching sequences: an approach drawing upon the concept of learning demand and a social constructivist perspective on learning. *Studies in Science Education*, **38**, 115–142.

Mortimer, E. F. and Scott, P. H. (2003) *Meaning making in secondary science classrooms*. Maidenhead: Open University Press.

Ogborn, J., Kress, G., Martins, I. and McGillicuddy, K. (1996) *Explaining science in the class room*. Buckingham: Open University Press.

Further reading

Alexander, R. J. (2005) *Towards dialogic teaching: rethinking classroom talk*. 2nd edn. York: Dialogos.

Chapter 21

Teachers' and pupils' questions

Questioning is a key feature of scientific activity and of teaching science. Asking questions leads

Wynne Harlen

scientists to seek answers through enquiry and so develop understanding of the world around. Pupils' scientific activity, too, is stimulated by questions, sometimes implicit rather than explicit, sometimes raised by the teachers and sometimes by the pupils. What is important is the way that a question is accepted by the class and that the learner sees it as a question worth answering and is motivated to seek an answer. It is in helping this search for answers through scientific activity that the role of teachers' questions is so important. The chapter begins with these, and turns later to how to encourage and deal with the questions that pupils ask.

Questions for different purposes

There are several reasons for giving attention to the questions teachers ask. First, they are by far the most common form of communication between teachers and pupils. Second, they have the potential to stimulate pupils' thinking and guide their effort productively. Third, the questions often fail to do this because they are not appropriately worded. For example, research shows that the overwhelming majority of teachers' questions are 'closed' and a large proportion of these ask for facts. Whilst occasional questioning of what the pupils know is expected, often teachers ask a factual question when what they really want is the pupils to give their ideas or think things out. Finally, changing questioning is one of the most effective steps to take in improving teaching.

Teachers ask a number of different kinds of questions for different purposes, such as for class control, checking on whether instructions have been understood or routines followed, or asking for information. The questions that are our concern here are those that ask about pupils' ideas or encourage the use and development of enquiry skills. For these questions to be effective their form, content and timing need to be appropriate for their purpose. These three aspects are interconnected and all need to be considered in framing questions. Box 21.1 illustrates how just small changes in wording can make a difference.

The examples in Box 21.1 indicate the difference the form of a question (open/closed; person-centred/subject-centred) can make to how pupils respond. They also show that the content of the question has to reflect the kind of response intended. If the intention of the question is to encourage pupils to use enquiry skills then the question needs to indicate the skill that is required. For example:

- *What would you like to find out about inherited features?* (raising questions)
- *Why is copper an example of a metal?* (classification)
- *What's similar and what's different between a block of wood and a block of steel?* (comparison)
- *What do you think will happen if we decrease the voltage across the motor?* (prediction)
- *What could you do to find out what makes a difference to the rate of growth of a crystal?* (investigation)
- *What have you found out about the link between the position of the torch and the size of the shadow?* (interpretation)

Timing is also important. When starting a new topic, pupils need time to explore and relate new experiences to existing ones before they can be expected to explain what is going on. So, *'How can you make different sounds?'* should come before *'How do you think these sounds are produced?'*

A further important point about teachers' questioning concerns giving pupils time to answer. Research (Budd Rowe, 1974) showed that, after asking a question, teachers frequently wait no longer than one second before intervening again if no answer is forthcoming. When they were advised to increase the 'wait' time to eight to ten seconds after asking questions that required explanations, the pupils' answers were longer and more thoughtful. The 'wait' time is necessary not only to allow the pupils to think and to formulate their answers, but to convey the message that the teacher is really interested in their ideas or their skills and will listen to their answers carefully. It also slows down the discussion, giving the teacher time to phrase thoughtful questions and the pupils time to think before answering. The whole exchange is then more productive in terms of giving teachers access to pupils' real understanding and not just their first superficial thoughts. A teacher's experience of changing this aspect of her questioning, as a result of work described by Black *et al.* (2002), is reproduced in Box 21.2.

Encouraging and responding to pupils' questions

Another part of the teacher's role in relation to questions is responding to the questions that pupils ask. There is direct benefit to pupils' thinking in encouraging them to ask questions. In addition there is value to teachers, as through their questions pupils reveal the limits of their understanding and the nature of their own ideas. By no means all of their questions will be ones that

Box 21.1

The wording of teachers' questions

Consider a situation in which key stage 3 (junior secondary) pupils have been setting up circuits with a battery and two bulbs, one circuit with the bulbs in parallel and the other with the bulbs in series. To find out the ideas the pupils have for explaining the difference in the brightness of the bulbs in the two circuits, the teacher might ask questions such as:

1   *Explain to me what is happening when the wires are connected to complete the circuit.*
2   *Why does the brightness of the bulbs differ in the series and parallel circuits?*
3   *What causes the bulbs to light up?*
4   *What difference would it make if we reverse the connections to the batteries?* etc.

Or (s)he might ask:

5   *What do you think happens when the wires are connected to complete the circuit?*
6   *Why do you think there is a difference in the brightness of the bulbs in the series and parallel circuits?*
7   *What do you think causes the bulbs to light up?*
8   *What difference do you think it would make if we reverse the connections to the batteries?*
9   *What are your ideas about the current running through each bulb in the two circuits?* etc.

Or, again (s)he might ask:

10 *What could you do to find out if there is a difference in the current going through the bulbs?*
11 *What do you think will happen if you take out one of the bulbs in each circuit?*
12 *What do you think you would need to do to make the bulbs in this [series circuit] as bright as the ones in the other circuit?*
13 *What do you see when you look at the bulb with a hand lens?*

The first set of questions (1–4) are open in form, as opposed to closed questions where a short one-word answer is all that is required. However, these questions ask directly for *the* answer, not the pupils' ideas about what is happening. By contrast, the second set (5–9) are expressed so as to ask for the pupils' ideas, with no suggestion that there is a right answer. They are described as 'person-centred' as opposed to 'subject-centred' questions. All the pupils should be able to answer the second set, while only those who feel that they can give the right answer will attempt to answer the first set. Thus the open, person-centred questions are preferred for eliciting pupils' ideas.

The questions in the third set (10–13) are also expressed as open, person-centred questions, but they are more likely to lead to *action* and to the use of enquiry skills rather than to the expression of ideas because they do not ask for explanations. So the content of these questions makes them useful for finding out about pupils' ability to observe or investigate or use other skills.

Evidently small changes in wording of a question can have a big impact on how pupils respond.

Box 21.2

A teacher's experience of changing her 'wait' time

Increasing waiting time after asking questions proved difficult to start with – due to my habitual desire to 'add' something almost immediately after asking the original questions. The pause after asking the questions was sometimes 'painful'. It felt unnatural to have such a seemingly 'dead' period, but I persevered. Given more thinking time students seemed to realise that a more thoughtful answer was required. Now, after many months of changing my style of questioning, I have noticed that most students will give an answer and an explanation (where necessary) without additional prompting.

(Quoted in Black *et al.*, 2002, p. 5)

lead to scientific activity. So teachers need to be prepared to respond to, though not necessarily to provide an answer to, the variety of questions that pupils ask. We will come to how to deal with different kinds of questions later; first it is important to get the questions flowing.

Some teachers report that their pupils don't ask questions, so they don't get the opportunity of satisfactory answers. The likely reason for ceasing to ask questions is repeated experience of not having any, or any satisfying, answers. The problem may well have its roots at the primary level and it is there where teachers can take action to encourage questions. In secondary science classrooms pupils may be deterred from asking questions for fear of their questions being ridiculed by peers or dismissed as irrelevant by the teacher who is intent on 'covering' specific content.

Encouraging questions

Questions arise from curiosity, so the first point is to have materials, activities, events and sometimes people, to stimulate interest and questions. The materials need not be novel. Often displays of familiar things, such as food products or household tools to which pupils can relate, are more effective in generating questions than the unfamiliar items provided in kits from scientific suppliers. Provision for pupils to bring in materials and objects to display means that these have built-in interest likely to be shared by other pupils. The task of collecting the objects generates some questions and focuses on the topic in advance of the lesson, as illustrated by the example in Box 21.3.

Given a stimulus, questions can be elicited through:

- brainstorming as a whole class – the public acceptance of all questions of whatever kind will encourage those at first reluctant to express their questions;
- snowballing – raising questions in pairs or small groups, and then sharing with merged groups and then the whole class;
- a question box or board where pupils can post or pin up their questions anonymously;
- deciding the most useful questions to ask a visitor or during a visit out of school;

Box 21.3

Questions from everyday objects

Mike, a trainee teacher, complained to his tutor that he was restricted in teaching about materials because his placement school did not have any 'materials kits'. On the suggestion of his tutor, Mike invited members of the class to select an object from around the room (furniture, clothing, stationery, etc.) and ask any question relating to what it was made of. This raised many interesting questions to investigate further, enabled Mike to recognise that some pupils confused objects with the materials from which they were made, and provoked discussion of whether air is a material and whether a sample of air becomes an object when it is enclosed in a bottle. This lively introduction engaged the pupils' attention for the more conventional study of classifying materials.

- discussing different kinds of questions and involving older pupils in categorising them in the way suggested below for teachers;
- using question stems as prompts to construct questions.

All of these will not only lead to really useful information for the teacher about what pupils want to know and what their current thinking is, but also make clear to pupils that questioning is valued. Holding regular question-raising sessions where pupils can say what they would like to know about a topic they are working on can provide opportunity for pupils to find answers to their own questions. Such sessions can serve as a good stimulus when starting on a topic. Displaying the questions, reviewing and adding to them at intervals, enables pupils as well as teachers to be more aware of their developing understanding.

As we have said, the easiest way to suppress questioning is to ignore questions, sweep them aside or make pupils feel foolish for asking. So handling questions in a way that takes them seriously, even if they can't be answered, is essential.

Handling pupils' questions

A useful first step when deciding how to respond to a pupil's question is to think about the kind of question it is and why it is being asked. Not all children's questions, as parents and teachers well know, are asked because of real interest in the answers. Some are attention-seeking, some delaying tactics, some probing for hints about what the teacher has in mind. Some questions are really expressions of interest or wonder that are put in the form of questions, but to which no answer is really expected. For example, young pupils looking at a bird's nest asked *'How do they weave it?'* Rather than begin to answer this question by focusing their attention on how it might be done, the teacher judged it to be an expression of wonder in which she joined by saying *'Yes, it is wonderful, isn't it?'*; the children's attention quickly moved on to other features of the nest.

Among the genuine questions there are likely to be ones that can be classified as falling into one of these four types:

- **Factual questions:** those asking for simple facts, e.g. *'What's the name of this rock?'*, *'How long does it take for a bird's egg to hatch?'*, *'How many kinds of woodlice are there in Britain?'*

- **Investigable questions:** those that could be answered, at least in part, by observation or investigation by the pupils, e.g. *'What would happen if we plant the seeds/bulbs upside down?'*, *'Which of these rocks is the hardest?'*, *'Do all fuels contain the same amount of energy?'*, *'Do maggots move faster if they get hot?'*
- **Complex questions:** those that require complex answers and reference to concepts that are beyond the understanding of the pupils, e.g. *'How do satellites stay in the sky?'*, *'Why do you see colours when there is oil in a puddle?'*, *'How do hibernating animals survive extreme temperatures?'*, *'How do tap dancers do it [move so fast]?'*
- **Philosophical questions:** those that may be philosophical, e.g. *'Why do birds only have two legs?'*, *'Why do we have day and night?'*, *'Is it cruel to investigate woodlice in science lessons?'*, *'Does light travel faster than God?'*

Each of these types is best handled in a different way and knowing some ways of doing this can take the anxiety out of encouraging pupils to ask questions.

Factual questions

These are questions that cannot be answered by the pupils' enquiry into the objects themselves because they refer to names, conventions and factual information. They can be answered immediately if the teacher knows the answer, or later when the teacher can look it up or can help the pupils find it by using reference sources – books, CD-ROMs, the Internet. Suitable questions can be displayed on a notice board, as *'This week's interesting questions'* to encourage other pupils to seek out answers.

Investigable questions

These are the questions of most value in science education. It is important for the teacher to recognise them and to resist the temptation to give the answer, which may seem obvious but it is of more value to the pupils if they find it for themselves. There is often the need for some discussion of the question before it can be investigated. Turning a vague 'which is best' type of question into an investigation involves deciding what 'best' means in a particular case and whether the comparison is, for example, between types of material, or specific objects, or pieces of material (see 'How clear is your question?' in Goldsworthy, Watson and Wood-Robinson, 2000, pp. 37–41).

It is quite likely that a question that can be profitably investigated by the pupils comes up at an inconvenient time. In that case it should be stored, perhaps on a list on the classroom wall of *'Things to investigate'*, to be taken up at a later time. One teacher, working with pupils with learning difficulties, had a section of her board permanently headed *'Not relevant just now'* to jot down pupils' questions to be considered later. This is a way of acknowledging that the pupils' questions are valued – but it is important that they are not forgotten.

Complex questions

These may well seem the most difficult questions to handle, particularly because the teacher may not know the answer and if (s)he does, will realise that the pupils would not understand it. Giving complex answers may well send the message to pupils that science is difficult, and if they often find their questions met by answers they can't understand they are likely to stop asking questions. To prevent this, the question has to be discussed and can often be turned into one that pupils can investigate. For instance, the question about colours seen in an oil film can lead to investigations about where the oil is, that it floats on water, and about whether the thickness of the oil film makes a difference to the colours. This technique of 'turning' was suggested by Jelly (2001) who gave the example in Box 21.4. Jelly admits that the outcome is not a complete answer to the pupil's question, but it often satisfies the curiosity for the moment and underlines the message that in science answers can be found by enquiry.

Box 21.4

Example of 'turning' a question

Consider a situation in which children are exploring the properties of fabrics. They have dropped water on different types and become fascinated by the fact that water stays 'like a little ball' on felt. They tilt the felt, rolling the ball around, and someone asks 'Why is it like a ball?' How might the question be turned by applying the 'doing more to understand' approach? We need to analyse the situation quickly and use what I call a 'variables scan'. The explanation must relate to something 'going on' between the water and the felt surface, so causing the ball. That being so, ideas for children's activities will come if we consider ways in which the situation could be varied to better understand the making of the ball. We could explore surfaces, keeping the drop the same, and explore drops, keeping the surface the same. These thoughts can prompt others that bring ideas nearer to what children might do.

(Jelly, 2001, pp. 44–45)

Philosophical questions

These questions, also, require some discussion with the pupils asking them. Only then will it be possible to decide whether *'Why do we have day and night?'* means *'Who decided this?'* or *'What causes day and night?'* Frequently the question will be rephrased to make it clear that it falls in one of the other categories; if not, then it is only possible to agree that it is an interesting question but one to which no one can give a definite answer.

Discussing questions with pupils

The categories just suggested for teachers to use in deciding how to respond to pupils' questions can be shared with pupils to help them begin to work out how to answer their own questions. The differences can be explained simply, perhaps by taking a collection of questions and asking them to decide: which can be answered by looking up in a book or other reference source; which can be answered by observation or investigation; and which can't be answered by science. Investigable questions may be further considered, in terms of what kind of investigation would furnish an answer. The AKSIS project developed activities, for both primary and secondary pupils, using model questions to be supplemented by the pupils' own, to discuss how they can find answers by different kinds of scientific enquiry (Goldsworthy *et al.*, 2000, pp. 27–35) (see also Chapter 25). This was adopted and adapted in the Key Stage 3 Strategy materials (DfES, 2002). Secondary pupils may be able to take this further, to develop understanding of what science is about, the nature of the knowledge it provides and its limitations in terms of the kinds of questions that we can answer through scientific activity. What is important is that questions, and particularly questions generated by pupils, are at the centre of science learning so that curiosity is stimulated and discussion takes a major role in science education.

References

Black, P., Harrison, C., Lee, C., Marshall, B. and Wiliam, D. (2002) *Working inside the black box*. London: nferNelson.

Budd Rowe, M. (1974) Wait time and rewards as instructional variables, their influence on language, logic and fate control. *Journal of Research in Science Teaching*, 11, 81–84.

DfES (2002) *Key Stage 3 National Strategy: Science: Scientific enquiry notes for tutors*. Ref. 0348/2002. London: Department for Education and Skills.

Goldsworthy, A., Watson, R., Wood-Robinson, V. (2000) AKSIS project. *Developing understanding in scientific enquiry*. Hatfield: Association for Science Education.

Jelly, S. J. (2001) Helping children to raise questions – and answering them. In *Primary science: taking the plunge*, ed. Harlen, W. 2nd edn. Portsmouth, NH: Heinemann.

Chapter 22

Assessment for learning and assessment of learning

All pupil assessment involves collecting evidence of pupils' achievements, interpreting the evidence and using it for a defined purpose. This chapter is about carrying out this process for two main purposes: helping learning and reporting on learning. These are described as formative assessment, or assessment *for* learning, and summative assessment, or assessment *of* learning. The first section provides a rationale for the importance of formative assessment and considers what implementing it involves. This is followed by a discussion of how summative assessment differs from formative assessment and the relationship between the two. Other purposes for which pupils are assessed, not considered here, are for accountability, for monitoring standards over time and for research. In these cases, the purpose of the assessment is not to make decisions about individual pupils, although using assessment information for these other purposes can and does affect pupils through impact on teachers and the curriculum, a point revisited briefly at the end of the chapter.

Wynne Harlen

Why assessment for learning?

Using assessment to help learning is logically necessary for teaching that aims for understanding. It is particularly appropriate in science, but the argument applies to any other learning where the aim is for learners to construct meaning through their own thinking and actions. In science education, the aim is to enable pupils to build scientific understanding through direct interaction with, and thinking about, materials, events and phenomena in their environment. The emphasis is on understanding, which, on the basis of modern views of learning, requires action by the learner. It is recognised that learners 'do the learning' by constructing meaning from their experiences and making sense of the world in terms of concepts and mental models. It is now well known from a considerable body of research (for example the research of the CLIS and SPACE projects) that learners construct their own understanding of their experiences, and that these ideas may be in conflict with the widely held ideas about events. The way in which learners come to revise and reconstruct their understanding to bring it more into line with accepted scientific ideas is through interaction with their environment and with the ideas of others. This is elaborated in the socio-cultural view of learning based on the ideas of Vygotsky (1962) and Lave and Wenger (1991) among others (Bransford, Brown and Cocking, 1999) (see also Chapter 20).

Box 22.1

Key features of formative assessment

As a result of a thorough review of research on classroom assessment, Black and Wiliam (1998a,b) concluded that the use of assessment for formative purposes can lead to substantial gains in learning when it includes certain key features. These are:

- the provision of effective feedback to pupils;
- the active involvement of pupils in their own learning;
- adjusting teaching to take account of the results of assessment;
- a recognition of the profound influence assessment has on the motivation and self-esteem of pupils, both of which are crucial influences on learning;
- the need for pupils to be able to assess themselves and understand how to improve.

Perhaps the most significant finding from the research is that the practice of formative assessment benefits all pupils, but the increase in levels of achievement is particularly marked for lower achieving pupils. Thus the effect is to decrease the gap between the higher and lower achieving pupils.

Black and Wiliam acknowledged that such practices require large shifts in teachers' perceptions of their roles in relation to their pupils, but that considerable gains in achievements are possible as a result.

When learning is understood in this way, the pupils are at the centre of the process. It follows that the more they know about what it is intended should be learned – the learning goals – and about where they have reached in relation to these goals, as well as about what further needs to be done to reach the goals, the more they can direct effort usefully for learning. The role of the teacher is to assess where pupils are in relation to the goals, to decide on appropriate next steps, to help the pupils take these steps and, importantly, to involve the pupils in these processes. These actions together comprise formative assessment or assessment for learning:

the process of seeking and interpreting evidence for use by learners and their teachers to decide where the learners are in their learning, where they need to go and how best to get there. (Assessment Reform Group, 2002)

There is, moreover, convincing research evidence that formative assessment has a positive impact on learning. The value of using assessment in this way was the main message from a review of research on classroom assessment conducted by Black and Wiliam (1998a,b). Box 22.1 summarises the main findings.

Implementing formative assessment

How are the essential features, indicated in Box 22.1, put into practice? First it is important to emphasise that formative assessment is not something added to teaching, but is integral to it. Like teaching, it does not happen at infrequent intervals, as in the case of summative assessment. It is a cyclic process; the effect of decisions at a particular time is to alter the learning activity, hopefully towards achievement of the goals, and to lead to a further activity, where again evidence is gathered and interpreted to decide the most useful further steps, and so on. This can be represented as in Figure 22.1.

We can break into the cycle at activity **A**, related to a clear goal of learning. This provides opportunity for teacher and pupils to gather evidence about the pupils' current understanding or skills in relation to the goal. Evidence can be gathered in a range of ways, such as questioning, discussion, review of what pupils write or draw about what they know and can do, and other methods designed to gain access to the pupils' existing understanding. The evidence is then interpreted in terms of the goals of the activity, but also taking into account such things as a pupil's recent progress and effort put in. This means the judgement is pupil-referenced (ipsative) as well as criterion-referenced.

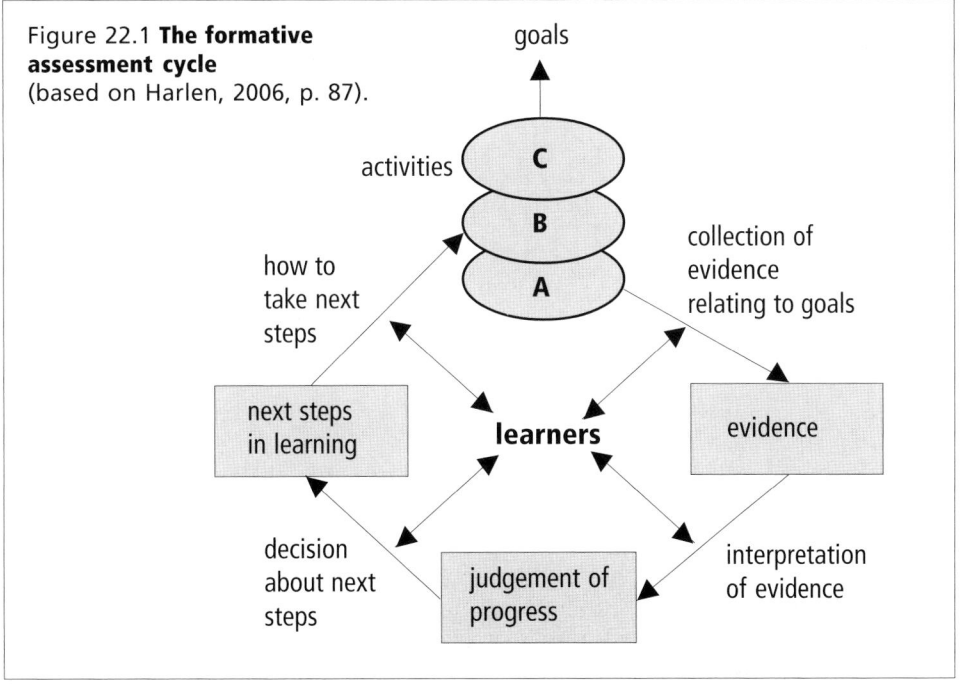

Figure 22.1 **The formative assessment cycle** (based on Harlen, 2006, p. 87).

In the next part of the cycle the judgement of where the pupils have reached is used to decide the next steps. This decision requires a clear grasp on the part of the teacher of the goals of the activity and of the course of progress towards them. Once the next steps have been identified the teacher, together with the pupils involved, decides how to take them. This can't be planned in detail in advance, since the purpose of assessing within teaching is to guide decisions about how to help learning. However, teachers can, of course, be equipped with a range of strategies – a tool-box, if you like – from which they select according to the nature of the step that needs to be taken. The outcome of the process is the next learning activity, **B** in Figure 22.1, which takes pupils further towards achievement of the goals. The process then continues in a cycle, leading to activity **C**, and so on. This is, of course, a model and, although described as a series of separate actions, in practice the processes within the cycle often run together.

In all steps there is a role for the pupils who, through participating in the decisions, will understand what they need to do and will be committed to making the effort that is required. Chapter 23 and other chapters in this book deal with several of the features of formative assessment identified in Box 22.1. Here we consider feedback.

Feedback and formative assessment

The cycle depicted in Figure 22.1 is one in which evidence is fed back into teaching and learning. This feedback helps to regulate teaching so that the pace of moving toward a learning goal is adjusted to ensure the active participation of the pupils. As with all regulated processes, feedback into the system is the important mechanism for ensuring effective operation. Just as feedback from the thermostat of a heating or cooling system allows the temperature of a room to be maintained within a particular range, so feedback of information about learning helps to ensure that new experiences are neither too difficult nor too easy for pupils. In the case of teaching, the feedback is both to the teacher and to the pupils.

Feedback to the teacher is needed to inform decisions about where pupils are and what are their appropriate next steps. For these decisions the teacher needs a clear view of progression in the ideas or skills that are the goals of learning. Pupils obtain feedback directly from self-assessment of their own work, from the teacher and from other pupils.

Formative feedback

Since much of the communication between teacher and pupils is through marking written work, the form of the feedback given in this way is of considerable significance if pupils are to become involved in taking their next steps. Research shows that, although all feedback through marking is intended to help learning, much of it does not have this effect (Kluger and DeNisi, 1996). Some of the most influential studies on feedback by marking have been carried out by Ruth Butler. Box 22.2 summarises one of these studies.

Of course not just any comment will provide useful feedback. Experience shows that it is important for it to be non-judgemental and to show where pupils need to make improvements or direct their future effort. Comments of the type *'Well done!'*, *'A good effort'*, *'Try to draw more carefully'* or *'Always put*

Box 22.2

Research into feedback that promotes learning

In this study by Ruth Butler (1987) the effects of different types of feedback by marking were compared. Using a controlled experimental design she set up groups which were given feedback in different ways. Pupils in one group were given marks, or grades only; those in another group were given only comments on their work and the third group received both marks and comments on their work. These conditions were studied in relation to tasks some of which required divergent and some convergent thinking.

The result was that, for divergent thinking tasks, the pupils who received *comments only* made the greatest gain in their learning, significantly more than for the other two groups. The results were the same for high and low achieving pupils. For convergent tasks, the lower achieving pupils scored most highly after *comments only*, with the *marks only* group next above the *marks plus comments* group. For all tasks and pupils, *comments only* led to higher achievement.

(Quoted from Harlen, 2006, p. 174)

the date on your work' do little to advance learning. Black *et al.* (2003, p. 45), working with secondary teachers, quote examples of more useful comments:

Richard, clear method, results table and graph, but what does this tell you about the relationship?

Go back to your notes from the 29th September and look up where chlorophyll is and what it does.

Well explained so far but add reasons why the Haber process uses these conditions.

Harlen (2006) quotes examples of primary teachers' marking in which children respond to teachers' written comments on their work. For instance, one child wrote and drew about making a switch but without making clear how it would be connected into a circuit. The teacher's question about where the wires would be attached was answered by the child before going on to the next activity.

Such comments require time for pupils to read and respond. A regular time set aside for this is important not only to consolidate or correct the work but to convey the message that responding to the comments is part of their learning. Moreover, pupils pick up the value of these kinds of comments and use them in giving feedback to each other when they have opportunity for peer-assessment (see Chapter 23).

Box 22.3 summarises some useful advice on feedback drawn from primary and secondary practice (e.g. Evans, 2001; Black *et al.*, 2003).

Summative assessment: assessment of learning

The purpose of summative assessment is to provide a summary of achievement at a particular time. The information needed for this purpose is much less detailed than that needed for formative assessment and for this reason alone it cannot guide teaching and learning in detail. Moreover, it provides information after the event, while formative assessment is an ongoing part of teaching and

Box 22.3

Some guidelines for feedback to help learning

- Don't give judgemental comments and particularly not scores or grades since these divert attention from the learning and lead to pupils comparing themselves with others.
- If regular grades or marks are required by the school policy, keep them in a record book but don't put them on pupils' work.
- Comment only on certain features, relating to the goals of the work, telling pupils that this is what you are doing.
- Consider carefully whether to comment on neatness, spelling, etc., unless these were specifically goals of the work.
- Emphasise how to improve by pinpointing aspects that need attention.
- Mark selectively, giving attention to work where pupils are required to think, rather than just record. Acknowledge that other work has been completed using a signature or stamp or sticker (not a tick, which is judgemental).
- Give time for pupils to read and discuss comments, reflect on them and respond as necessary.

can affect the learning process. Summative information is used for two main purposes, which we can call 'internal' and 'external':

- **Internal purposes** are for school records and for informing other teachers, parents or carers and the pupils themselves about what pupils have achieved at a particular time, generally the end of a term or half-year.
- **External purposes** are for providing those outside the school with information for selection, certification or to give public acknowledgement of achievement.

All teachers are involved in assessment for internal purposes, producing or contributing to records of pupils' achievement and reporting to parents or carers and others on progress. Those receiving this information will wish to know what has been achieved in relation to levels or standards that apply to all pupils. Thus the evidence has to be judged against the same criteria in the same way. Levels, as in the English National Curriculum and its equivalents in other countries, are a short-hand for the achievement that they represent.

To ensure consistency in assessment judgements from one occasion to another and one teacher to another (reliability), some form of moderation is necessary. This can take various forms but the most productive involves teachers discussing samples of pupils' work, comparing judgements and clarifying with each other the operational meaning of the level descriptions or other criteria. Such meetings have the added advantage of enabling teachers to share understandings of certain goals of learning and how to achieve them. Box 22.4 brings together some of these points in comparing the characteristics of summative and formative assessment.

Using pupil achievements for other purposes

Summative assessment for external purposes is often conducted, at least in part, through special tasks, tests or examinations. These can only cover a limited sample of what pupils can do. When there are 'high stakes' attached to the results, there is a well-recognised consequence that the content of the tests becomes the focus of teaching. The high stakes can be for the pupils, in terms of grade levels needed for entry to higher education, for instance. But they can also apply to teachers and schools when, as in England, pupil achievement data are aggregated at the school level and used for creating league tables based on pupil performance.

The practice of holding schools responsible for raising levels of achievement as measured by tests, with significant implications if targets are not met, means that the tests dominate the curriculum and teaching. Research (reviewed by Harlen and Deakin Crick, 2003) shows that even when not teaching directly to the tests, teachers report changing their approach. They adjust their teaching in ways they perceive as necessary because of the tests, spending most time in direct instruction of facts to be tested and less in providing opportunity for pupils to learn through enquiry and problem-solving (Johnston and McClune, 2000). They also administer frequent practice tests, which take up valuable learning time and are demotivating, especially for lower achieving pupils. The consequence is that the gap between the higher and lower achieving pupils widens. When in the grip of summative testing, teachers make little use of assessment formatively and provide fewer opportunities for enquiry-based science.

Box 22.4

Comparing characteristics of summative and formative assessment

Formative assessment ...	Summative assessment ...
• is an integral part of teaching for understanding. It is not optional; it cannot be taken away without changing the whole nature of the teaching and learning.	• takes place at certain intervals when achievement is to be reported.
• relates to progression in learning but takes individual progress and effort into account; that is, it is both criterion-referenced and pupil-referenced.	• relates to progression in learning judged against publicly available criteria.
• leads to action that supports further learning.	• gives results for different pupils that are based on the same criteria so can be compared and combined if required.
• can be used in all learning contexts.	• requires methods that are as reliable as possible without endangering validity.
• provides information about all learning outcomes.	• involves some quality assurance procedures such as moderation.
• involves children in assessing their performance and deciding their next steps.	

Concluding comment

This chapter has discussed assessment for different purposes. Formative and summative assessment are not different methods or types of assessment, but are defined by the purpose they serve. A teacher-made classroom test could be used to inform teaching, without any reference to levels, or it could be used to provide a grade or level for end of year or stage reporting. Assessment is only formative if it is actually used to help learning. Once evidence is gathered and used for helping learning it can later be reinterpreted and used to summarise learning. However, there is less opportunity for information gathered for summative assessment to be used formatively.

We have also noted evidence that using pupil achievement results from tests for school evaluation leads to inappropriate 'teaching to the test'. The evaluation of schools (see Chapter 12) must be based on far wider evidence than the achievements of pupils in external tests. Indeed, the criteria for evaluating a school ought to include how well it is using assessment to help learning and that it is providing summaries of achievement as needed and not more frequently, which would inhibit the formative use of assessment.

References

Assessment Reform Group (2002) *Assessment for learning: 10 Principles*. Available from The Institute of Education, University of London and from the ARG website: www.assessment-reform-group.org

Black, P. and Wiliam, D. (1998a) Assessment and classroom learning. *Assessment in Education*, **5**(1) 7–74.

Black, P. and Wiliam, D. (1998b) *Inside the black box: raising standards through classroom assessment*. London: nferNelson.

Black, P., Harrison, C., Lee, C., Marshall, B. and Wiliam, D. (2003) *Assessment for learning: putting it into practice*. Maidenhead: Open University Press.

Bransford, J. D., Brown, A. L. and Cocking, R. R. ed. (1999) *How people learn: brain, mind, experience and school*. Washington, DC: National Academy Press.

Butler, R. (1987) Task-involving and ego-involving properties of evaluation: effects of different feedback conditions on motivational perceptions, interest and performance. *Journal of Educational Psychology*, **79**, 474–482.

Evans, N. (2001) Thoughts on assessment and marking. *Primary Science Review*, **68**, 24–26.

Harlen W. (2006) *Teaching, learning and assessing science 5–12*. 4th edn. London: Sage.

Harlen, W. and Deakin Crick, R. (2003) Testing and motivation for learning. *Assessment in Education*, **10**(2), 169–208.

Johnston, J. and McClune, W. (2000) Selection project sel 5.1: Pupil motivation and attitudes – self-esteem, locus of control, learning disposition and the impact of selection on teaching and learning. In *The effects of the selective system of secondary education in Northern Ireland*. Research Papers Volume II, pp. 1–37. Bangor, Co. Down: Department of Education.

Kluger, A. N. and deNisi, A. (1996)The effect of feedback intervention on performance: a historical review, a meta-analysis and a preliminary feedback intervention theory. *Psychological Bulletin*, **119**(2), 254–284.

Lave, J. and Wenger, E. (1991) *Situated learning: legitimate peripheral participation*. Cambridge: Cambridge University Press.

Vygotsky, L. S. (1962) *Thought and language*. Cambridge MA: MIT Press.

Chapter 23 — Pupils' self- and peer- assessment

In the move towards pupils taking more responsibility for their learning, self-assessment has an important part to play. Teachers need to communicate to their pupils how to recognise the goals of successive steps in learning and how to judge the quality of their own work in attaining those goals. This chapter describes some strategies to help learners to recognise the criteria for quality that tasks demand, and to facilitate pupils' truthful reflection on their endeavours.

Chris Harrison

The value of self-assessment

The case for pupil self-assessment is based both on theoretical arguments relating to how people learn and on practical experience. A constant theme in the chapters of this book is emphasis on the active involvement of learners if there is to be learning with understanding. Learners 'do' the learning by constructing meaning from their experiences and interactions with others, using existing ideas. It follows that the more learners know about what it is intended should be learned – the learning goals, about where they have reached in relation to these goals, and about what further needs to be done to reach the goals, the more they can direct effort usefully for learning. It is for this reason that learners are put at the centre of Figure 22.1 in Chapter 22, in the cycle of events in which information about where pupils are in relation to learning goals is used to decide how to take their next steps in learning.

What is self-assessment?

Self-assessment is an active reflective activity, to inform the learner through his/her own judgements. Teachers have not found it an easy task to develop self-assessment skills in pupils. In asking a pupil to self-assess, we are calling on a range of skills that need developing and nurturing or to be introduced through direct teaching. Pupils need to acquire skills similar to those of their teacher. Self-assessment requires tools to evoke evidence, understanding to interpret this evidence and time to weigh up the analysis and reach judgements The first hurdle that teachers have to overcome is that learners need to realise that they have a role to play in learning and need to be active within the assessment process.

By reflecting on their learning, pupils gain both directly from the task in hand but also more generally in their learning behaviours (see also Chapter 26). David Boud (2003) believes that this contributes to personal development because self-assessment:

is as much concerned with planning learning and the existing learner practices as it is with recording achievements or checking understanding. ... Self assessment has great potential when it is seen from the point of view of contributing to student learning and when it is used to engage students more deeply in the subject areas being studied.

There are four main aspects to self-assessment:

- self-monitoring and checking progress (*Where am I and how far have I come?*);
- diagnosis and recognition of learning needs (*What can I now do and what do I need to take the next step?*);
- promoting good learning practices (*What am I doing that is successful?*);
- linking learning practices (*Can I adopt, adapt or influence my learning techniques in other areas?*).

In reality, these four aspects interlink. However, the degree to which one aspect can influence and benefit another depends on the emphasis that the teacher gives to it and the classroom climate in which the activities are carried out. If learners are asked to self-assess in the closing minutes of a lesson or open themselves up to ridicule from their peers by the revelation of their inadequacies, or feel that their teacher will underrate them if they admit to less than full understanding, then there is little chance of self-assessment skills developing.

Assessment and learning

Teachers utilise a repertoire of questions and activities to elicit responses from pupils that enable the teachers to decide on the next steps in learning. The assessment activity takes place alongside the learning and is used as a tool to diagnose current understanding and advise the pupils on what they might do to improve their learning. This ensures a feedback mechanism to prompt future learning (see Chapter 22). In the last decade, there has been a move to a competency-approach to learning, where clear criteria are used to determine success; making criteria explicit is crucial in formative assessment. Self-assessment is an essential component of successful formative assessment in the classroom because it can help pupils gauge suitable targets for their learning. The learning has to be done *by* them; it cannot be done *for* them (Black *et al.*, 2003, Black and Harrison, 2004).

Helping pupils evolve a means of setting their own targets begins the process of self-assessment. Pupils need to acquire similar skills to those of their teacher to find out where their leading edge of learning is and where they need to head

Box 23.1

A productive self-assessment incident

from the King's Medway Oxford Formative Assessment Project (KMOFAP)

A teacher, Tom, gave the following written feedback to a pupil:

Good range of substances and you know which are solids, liquids and gases. Try using the terms atom and molecule instead of particle all the time.

The pupil made a second attempt at the work, using the teacher's advice, and then responded to the teacher's comment with the following note:

I think I've done it sir except for line 3. Can chlorine be a molecule because it's an element and I thought elements were made of the same type of atoms?

(Black and Harrison, 2004)

next. Pupils can then begin to see how the advice from their teacher will help them improve. They also begin to form an idea of what quality looks like within a piece of work, to form frameworks for assessing their own work and apply assessment criteria to new pieces of work. Through this process, learners become more aware of what they need to do to improve, and as a consequence are often more motivated to learn.

On rare occasions, self-assessment arises naturally as part of the learning process, as described in Box 23.1. Here the teacher's written comment helped the learner see where she was at in her learning and also where she needed to go next to improve. On trying to do this, the learner began to understand the problem she was having moving towards the point that the teacher had suggested. She was then able to pinpoint her problem and what she needed help with from the teacher. If pupils were able to do this on a more regular basis, then teaching would be a much easier task. We need to create more opportunities for pupils to reflect on their work and to be proactive in moving their own learning forward.

Pupils need to understand the targets for the piece of learning and the criteria of quality that the product demands as they carry out the work. The product may be a tangible outcome in the form of a piece of writing, or it may be a new understanding in the mind of the learner. They then need to look critically at their emerging product and judge it against the assessment criteria so that they can shape and fashion it as it evolves. The pupils are therefore working with a picture in their heads of what a particular task demands and what learning they are hoping to achieve. Royce Sadler (1989) describes a gap-closure model in that learners need to seek evidence of the desired learning goal, their current position in relation to that goal and some understanding of a way to close the gap between the two (compare *'learning demand'* in Chapter 19). New understanding has to be recognised and assimilated into pre-existing ideas so that they make sense. Realising that there are new goals for learning is an essential part of this process if learners are to be productive.

Figure 23.1 illustrates the processes that are necessary to close the learning

Figure 23.1
**Closing the
learning gap.**

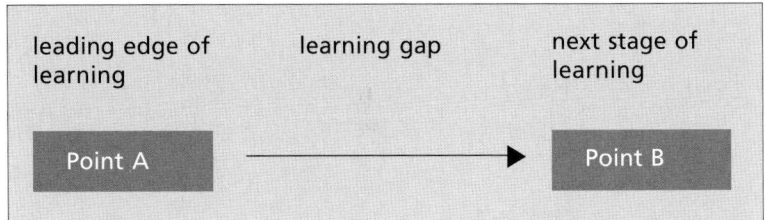

gap. First, it is important that pupils recognise where they are in their learning (point A), that is, what can I do and what do I know about this area of science so far? Then, they need some idea of where to head next in their learning (point B), that is, where to target their efforts. The teacher's role is to set up the activities to help the pupils move from point A to point B, but ultimately it is the pupil who has to put in the work and make this transition to close the learning gap, and recognise when it is completed satisfactorily. In other words, self-assessment is an essential component of learning (Black *et al.*, 2003).

Recognising standards of quality

It is very difficult for someone to look closely at their own work and be objective in applying assessment criteria. First, there is a problem in understanding fully what the assessment criteria mean in relation to the piece of work. Can the learners be sure that their interpretation is an accepted quality example of the set of criteria?

It takes teachers several attempts to become conversant in applying criteria for a new assessment task. Some teachers work through a range of pupils' answers to get a feel for the essence of quality in a particular context. So it makes sense for learners to undergo a similar experience if they need to identify how criteria for quality apply in their own work. This can be achieved through three main routes:

● assessment of anonymous work;

● peer-assessment;

● ipsative assessment.

Assessing anonymous work

When pupils look at anonymous work they have no loyalty towards whoever produced it and so they can focus on the characteristics of the piece rather than be concerned about the feelings of the person who did the work. This allows them to make judgements about how well the task has been completed and to recognise the attributes that illustrate or detract from this. It can be useful to present learners with a list of criteria, so that they can see whether specific criteria are displayed in a piece of work. Care has to be taken that learners do not approach this with a checklist mentality: the aim is not simply that they can spot aspects of a criterion, but that they gain an understanding of what a good example looks like in the reality of that particular task. Another approach is to take one criterion from the list and ask pupils to discuss how this is displayed in a variety of pieces of work. Then they get a feel for its scope and range before they attempt to exemplify it through their own work. Yet another way is to get pupils first to identify and articulate what quality for the task looks like and then to devise the criteria that make up that judgement. To do this, the teacher needs to present pupils with six to ten pieces of work that show a range of attainment, including some pieces that she would class as good or quality products. Pupils can rank them, select the best three, or have some other way of sorting and comparing the pieces, but, in doing so, they need to discuss both in groups and as a whole class the reasons for their particular choices. From this the criteria for quality emerge, and learners have some sort of picture of what a finished piece of work might look like. When they start to construct their own attempt they can direct their efforts more effectively and judge their achievement.

This approach is valuable because the interchange will be in language that pupils themselves naturally use, and because pupils learn by taking the roles of teachers and examiners of others (Sadler, 1989). Also, by placing the central focus of the work with the learners, the teacher can be free to observe what is happening and so choose and frame helpful interventions.

Peer-assessment

A second way of approaching an understanding of quality is through peer-assessment. Peer-assessment is uniquely valuable because pupils may accept, from one another, criticisms of their work that they would not take seriously if made by their teacher. Again, it uses the pupils' own kind of language. However, because there is more of an emotional involvement, pupils need to be trained in how to look carefully at a piece of work completed by a classmate and also in how to respond to this peer once they have made a judgement. This takes time but can be achieved if it becomes a regular part of classroom practice. Many teachers begin this by asking pupils to peer-assess simple tasks. One teacher, Rose, reported on the use of both self- and peer-assessment of homework:

> We regularly do peer marking – I find this very helpful indeed. A lot of misconceptions come to the fore and we then discuss these as we are going over the homework. I then go over the peer-marking and talk to pupils individually as I go round the room. ... Pupils regularly read their own work or another pupil's as a matter of course. This has made them realise how important it is to write clearly. Previously I would have said that I could not read their work – their peers saying they cannot read the writing has more of an impact. (Black *et al.*, 2002)

This extract shows that involving pupils in this way helps them to take responsibility for their own and one another's learning, although they might first look at surface features, such as legibility, and take some time to learn to look also at the quality of the content. These peer-assessment skills also need good models of feedback from the teacher when she assesses their work, as the learners adopt similar models with one another. So, for example, if teachers highlight in written work in different colours, one for quality aspects and another for areas that need attention, learners are apt to do the same when they assess one another's work. What is striking about peer-assessment, and to some extent assessment of anonymous work, is that pupils are able to recognise mistakes in others' work, whereas their closeness and attachment to their own work cloud their recognition of their own similar mistakes until they see them in the work of others. Likewise, they are able to see attributes in other pupils' work that they have not yet aspired to and achieved, but they begin to get an inkling of how these might feature in their own work. So peer-assessment can apprentice learners into improving the quality of their output and leads to them becoming more reflective about their own work.

Peer-assessment is now successful in many classrooms where the classroom environment is supportive of such practices. It helps if pupils develop a language that focuses on assessment, so that when they swap work in pairs they know what sort of questions to ask. Questions and prompts need to promote thinking and start a discussion that helps each of the learners develop their reflective and self-assessment skills. To do this, questions need to encourage analysis, judgement and justification as well as help the learners see what improvements might be made; again, pupils learn from teachers modelling these. Useful questions to focus learners on being reflective about their work and so prompt discussion about improvement are:

What do you think you have done well?
What were you trying to do in this section?
Can you tell me why you used this example?
Why did you do this, in this kind of way?
Which bits were you unsure about?
What would you change if you did it again?
What could you add to strengthen this part?

Ipsative assessment

The third way of developing self-assessment skills is through ipsative assessment. This is where pupils need to compare what they are producing with pieces of work that they have previously completed. In this way, they can map and instigate their own progress as they continually try to improve the quality of their work from piece to piece. It is more direct, but more difficult, than the other two methods as it is not mediated through considering the work of others and so there is a potentially high emotional response involved.

In most classrooms, teachers use a mixture of the three routes. Many establish the supportive environment, language and reflection skills through looking at anonymous work and through peer-assessment, before they progress on to the more tricky ipsative approach.

Self-assessment tools and processes

How can teachers help pupils develop self-assessment skills? Many of the teachers that we, in the King's College Assessment for Learning team, have worked with have benefited from developing their own approaches. Some of the types of tools that teachers might use are outlined below.

- Prior to starting a new activity, the teacher uses KWL (Know, Want to know, Learnt) routines and grids to help focus learners on their achievements and goals.
- During or immediately after an activity, the teacher might use a means of pupils charting their confidence level in a piece of work, such as a 'traffic-light' system, or a thumb tool or a smiley face to indicate aspects or answers

about which they are confident, unconfident or partially confident. This begins the pupils' reflective process needed for self-assessment and helps create the right environment because the judgement is in their hands. The next step is to bring their ideas of quality to the fore through discussion about their judgement. Then the final decision about next steps becomes reciprocal, between the pupil and their peers or teacher.

- Coming back to pieces of work several days or weeks later, teachers can help pupils look through the work using either a reflection sheet or a learning diary. Questions focus the learner on what to consider, for example, what they found easy/hard in the work, which bits they are proud of or where they feel they can now do better. This helps learners realise where they need to focus their future efforts and so it becomes prospective rather than simply a retrospective exercise.

In attempting any of these approaches it is essential to bear in mind that these tools and processes are designed to engage the learner in being reflective, both about the task in hand and more broadly about the way they learn. Self- and peer-assessment therefore encourage a deep rather than a surface approach to learning. However, there are no guarantees; by its nature self-assessment is individualistic and so learners may not respond in ways expected by the teacher. This puts the onus on the teacher to be even more careful in his/her approach. The targets that learners set must become focused on learning and improvement and not simply on tricks and additions that improve performance without affecting underlying understanding. Such practices take time and effort to evolve and should form part of regular collaborative classroom practice rather than be limited to termly or yearly summary reflections.

References

Black, P., Harrison, C., Lee, C., Marshall, B. and Wiliam, D. (2002) *Working inside the black box: assessment for learning in the classroom*. London: nferNelson.

Black, P., Harrison, C., Lee, C., Marshall, B. and Wiliam, D. (2003) *Assessment for learning: putting it into practice*. Maidenhead: Open University Press.

Black, P. and Harrison, C. (2004) *Science inside the black box*. London: nferNelson.

Boud, D. (2003) *Enhancing learning through self-assessment*. London: RoutledgeFalmer.

Sadler, R. (1989) Formative assessment and the design of instructional systems. *Instructional Science*, **18**, 119–144.

Further reading

Association for Achievement and Improvement through Assessment (AAIA) *Self-assessment*. Excellent downloadable booklet available on: http://www.AAIA.org.uk

Chapter 24

Investigations, scientific literacy and evidence

In the previous edition of this book, we put forward the notion that ideas about scientific evidence had not been afforded

Richard Gott and **Sandra Duggan**

sufficient weight in the science curriculum. Seven years on, the National Curriculum now shows more signs of recognising the significance of the issue but there is much debate about how to teach, and how to assess, this area of the curriculum. In this chapter, we argue that one way forward may lie in carefully selected activities designed to engage pupils with real but accessible scientific data.

Scientific literacy and education

There is increasing international recognition that science education, pre A-level, should be primarily about developing 'scientific literacy'. For example, in the US, the American Association for the Advancement of Science, in Canada, the Council of Ministers of Education, and in the UK, *Twenty First Century Science* (see websites and Chapter 1), all focus on the need to develop a scientifically literate society able to interact with the innovations in science and technology that confront us all in our everyday lives. There are also concerns about the more general issue of the 'public understanding of science', which have become a factor in any curriculum discussion. One of the main problems in all this debate is that there is a lack of agreement about what being scientifically literate actually means and, consequently, a lack of clarity about what to teach, and how, in order to provide the sort of science in schools that will lead to a scientifically literate population or to a public that understands, and can articulate with, science.

DeBoer (2000) offers a range of definitions of scientific literacy, from those that equate scientific literacy simply with being educated in science, to those that focus on the ability to participate in informed democratic decision-making about issues that involve science. Other definitions focus on scientific literacy as a way of learning about science for its aesthetic appeal, or associate it with technological literacy. DeBoer concludes that one common factor is that all the definitions generally imply a broad and functional *understanding* of science for *general* education purposes (as opposed to education for careers in science), which define what we need to know *'in order to live more effectively with respect to the natural world'*.

Taking DeBoer's review one step further, we suggest that these definitions have another common theme in that the majority refer, *inter alia*, to *understanding scientific evidence* as being a significant part of scientific literacy. A House of Commons report (2002), in addressing the question *'What science do all students need?'*, endorses this view:

> What is important is not that citizens should be able to remember and recall solely a large body of scientific facts, but that they should understand how science works and how it is based on the analysis and interpretation of evidence. (para. 86)

Similarly, the Programme for International Student Achievement (OECD, 2004) defines scientific literacy as:

> the capacity to use scientific knowledge, to identify questions and to draw evidence-based conclusions in order to understand and help make decisions about the natural world and the changes made to it through human activity. (p. 286)

What does understanding evidence involve and why does it matter?

Some years ago, we published a tentative list of constituent ideas, 'concepts of evidence' (see website), which, we suggest, go some way to defining 'procedural knowledge' and underpin an understanding of scientific evidence. To judge, weigh up or evaluate evidence we need to be able to understand the ideas that lie beneath the concepts of reliability and validity. These include ideas such as the purpose of control variables, of repeatability and of accuracy and precision. An extensive list can be viewed on our website, a list which has been validated in various ways, some of which will be touched on later in this chapter.

Science relies absolutely on evidence. This is its defining characteristic – theory must accord with reality. An understanding of scientific evidence matters for understanding science as a discipline but also, and arguably more importantly, because understanding evidence is essential for engaging with scientific issues in everyday life and for employment in science and science-related occupations.

Evidence and everyday life

Case studies of how the public interact with science have shown that, when the need arises, most people can acquire the scientific information they need in order to act. Layton *et al.* (1993) used the phrase *'instrumental science'* to describe the acquisition of relevant conceptual knowledge. In one piece of research (Tytler, Duggan and Gott, 2001a, b) we sought to pin down what sort of science people need in adult life. We found that activists involved in local issues admitted that they had little prior knowledge about the matter of concern (in this case, emissions from a cement kiln) but that they gleaned the information from reading, talking to people and from the Internet. The last was used not only for information but also to contact other groups with similar concerns. Similarly, on the issue of parents' decisions about immunisation (Duggan and Gott, 2002), the parents we interviewed demonstrated that they were well able to seek out relevant information. What mattered with regard to people's ability to use and act on the knowledge they gained, was their understanding of the evidence. Issues such as sampling procedures, validity of design and measurement and significance of risk were critical both in community action and in personal decision-making. But we found that it was only those who had a thorough training in science who were confident enough to challenge 'expert' opinion.

Employment in science and science-related occupations

The Council of Science and Technology Institutes (CSTI, 1993) sought the views of employers in industries where science and maths are used and found that of the 30 per cent of the workforce using science or maths in some aspect of their work, only 4 per cent are engaged in 'pure science', the rest being employed in applied science and engineering. One of the three key requirements for employees was 'a central core' of skills, defined as the ability to: generate one's own ideas, hypotheses and theoretical models and/or utilise those postulated by others; design and conduct experiments, trials, tests, simulations and operations; and evaluate the resulting data. Coles (1997), interviewing scientists employed in the private and public sector across a wide range of scientific fields and at different professional levels, came to broadly similar conclusions, finding that weighing evidence and developing scientific habits of mind (logical thinking, scepticism) were often valued ahead of any specific scientific knowledge, understanding or skills.

Our own research has attempted to delve below 'the things that scientists do' in a search for the understandings that are necessary, if insufficient, pre-conditions. Our aim is to determine what *underpinnings* must be *taught* so that pupils can better fulfil the requirements of the workplace. In a small exploratory study in six local industries (Gott, Duggan and Johnson, 1999), we found that, not surprisingly, the knowledge of scientific facts and concepts required in each industry was highly specialised and most of it tended to be acquired, at least at the mid to lower levels, 'on the job'. But, when questioned carefully, the majority of these industries also cited many aspects of evidence, such as accuracy and error, as being fundamental.

Evidence in the science curriculum

How can ideas about evidence be taught in science in schools? The most obvious place is in practical investigative work, which has become an established part of the National Curriculum for Science in the UK since its introduction in 1989. However, we have argued that practical work is a means rather than an end in itself, and that we need to be quite clear about the purpose of each practical – what it is that pupils are supposed to understand as a result of carrying it out. We need, therefore, to think very carefully about 'what' to teach. For key stage

4 this is synonymous with the revised National Curriculum to be taught for GCSE, with a section of the Programme of Study called 'How science works'. This is reproduced in Box 24.1 (see also Chapter 8).

We can see that ideas about evidence permeate the Programme of Study

Box 24.1

How science works (National Curriculum 2006: Key Stage 4 Programme of Study)

(This is the latest available version at the time of writing)

Data, evidence, theories and explanations

1 Pupils should be taught:

a *how scientific data can be collected and analysed*

b *how interpretation of data, using creative thought, provides evidence to test ideas and develop theories*

c how explanations of many phenomena can be developed using scientific theories, models and ideas

d that there are some questions that science cannot currently answer, and some that science cannot address.

Practical and enquiry skills

2 Pupils should be taught to:

a *plan to test a scientific idea, answer a scientific question, or solve a scientific problem*

b *collect data from primary or secondary sources, including using ICT sources and tools*

c *work accurately and safely, individually and with others, when collecting first-hand data*

d *evaluate methods of collection of data and consider their validity and reliability as evidence.*

Communication skills

3 Pupils should be taught to:

a *recall, analyse, interpret, apply and question scientific information or ideas*

b *use both qualitative and quantitative approaches*

c *present information, develop an argument and draw a conclusion, using scientific, technical and mathematical language, conventions and symbols and ICT tools.*

Applications and implications of science

4 Pupils should be taught:

a about the use of contemporary scientific and technological developments and their benefits, drawbacks and risks

b to consider how and why decisions about science and technology are made, including those that raise ethical issues, and about the social, economic and environmental effects of such decisions

c how uncertainties in scientific knowledge and scientific ideas change over time and about the role of the scientific community in validating these changes.

and, compared to previous versions, there is also a move to include societal issues in relation to the understanding and use of evidence (in bold). The italicised items are ideas that *could* be addressed through practical work although they could also be taught in other ways, for instance by demonstration, chalk and talk or ICT – that is a matter for the teacher to decide. The key to whether this kind of autonomy is given to the teacher will depend on the form that the assessment scheme takes. The curriculum in general in the UK is widely regarded as 'assessment driven', a view endorsed in relation to science by the House of Commons Science and Technology Committee (House of Commons, 2002):

> *Any changes to the National Curriculum will have limited impact on the way science is taught in schools if the assessment is not changed too.* (para 71)

It follows that any attempt to change the curriculum must be directly tied to a less rigid assessment scheme. It is to that issue we now turn.

Assessing ideas about evidence

One of the three awarding bodies in England, AQA (Assessment and Qualifications Alliance), has used concepts of evidence as the basis of a unit in their general GCSE specifications for *How science works*. AQA explicitly states that it regards '*how science works in the world at large as well as in the laboratory*' as '*a separate body of knowledge, understanding and skills*' and includes understanding social aspects of scientific evidence.

How science works is assessed partly by a centre-assessed unit which comprises:

1   An **Internal Skills Assignment** or ISA. Each ISA centres on a practical investigation drawn from an approved, but not fixed-for-all-time, list, including fieldwork investigations, carried out in normal lessons. These investigations are not directly assessed as they are being carried out (although teachers may assess pupils' practical and safety skills on a simple 'can-do' basis) but via an externally set, internally assessed examination which is a written test of:

- the pupil's understanding of the data from his/her own investigation, which they bring to the session with them;
- the pupil's understanding of *other* data relating to the same topic as the pupil's own investigation. This will include questions on the analysis and evaluation of the data.

2   A **Practical Skills Assessment** of the pupil's practical abilities over the whole course, which will be done by the teacher. This will be a holistic assessment of the pupil's ability to work safely and to manipulate apparatus skilfully.

In addition, questions addressing *How science works* will be integrated into the externally assessed written papers that test both the substantive content and the application of procedural knowledge. We see, then, that there is now a significant emphasis on these ideas, and teaching them will be a matter of immediate concern.

A note on the reliability and validity of these methods of assessment

In a review of methods of assessing practical work (Gott and Duggan, 2002), we noted that, while the assessment of this part of the National Curriculum was reliable, its validity was questionable for two reasons:

- The assessment criteria had narrowed the choice of suitable investigations because only a few investigations allowed pupils the opportunity of achieving the higher levels. This also had the effect of decreasing the number of investigations that pupils undertook. The assessment criteria also caused the students to approach it in a routinised way which is in direct opposition to the spirit of open-ended 'creative' investigative work.
- Tackling the problem of assessing procedural knowledge was undermined because a significant proportion of the 'marks' was allocated to explanation of underlying substantive issues such as particle theory or Ohm's law.

Our review concluded that there is no easy solution to the assessment problem because we do not know enough about the validity of alternative methods of assessment. We found many unanswered questions.

The AQA specifications, described above, are an attempt to improve assessment by using a much broader approach than before through employing a number of different methods of assessment. In addition, by explicitly recognising procedural knowledge, the specifications focus clearly and directly on assessing ideas about evidence. Questions still inevitably remain about the validity of these methods of assessment. A potential problem is that a standard handful of routinised well-practised investigations will again emerge. QCA has stipulated that the investigations must be in the context of the substantive parts of the curriculum, which is somewhat restricting (we have tried to list the possibilities!). This suggests that the idea of procedural knowledge as difficult content in its own right may not have been thoroughly appreciated.

Teaching ideas about evidence

How can teachers respond to these changes in the assessment system? Our suggestions are represented in Figure 24.1. We have argued that a real engagement with issues requires us to consider the quality of each and every datum, then the quality of the data set (A and B in diagram) and the pattern and

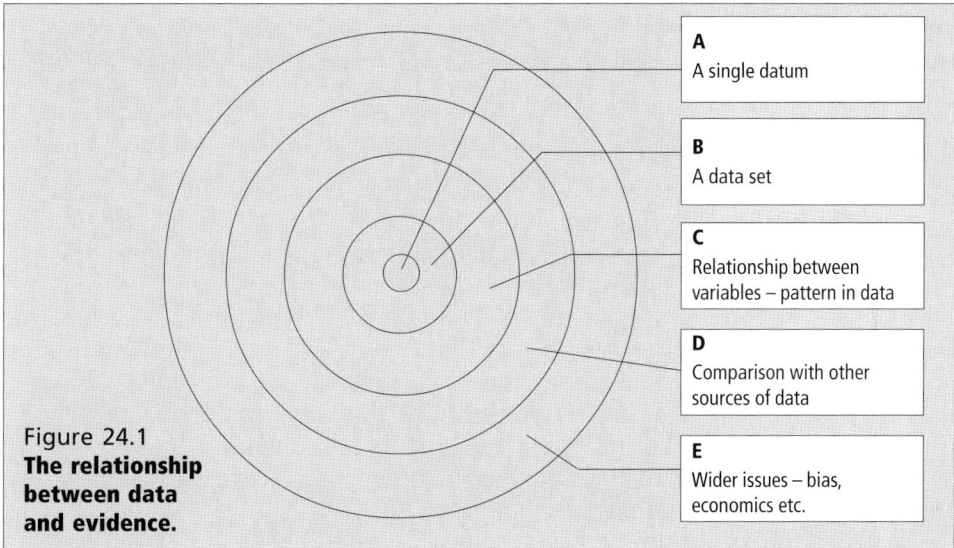

Figure 24.1
The relationship between data and evidence.

A
A single datum

B
A data set

C
Relationship between variables – pattern in data

D
Comparison with other sources of data

E
Wider issues – bias, economics etc.

relationships (C) that can then be identified within it, and finally the coherence of that data with those from other experiments (D). Once we have established that, then we can weigh that evidence against societal and economic factors and decide on its value (E). But issues of genuine public concern may be unlikely to provide us with the opportunity to do this at first hand. Global warming for instance, whilst a 'hot topic', is based on complex models that make predictions on limited evidence. As such, while it could be a good topic for debate about how political issues relate to science, we need examples where more accessible data can be brought to bear on simpler issues where the problems associated with checking data and evidence can be addressed.

To illustrate the point, let us take an example of the recent spate of reports concerning sex changes in fish downstream of a sewage outfall. The finger has been pointed at contraceptive pills as a key element in the pollution. We cannot replicate this in the lab, but we can go out and consider pollution in a stream. We can think about sampling strategies, sensitivity of instruments and so on, even if the pollution we can detect is not a hormone but, say, some pollutant that affects oxygen levels or nitrates. We could also envisage looking at the effects of pollution on water plants (e.g. duckweed) in a controlled experiment in the lab. Having gained this kind of practical experience, we could then turn to secondary data on pollution in the river and ask pertinent questions about sampling and measurement and so on. The final step would be, of course, to discuss that evidence in the light of the impact on all of us of such sex changes, including the distinct possibility that we might all go the way of the fish sometime in the future.

We can think of other such issues – pollution from industrial chimneys (Tytler *et al.*, 2001b), or vehicle exhaust emissions in cities – that may be approachable in similar ways. They would each form a small project or 'case study', taking up perhaps a week or more and involving investigations in the field and in the lab, analysis of secondary data and discussions of more political aspects.

What we should try to avoid are discrete and unconnected subsets (E alone in our diagram) where there is a danger of reducing the debate to politics and citizenship. This is acceptable in small doses provided we know what we are doing and realise that the evidence may not be 'scientific'; the 'bulls eye' of the data (Figure 24.1) is missing!

Concluding remarks

There are two overriding issues to consider: the nature of what we decide to teach, and the freedom for teachers to develop their own ways of doing it to suit their personal styles and the teaching situation they find themselves in.

The first requires encouraging pupils to collect and handle their own evidence and to deal with 'messy' data as an essential first step on the way towards informed decision-making. We believe that developing a critical awareness of the status and reliability of evidence should be a crucial aim of science education and that pupils should leave school with, at the very least, a belief in their ability to understand data and make judgements based upon it, if they so wish, or make quite different judgements based on other criteria but accept, knowingly, the consequences of so doing.

The second requires that the assessment scheme be less constraining than it is now so that teachers are liberated to teach ideas about evidence in the way they think best. We must see each practical as a way of teaching ideas – whether it is ideas about reliability or about Newton's laws. We can then assess understanding of those ideas in the most economical way.

References

Coles, M. (1997) Science education – vocational and general approaches. *School Science Review*, **79**(286), 27–32.

CSTI (1993) *Mapping the science, technology and mathematics domain*. London: Council of Science and Technology Institutes.

DeBoer, G. E. (2000) Scientific literacy: another look at its historical and contemporary meanings and its relationship to science education reform. *Journal of Research in Science Teaching*, **37**, 582–601.

Duggan, S. and Gott, R. (2002) What sort of science education do we really need? *International Journal of Science Education*, **24**, 661–679.

Gott, R. and Duggan, S. (2002) Problems with assessment of performance in practical science: which way now? *Cambridge Journal of Education*, **32**, 183–201.

Gott, R., Duggan, S. and Johnson, P. (1999) What do practising and applied scientists do and what are the implications for science education? *Research in Science and Technological Education*, **17**, 97–107.

House of Commons Select Committee on Science and Technology (2002) *Science education from 14 to 19*. London: The Stationery Office.

Layton, D., Jenkins, E., MacGill, S. and Davey, A. (1993) Inarticulate science? *Perspectives on the public understanding of science and some implications for science education*. Nafferton: Studies in Education Ltd.

OECD (2004) *Learning for tomorrow's world: first results from PISA 2003*. Organisation for Economic Co-operation and Development.

Tytler, R., Duggan, S. and Gott, R. (2001a) Dimensions of evidence, the public understanding of science and science education. *International Journal of Science Education*, **23**, 815–832.

Tytler, R., Duggan, S. and Gott, R. (2001b) Public participation in an environmental dispute: implications for science education. *Public Understanding of Science*, **10**, 343–364.

Websites

American Association for the Advancement of Science (Partnership for Scientific Literacy): http://www.project2061.org/publications/articles/psl/default.htm

Concepts of Evidence: http://www.dur.ac.uk/richard.gott/Evidence/cofev.htm (The website also has downloadable versions of this fuller version, together with a slimmed down option matched to the 2006 GCSE specifications, by a group of teachers.)

Council of Ministers of Education *Common Framework of Science Learning Outcomes*: http://www.cmec.ca/science/framework/Pages/index.htm

National Curriculum: http://www.qca.org.uk/downloads/10340_science_prog_of_study_from_2006_ks4.pdf

Twenty First Century Science: http://www.21stcenturyscience.org/newmode/literacy.asp

Chapter 25

Better scientific enquiries

Most teachers believe that scientific enquiries are worth doing to help pupils learn science, but they are not satisfied with our current offerings in scientific enquiry. In this chapter we

Rod Watson, Valerie Wood-Robinson and **Labrini Nikolaou**

address the following aspects of scientific enquiry: improving the balance of kinds of enquiries used in our schools; explicit teaching of the knowledge and understanding underpinning the use of skills and processes in scientific enquiry, using a mixture of stand-alone activities and whole enquiries that have specific and limited educational objectives; and improving the quality of dialogue within enquiry lessons.

What is scientific enquiry?

Teachers have identified (Watson and Wood-Robinson, 1998) the following two characteristics of scientific enquiries:

- In scientific enquiries pupils have to make their own decisions either individually or in groups: they are given some autonomy in how the enquiry is carried out.

- A scientific enquiry must involve pupils in using procedures such as planning, measuring, observing, analysing data and evaluating methods. Not all enquiries will allow pupils to use every kind of investigational procedure, and enquiries may vary in the amount of autonomy given to pupils at different stages of the investigative process.

Most teachers, represented by those involved in the ASE King's Science Investigations in Schools (AKSIS) project, feel that the range of enquiries in use is too restricted and that they often give too little initiative to pupils (Watson, Goldsworthy and Wood-Robinson, 1999a). There is also concern that too much reliance is placed on learning skills and processes by doing, rather than being taught them explicitly. As Lederman puts it:

Student knowledge about enquiry ... does not occur by accident. Students do not develop such understandings simply through experiencing enquiry any more so than we would expect them to develop understandings of photosynthesis simply by watching plants grow. (quoted in Abd-el-Khalik et al., 2004, p. 403)

Kinds of scientific enquiry

There is no one way of carrying out scientific enquiry. Since the introduction of the UK Science National Curriculum there has been much criticism of the limited nature of scientific enquiries being used (Watson, Goldsworthy and Wood-Robinson, 2002). The 'fair test' has come to dominate much enquiry work. In the fair test the experimenter changes an independent variable (e.g. the amount of light shining on pond-weed) and measures what happens to a dependent variable (e.g. the amount of oxygen released from the plant), whilst other relevant variables are held constant (e.g. temperature). This is an important kind of enquiry but it is not the only one. We have categorised enquiries described by teachers, in response to a questionnaire, into six kinds. Table 25.1 shows the results of the analysis. Particularly in the secondary schools, fair testing dominated to the exclusion of other kinds of enquiry. Moreover, the range of fair tests used was very restricted. For example, pupils studied variables affecting solubility or rate of dissolution (usually of sugar) over and over again.

Table 25.1 **Kinds of enquiry carried out with children aged 7–14.**

Kind of enquiry	Age 7 to 11 key stage 2 ($n = 464$) %	Age 11 to 14 key stage 3 ($n = 572$) %
Classifying and identifying	9	2
Fair testing	50	82
Pattern seeking	2	2
Exploring	16	3
Investigating models	0	0
Making things or developing systems	12	4
No response or insufficient detail	*11*	*7*

Since our 1999 study, there have been a number of initiatives to try to achieve a more balanced curriculum. The Science National Curriculum for England (QCA, 1999) was worded to encourage a greater variety of enquiries. Kinds of enquiry were exemplified in the QCA *Scheme of Work for Key Stage 3* in module M (QCA, 2000) and further emphasised in the Key Stage 3 National Strategy *Framework for teaching* (QCA, 2002, pp.11–13). An impediment to change has been the GCSE coursework examination criteria, but the introduction of a new

National Curriculum specification for key stage 4 in 2006 has led to the development of new GCSE curricula, some of which include a wider variety of enquiries (see Chapter 24).

So what is this variety of enquiries? The six categories of enquiry are described below (adapted from Watson *et al.*, 1999a):

- **Classifying and identifying**

  Examples: *What chemicals are in this green rock? How can we group these spiders?*

  Classifying is a process of arranging a large range of phenomena, either objects or events, into manageable sets. Identifying is a process of recognising objects and events as members of particular sets, possibly new and unique sets, and allocating names to them.

- **Fair testing**

  Examples: *What is the effect of exercise on heart rate? How does the rate of reaction of sodium thiosulfate solution with an acid change with different concentrations of the acid?*

  These enquiries are concerned with observing and exploring relationships between variables. The values of an independent variable are changed and the effects on a dependent variable noted. Other variables are controlled, for a 'fair test'.

- **Pattern seeking (surveys)**

  Examples: *What causes the variation over time in levels of air pollution? What affects how far people can throw a tennis ball? What factors caused five people in the same village to develop CJD?*

  The dependent variable is identified first, that is, an effect is noticed and the enquiry is structured around finding a possible cause for the effect. These enquiries often involve observing and recording natural events as they occur and so it is not possible to control variables: instead, consideration has to be given to sample characteristics. Other pattern-seeking enquiries are surveys, which are used in genetics, epidemiology, psychology, sociology, meteorology, astronomy and ecology.

- **Exploring**

  Examples: *How does the size of the hole in the ozone layer over the Antarctic change over time? Is there a pattern in hourly measurements of the concentration of nitrogen dioxide in the air in central London?*

  These enquiries involve careful observations of objects or events. Often the observations are taken over time and recorded to see how certain features change. Explorations can be the start of other enquiries, which seek to explain patterns noticed.

- **Investigating models**

  Examples: *Why does the population of ladybirds in the school nature trail change? Why do the bubbles in a fizzy drink get larger and faster as they rise up the glass?*

  In many enquiries, after analysing their data pupils use their current knowledge and understanding to explain the data. Investigating models is different. Different explanations are considered and data are sought to support or refute explanations. Testing models is difficult and may lead on to one or all of the preceding types of enquiry, but which approach is chosen depends on decisions made about what would count as evidence to test the model.

- Making things or developing systems

  Examples: *Devise a way of retrieving pure salt from salt that has been spilt on the soil. Design a regime to improve your fitness and to evaluate its effectiveness.*

  In these enquiries pupils design an artefact or system to meet a human need. Some technological enquiries involve a high level of scientific knowledge or have a strong emphasis on scientific procedures and so can be classified as scientific enquiries.

What would be an appropriate balance between these kinds of enquiry? That depends on the age of the pupils. At secondary level the emphasis on fair testing needs to be reduced considerably to make space for more:

- **classifying and identifying enquiries**. Classification should be more complex than simply classifying into two groups like conductors or non-conductors.
- **pattern-seeking enquiries**. Some biological enquiries could move out of the laboratory and into the field, so that, for example, woodlice are no longer confined to wandering around four different artificial environments in choice chambers in the laboratory but instead are studied in their natural habitats. Greater emphasis on pattern-seeking implies more use of secondary sources.
- **investigating of models**. An increase in the use of investigating models is perhaps the hardest of the shifts to achieve. Generating an explanation for, or a model of, a phenomenon and collecting evidence to test the model is time-consuming and hard for the pupils to do and for teachers to teach. Nevertheless, we recommend that time should be set aside for extended enquiries of this type as they provide an opportunity to explore the relationships between evidence and scientific explanations.

Explicit teaching of scientific enquiry

We found (Watson, Goldsworthy and Wood-Robinson, 1999b) that primary and secondary pupils, of quite different ages, were carrying out enquiries with similar levels of procedural demand and attaining similar levels of performance. When we asked teachers when pupils were taught particular procedures, like aspects of graphing, the normal reply was, '*They will have studied this last year*'. It seemed that for some scientific procedures no teachers took responsibility for actually teaching them. Not surprisingly, when we taught specific skills and procedures (e.g. graphing skills, see Goldsworthy, 1998), pupils' skills in constructing and understanding graphs improved. We also carried out a series of 34 in-service training courses in different primary schools (Goldsworthy, 2002). Teachers learnt new techniques for explicit teaching of specific aspects of enquiry and tried them out in their own classrooms. This resulted in a significant improvement in the quality of pupils' work. These studies lead us to the rather unsurprising conclusion that teaching can result in learning!

Explicit teaching of enquiry can take place either through stand-alone activities or as an integral part of whole enquiries. In recent years, various stand-alone resources have been developed for the teaching of specific aspects of enquiry. These resources identify specific aspects of procedural knowledge understanding to be taught and provide teaching and learning activities for them (Foulds, Gott and Duggan, 1997, 1998, 1999; Goldsworthy, Watson and Wood-Robinson, 1999, 2000a, 2000b; Sang and Wood-Robinson, 2002). In addition, this approach has been promoted by the Key Stage 3 Strategy / Secondary National Strategy CPD training (see Chapter 9).

However, applying procedural understanding to a particular whole enquiry requires more than an understanding of the scientific procedures. It also requires pupils to understand the particular context. The dialogue in Box 25.1 indicates a lack of such understanding.

Box 25.1

Interview with a group of 14/15 year-olds

The pupils were investigating the effect of concentration on the rate of reaction of magnesium with dilute hydrochloric acid.

Interviewer: *How many different concentrations of acid are you using?*

Roma: *Five.*

Interviewer: *Why five?*

Terry: *We always do five.*

Interviewer: *Why do you always do five?*

Naomi: *Our teacher tells us to do five.*

Interviewer: *Why does your teacher tell you to do five?*

Naomi: [pause] *I don't know, that's what she says.*

Roma: *It's so that you have enough readings to draw a graph, to see the shape of the curve.*

Interviewer: *Why do you think five readings is enough?*

Roma: *Miss said that five was enough.*

Two aspects of procedural understanding are needed to decide on the number of different concentrations to use in the enquiry described in Box 25.1. They are:

● that in order to see the pattern in the results, a graph will be plotted and there should be sufficient points to see the shape of the line;

● that there is error in each reading. This error can be managed by either taking repeat readings and averaging, or by choosing a large number of concentrations and using the process of producing a line of best fit to smooth out the errors.

To decide how many measurements to take in this particular enquiry, pupils needed to combine procedural understanding with context-specific features. In this case, taking five readings may be just about enough to be able to draw a line through the points to see a pattern. However, with the technique being used, the errors in measuring the time taken for the magnesium to disappear were large, so either several repeat readings were needed for each concentration or many more than five concentrations were needed. Teaching this aspect of enquiry within the context of the whole enquiry is possible. However, when using whole enquiries it is important that the educational objectives for specific lessons should be *focused* and *limited*. It is simply not possible to teach all aspects of enquiry in one lesson.

Quality dialogue in scientific enquiry

A key feature of teaching enquiry is the quality of the dialogue generated. The dialogue in Box 25.2 shows how explicit teaching of one aspect of procedural understanding took place in an 'identification' enquiry called 'Mystery powders' (developed by the SEP–King's Enhancing Enquiries in School (SKEES) project – see website and Watson, 2006).

The class was an above-average group of 14 and 15 year-olds. They had spent the previous lesson revising the different groupings that chemicals can be placed in and the properties associated with those groups. In this lesson the pupils were given the problem in the fictitious context of the laboratory being flooded by a storm that washed the labels off some bottles of chemicals. The pupils' job was to design a way of identifying the chemicals *'so that the teacher can put the right labels back on each bottle'*. They were given thirteen bottles, labelled A to M, containing different solids and data cards describing the properties of the solids. Two aspects of procedural understanding associated with identification were being addressed in this lesson:

- deciding the criteria that can be used to judge good questions for identification;
- being able to arrange the questions in a suitable order in a key.

How can we decide whether this is good-quality dialogue? The dialogue in enquiry lessons should be focused on specific educational outcomes. It should aim to create a learning environment that supports pupils in making decisions for themselves in the open-learning contexts found in scientific enquiry.

Good dialogue should:

- **be purposeful** – the teacher plans and facilitates discourse with particular educational aims in view;
- **be constructive** – the teachers and students co-construct understanding based on each other's ideas; dialogue is therefore cumulative;
- **contain explanations of the teacher's and students' ideas** – students justify their ideas; teachers communicate that justification of ideas is important;
- **promote a supportive learning environment** – learning is seen as a collaborative process; teachers and students listen to one another and share ideas.

(Derived from Alexander, 2004, and Mercer *et al.*, 2004).

Using these criteria, what did the teacher do that affected quality? First, Mr Watt selected a challenging and interesting context. He made the purpose of the dialogue clear: to identify good questions (lines 1, 17). There is some evidence of the dialogue being cumulative but Mr Watt allowed the discussion of whether electrical conductivity was a good criterion for a question to fizzle out inconclusively (lines 4–12). After this the teacher refocused the pupils by saying that one criterion for a good question is that it divides the substances into roughly equal-sized groups (line 13). The dialogue is strong in explanation.

Box 25.2

Mystery powders

The lesson started with the pupils having to think up ten questions to identify a chemical that was in the teacher's head. They were only allowed to use questions that gave a yes/no answer. The teacher emphasised that the pupils had to choose their questions carefully. In their first four questions the pupils found out that the chemical had a melting point over 500 °C, was not soluble in water, did not conduct electricity when solid and was white. We join the dialogue after the fourth question:

1 **Mr Watt:** *Were all these good questions to ask?*

2 **Pupils:** *[many replies] No. Yes. It's ionic etc. ...*

3 **Mr Watt:** *OK. Denis?*

4 **Denis:** *Conduction when solid is a bad question because when it is yes ... Um ... It can only be no.*

5 **Mr Watt:** *Are there any in there which conduct when it is solid?*

6 **Denis:** *Yea, the metals. When it's a metal.*

7 **Mr Watt:** *So if you ask this question, conduction when solid ...?*

8 **Denis:** *It has to be a metal, when it's yes.*

9 **Mr Watt:** *And why is that?*

10 **Denis:** *Because when it's a liquid ... [stops talking]*

11 **Mr Watt:** *No, you are on the right lines. You are classifying there into metals and non-metals. Sadie?*

12 **Sadie:** *There are only metals and all of them are insoluble.*

13 **Mr Watt:** *OK. I think ... Which is the best question here to split our compounds into two sets?*

14 **Jordan:** *Ionic or covalent.*

15 **Mr Watt:** *From their properties. Tom?*

16 **Tom:** *Is it white?*

17 **Mr Watt:** *[strong confirming voice] That's the best question, I would say. Why is that the best question?*

18 **Tom:** *Because that's about half and half. About half of them are white.*

19 **Mr Watt:** *Which ones are white? Have a quick look at the cards. Which ones are white?*

20 **Many pupils:** *A, B, C, F.*

21 **Mr Watt:** *How many is that Tom?*

22 **Many pupils:** *Four. Five.*

23 **Mr Watt:** *So five of them are white. So with one question you split them.*

Mr Watt asked 'why' questions that promoted the use of the word 'because' (lines 4, 10, 18) and of complete sentences, rather than single words or short phrases (lines 8, 12 and 18). This short piece of dialogue indicates little about a supportive learning environment, although the longer dialogue, from which this is an extract, showed that the teacher frequently used the word 'we', that he encouraged many pupils to answer questions and that there was even one unsolicited question from a pupil.

Dialogue can be analysed in various ways (see Chapter 20). Teachers cannot readily analyse their on-going class exchanges while 'in the thick of it'. However, analysis of recorded dialogues from oneself, colleagues or research sources is useful for developing habits of quality dialogue in scientific enquiry lessons.

Better enquiries?

New courses are currently being introduced in schools offering opportunities for more up-to-date science curricula (see Chapters 1, 8, 24). These changes present opportunities for improving the quality of scientific enquiry in our schools, including the aspects discussed in this chapter.

Acknowledgement

Heekyong Kim assisted Rod Watson and Labrini Nikolaou in developing the framework for analysis of dialogue described in this chapter.

References

Abd-el-Khalik, F., Boulaoude, S., Duschl, R., Niaz, M., Treagust, D. and Tuan, H. (2004) Enquiry in science education: international perspectives. *Science Education*, **88**, 397–419.

Alexander, R. J. (2005) *Towards dialogic teaching: rethinking classroom talk*. 2nd edn. York: Dialogos.

Foulds, K., Gott, R. and Duggan, S. (1997) *Science investigations 1*. London: Collins.

Foulds, K., Gott, R. and Duggan, S. (1998) *Science investigations 2*. London: Collins.

Foulds, K., Gott, R. and Duggan, S. (1999) *Science investigations 3*. London: Collins.

Goldsworthy, A. (1998) Getting to grips with graphs. *Science Teacher Education*, **23**, 14–15.

Goldsworthy, A. (2002) *Investigations: AKSIS INSET: Making an impact*. Hatfield: Association for Science Education.

Goldsworthy, A., Watson, J. R. and Wood-Robinson, V. (1999) AKSIS project. *Investigations: Getting to grips with graphs*. Hatfield: Association for Science Education.

Goldsworthy, A., Watson, J. R. and Wood-Robinson, V. (2000a) AKSIS project. *Ymchwiliadau: Mynd i'r afael a graffiau*. Welsh Joint Education Committee Publications Scheme.

Goldsworthy, A., Watson, J. R. and Wood-Robinson, V. (2000b) AKSIS project. *Investigations: developing understanding*. Hatfield: Association for Science Education.

Mercer, N., Dawes, L., Wegerif, R. and Sanis, C. (2004) Reasoning as a scientist: ways of helping children to use language to learn science. *British Educational Research Journal*, **30**(3), 359–377.

QCA (1999) *Science: the National Curriculum for England*. London: QCA/DfES. Available at: www.nc.uk.net

QCA (2000) *Science: a scheme of work for key stage 3*. London: QCA/DfES. Available at: http://www.standards.dfes.gov.uk/schemes2/secondary_science/?view=get

QCA (2002) *Key Stage 3 National Strategy, Framework for teaching science: years 7, 8 and 9*. London: QCA/DfES. Available at http://www.standards.dfes.gov.uk

Sang, D. and Wood-Robinson, V. (2002) *Teaching secondary scientific enquiry*. London: John Murray.

Watson, J. R. (2006) *Beyond fair testing: teaching different types of scientific enquiry*. London: Gatsby Science Enhancement Programme.

Watson, J. R. and Wood-Robinson, V. (1998) Learning to investigate. In *ASE Guide to secondary science education*, ed. Ratcliffe, M. pp. 84–91. Cheltenham: Stanley Thornes.

Watson, J. R., Goldsworthy, A. and Wood-Robinson, V. (1999a) What is not fair with investigations? *School Science Review*, **80**(292), 101–106.

Watson, J. R., Goldsworthy, A. and Wood-Robinson, V. (1999b) One hundred and twenty hours of practical science investigations: a report of teachers' work with pupils aged 7 to 14. In *Practical work in science education – the face of science in schools*, ed. Nielsen, K. and Paulsen, A. C. pp. 112–121. Copenhagen: Royal Danish School of Educational Studies.

Watson, R., Goldsworthy, A. and Wood-Robinson, V. (2002) What is not fair with investigations? In *Aspects of secondary science teaching*, ed. Amos, S. and Boohan, R. pp. 53–59. London: RoutledgeFalmer.

Websites

SKEES (SEP-King's Enhancing Enquiries in School project): http://www.kcl.ac.uk/depsta/education/skeesproject.html

Chapter 26

Scientific thinking: how can we accelerate and generalise it?

This chapter challenges the 'delivery' view of teaching, arguing that children's ability to learn depends on their ability to process new information. A carefully constructed intervention programme can enhance this information-processing capability by setting challenges and encouraging pupils to be conscious of their own thinking. The investment of time for the development of higher-level thinking skills in the context of science repays itself in enhanced learning capacity across the curriculum.

Philip Adey

How children process information

Please Miss, why is the sea salty?

Well, there are many soluble salts in the earth. One of the most common is sodium chloride, which we call 'common salt'. Over millions of years of rain, a lot of salt gets dissolved out of the earth and flows into the sea. When water evaporates from the sea, it leaves the salt behind, so gradually the sea becomes more concentrated with salt.

This may be an accurate explanation, but 80 per cent of pupils switch off at this point; 10 per cent say *'Thank you'* and put their heads down, puzzled; 10 per cent ask *'What does dissolve mean?'*, *'Why does it evaporate?'*, *'What salts are there that are not common salt?'*, and so on. Whatever the response, not a lot of information has been transferred, in spite of the apparent (to a science teacher) clarity of the explanation.

People outside education sometimes believe that if a teacher knows

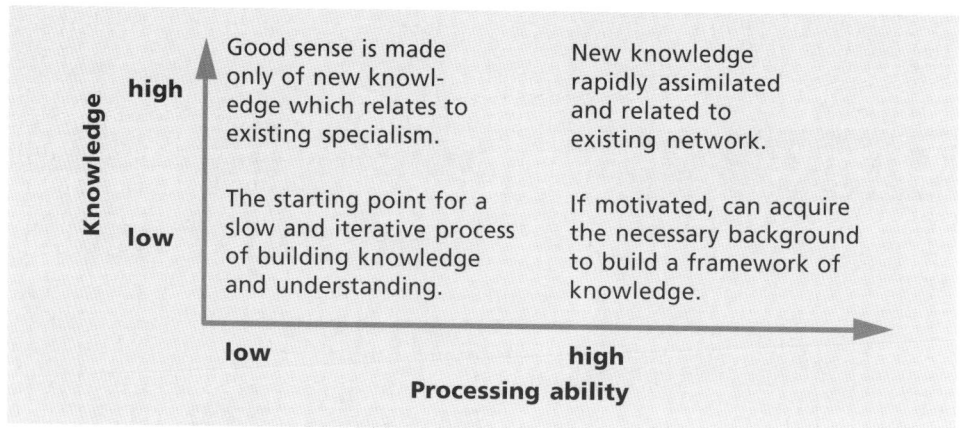

Figure 26.1 **Knowledge and processing ability.**

something, and a child does not, then all the teacher has to do is to tell the child what she knows. Anyone who has been a teacher knows that information (or knowledge) does not get transferred that easily. Where is knowledge? Is it in people's heads? In books? In the collective unconscious? Knowledge is in all these places but, unlike water, it cannot simply be poured from one place to another. This is because knowledge actually consists of an incredibly complex network of understandings deeply embedded in social and cultural assumptions. Knowledge is never a set of isolated items or 'facts', which a person or a book can pass on to a learner. Even apparently trivial bits of information such as *'The school is just south of the new supermarket'* may not have meaning for someone who is unsure which direction is south, or in a few years when the supermarket is no longer 'new'.

All information needs to be processed by the receiver. The effectiveness of this information-processing depends on (a) the existing network of understandings that the receiver already has, and (b) the power of his/her information-processing mechanism. If these are the two main controlling factors, there are four possibilities, summarised in Figure 26.1. (See also Chapter 19 for the role of existing knowledge on learning science concepts.)

Our ability to process information develops with age and experience. It involves a qualitative shift in the type of thinking available, a growth in the number of variables that can be held in the mind at once and acted upon. This is the basis of the stages of cognitive development described by Jean Piaget (Wadsworth, 1971; Boden, 1979). Children using what he calls concrete operations are able to understand relationships between two variables, and simple cause–effect relationships. But it requires a higher level of thinking, described as formal operations, to be able to handle fluently problems involving three or four variables. This is what is needed to understand how to control variables. Unless you can hold in your mind at one time the possible values of the variables length, mass and angle of swing of a pendulum, you cannot understand why it is necessary to hold two constant while you change the third. (Although young children can understand the concept of 'fairness' in a running race, on being encouraged to transfer this idea to a scientific investigation they think they have to routinely 'keep everything else the same', whether it is a relevant variable or not, because they cannot *understand* how to control variables.)

Likewise, proportional thinking requires that a ratio (two variables) be multiplied by a third variable to increase or decrease it by a given proportion. All three variables have to be held in the mind at once and manipulated independently. Such a demand on working memory is what characterises formal operations. In the National Curriculum for Science in England, demand for such formal thinking starts to be made at about levels 5 and 6, which form something of a natural barrier of difficulty for progression through the curriculum.

What is the status of different levels of thinking at which children process information? Do they form some sort of staircase up which all children ascend under the control of predetermined maturational development of the central nervous system? Although there certainly is an element in the process that depends on maturation, progress is very importantly influenced by the child's experiences. In other words, as teachers and as parents, we can have a real influence on the process of cognitive development.

How much does it matter?

Since the 1980s, education policy has been driven by a search for higher standards but there is little clear account of what counts as 'higher standards'. Most education professionals are sceptical of relying simply on test results, as tests often tap low-level rote knowledge rather than real understanding, and 'teaching to the test' may raise test grades but undermine good teaching. We believe that academic achievement can be improved, but to do so we must rely not so much on external controls or off-the-peg 'strategies', but on research and theoretical models of learning. Such models can inform the development of professional practice, and in this chapter I will show how teaching practice lies at the heart of genuinely improved academic standards, since this is the route to improving children's ability to process information to make meaning of what they encounter in the science lab.

Intervention

We need to distinguish here between the ideas of *instruction* and of *intervention*. The meaning of instruction is unproblematic: it is the provision of knowledge and understanding through appropriate activities. Instruction can be categorised by topic and domain and the end-product of instruction can be specified in terms of learning objectives.

Intervention is used here in the sense of intervening in the process of cognitive development, that is, in manipulating experiences aimed at maximising the rate of progression through the different levels of thinking. Both instruction and intervention are necessary to an effective educational system, but instruction has been emphasised to the neglect of intervention. It could be claimed that intervention offers the only route for the further substantial raising of standards in an educational world that has spent the last 50 years concentrating on improved instructional methods.

The theory and practice of increasing pupils' ability

To address directly the development of pupils' ability to process data does not mean trying to teach thinking skills like a set of rules. We have to provide the conditions under which the complex process of high-level thinking is most likely to develop. The term 'constructivism' is now well known in science education circles, meaning the need for pupils to construct their own knowledge and understanding. In cognitive intervention theory we also depend on constructivism, but we broaden its meaning to include the pupils' construction of their own higher-level thinking abilities.

Certain principles are built into activities designed to stimulate pupils' cognitive abilities. Some of these are described and exemplified below.

Challenge, otherwise known as cognitive conflict

Pupils' thinking is challenged, and they are supported in their problem-solving by carefully managed dialogue and resources.

In one activity, pupils are presented with a bunch of tubes varying in length, width and material, and asked to find which variable affects the pitch of the note you get when you blow across the tube. A typical 11-year-old will choose a short wide one and a long narrow one to compare. He may come to you and say *'I've found that wide tubes give lower notes than narrow tubes'*. This statement needs to be challenged, but the method of challenge is critical. It should be designed so that the pupil has the best possible chance of constructing the control of variables strategy for himself. Which of the two teachers' dialogues in Box 26.1 is more likely to achieve this?

Box 26.1	
Dialogue 1	**Dialogue 2**
T: *How do you know the width affects the note?*	**T:** *How do you know the width affects the note?*
P: *The wide one gives a deeper note.*	**P:** *The wide one gives a deeper note.*
T: *But look at the tubes, they have different lengths as well as different widths.*	**T:** *Look at the tubes. How are they different?*
P: *Oh yes.*	**P:** *They are different widths.*
T: *How can you tell whether it is the length or width or both?*	**T:** *Anything else?*
P: *??*	**P:** *Different lengths.*
T: *You can't, can you? If you change two things, you don't know which is having the effect, do you?*	**T:** *How do you know it is not the length that affects the note?*
P: *I suppose not.*	**P:** *Both the length and the width affect the note.*
T: *OK, go away and choose two tubes which have the same length, but different widths, and try those.*	**T:** *Maybe. But maybe it is just the width, or just the length. How could you tell whether it is length or width or both?*
	P: *??*
	T: *Go away and think about it, and try to find a pair of tubes that will prove whether it is really just the width that affects the note.*

Social construction

Pupils are encouraged to construct knowledge together, by expressing their understandings, listening and challenging each other, that is, generating high-quality argument. Social construction could be managed in the activity described above. It would happen when, for instance, the teacher asked different groups to tell the class what they had found out about the effect of width of tube on the note, probed for justification and examples of 'good pairs' of tubes, and asked other groups whether they agreed, or what different conclusions they had reached and why. This seems like a slow process in a world of 'delivering the curriculum', but it is central to the development of higher-level thinking that will give the pupils access to better understanding of all science concepts.

Reflection, otherwise known as metacognition

An important principle is to encourage children to be conscious of their own thinking strategies. In another activity, a pupil has been investigating the load and lift forces in a 'wheelbarrow' lever. A load is hung from one of the notches on a pivoted notched stick and a force meter at the other end measures the lift. She has recorded the lift as successive loads are added and calculated the ratio of load to lift for each. With quite a bit of help and discussion, and comparing results from other groups, she has established that the ratio is approximately constant. She has gone so far as to predict what the lift would be for a load that is too heavy to actually try. The dialogue in Box 26.2 ensues.

Box 26.2

Dialogue 3

T: *How did you do that?*

P: *What do you mean, how did I do that?*

T: *I mean, how did you get to that answer?*

P: *I just, well, worked it out.*

T: *Yes, but how did you work it out, what were you thinking?*

P: *Err, I just looked at the ratio, and I, err, timesed it.*

T: *Timesed what?*

P: *Timesed the ratio by the lift to get the load.*

T: *But you were supposed to find the lift. You didn't know what it was.*

P: *Well I tried different lifts until I found one, that when I timesed it, it gave the new load.*

The child is being encouraged to unpack her own thinking, to put on the table the process by which she reached an answer. This makes working explicit, so it becomes available for use again. It emphasises that the reasoning process is as important as the answer, although there may be many legitimate reasoning pathways to the same correct answer.

See also Chapters 20 and 25 for further examples of dialogue that can be challenging, constructive and reflective.

Bridging

The term bridging has two distinct meanings in this context. The first is the application of reasoning patterns (such as 'control of variables' or 'proportionality') to other places in the science curriculum where they are useful. The National Curriculum and QCA schemes of work offer hundreds of opportunities for using these reasoning patterns, and others such as equilibrium, probability and formal modelling. But the other meaning is to bridge the style of teaching one uses for the development of thinking into one's 'normal' science teaching, so that all your lessons include elements of challenge, of social construction, and of reflection on thinking (see Shayer and Gamble, 2001).

CASE

All these principles have been incorporated into the methods of 'cognitive acceleration' developed at King's College London, with demonstrable effects on pupils' academic achievement. CASE (Cognitive Acceleration through Science Education) has introduced a method of teaching that focuses not so much on good instruction leading to the development of content knowledge, but rather on intervention in children's ability to process information. In other words, CASE is a programme designed to help children to think more effectively. When they think better, they learn better, because they are better equipped to make better sense of their regular science instruction.

The CASE programme consists of a set of 30 activities (Adey, Shayer and Yates, 2001) designed to be used during the early secondary years at the rate of one every two weeks in place of a regular science lesson. It may seem that frequent special lessons for 'thinking', when direct coverage of curriculum content is set aside, makes it even more difficult to deliver the National Curriculum. But reflect for a moment on those words 'coverage' and 'deliver'. What view of knowledge do such words imply? They imply that knowledge is a packet that can be delivered, or a set of topics and material that can be covered in the sense of going over it. This is precisely the view of knowledge against which I argue and which has been discredited by constructivists. Time spent in encouraging the development of the general processing mechanism may immediately be lost from 'covering' the curriculum, but it provides learners with the tools with which they can learn more effectively in the future.

It is recommended that CASE lessons are quite specifically signalled to pupils as 'special', something different from regular science lessons. We are often asked whether they cannot be integrated into a complete work scheme. I cannot say categorically that such integration would not work, but all the evidence we have for the effect of CASE is with CASE taught as special activities about once every two weeks for two years. As a teacher one is operating in a different mode in CASE lessons. The objectives are to do with high-level thinking, while in your regular science lessons they are to do with the development of science knowledge and concepts. In a CASE lesson you need to lose sight of any particular information from the National Curriculum, and focus instead on the quality of argumentation and thinking evinced in your pupils.

Does it work ?

In a word, yes. It does. In our original research we asked ten schools to try CASE teaching in one or two early secondary classes for two years, and to identify matched 'control' classes who would follow their normal science curriculum. The CASE pupils made significantly greater gains in cognitive development over the two years of the experiment. More importantly, they demonstrated long-term effects on their ability to learn. They gained higher grades in GCSE than matched control pupils who had not had CASE intervention. When we published these data in 1991 they attracted many schools that wished to adopt the methods. At that time we started to run professional development courses for CASE, and also to train CASE trainers who have been working in many parts of the UK ever since. In 1996 we got the first GCSE data from those schools with which we started to work in 1991. These confirmed the original research results: CASE schools produced significantly higher 'value-added' effects. After taking account of the intake level of their pupils, CASE schools had much higher proportions of pupils achieving level 6 or above at key stage 3, and of pupils achieving grades A–C at GCSE, than non-CASE schools. This is not only in science, but in maths and English as well. It seems that the pupils' enhanced processing ability is general, and can be applied across the curriculum. Data from 1999 GCSE results demonstrate the reliability of the 1996 findings (Adey and Shayer, 1994; Shayer, 1999; Shayer and Adey, 2002).

Extending cognitive acceleration

The basic idea of cognitive acceleration has been extended to other subject areas and age groups. At key stage 3 there are programmes in mathematics (CAME), technology (CATE) and art, music and drama (ARTS). In primary schools there are science thinking programmes for years 1, 3 and 4 and maths programmes for years 1 and 2 and years 5 and 6 (Adhami, Johnson and Shayer, 1998; Adey, Robertson and Venville, 2001; Adey, Nagy et al., 2003; Hamaker, 2003). Individuals have extended the ideas to key stage 4 science.

Probably the majority of secondary school science departments in the United Kingdom have at some time obtained the curriculum materials (Thinking Science) and at least toyed with implementing CASE, but hundreds of schools have gone much further and participated in serious professional development to introduce the programme. Many local education authorities, also, have bought into CASE professional development programmes for their schools. CASE ideas play an important part in the Key Stage 3 Strategy, not only in science but also in the foundation subjects (see Chapter 9). It is hard to think of any other science teaching innovation, ever, that has had such a long shelf-life (1984 to the present), even if throughout this period it has been 'bubbling under' the mainstream rather than grabbing the headlines.

There is nothing magic about the CASE set of activities published as Thinking Science. What is magic is the use that teachers make of them, and learning how to do this is not a straightforward matter. Teaching for cognitive stimulation requires an unusual amount of concentration on questioning skills, managing group and whole-class discussions, and provoking reflective thinking in pupils, but these are strategies that can be learned by any teacher prepared to commit some time and energy to it. A number of university departments and independent consultants offer comprehensive professional development courses to schools and local authorities wishing to introduce CASE.

References

Adey, P. and Shayer, M. (1994) *Really raising standards: cognitive intervention and academic achievement.* London: Routledge.

Adey, P., Robertson, A. and Venville, G. (2001) *Let's think!* Slough: NFER-Nelson.

Adey, P., Shayer, M. and Yates, C. (2001) *Thinking Science: the curriculum materials of the CASE project.* 3rd edn. London: Nelson Thornes (available as print file and CD-ROM).

Adey, P., Shayer, M. and Yates, C. (2003) *Thinking Science professional edition.* Cheltenham: Nelson Thornes (same material as *Thinking Science*, with addition of *PowerPoint* and video-clips to run professional development for CASE).

Adey, P., Nagy, F., Robertson, A., Serret, N. and Wadsworth, P. (2003) *Let's think through science!* London: nferNelson.

Adhami, M., Johnson, D. C. and Shayer, M. (1998) *Thinking mathematics: the curriculum materials of the CAME project.* London: Heinemann.

Boden, M. (1979) *Piaget.* London: Fontana.

Hamaker, A. (2003) *CATE: Cognitive acceleration through technology education.* Taunton: Nigel Blagg Associates.

Shayer, M. (1999) Cognitive acceleration through science education II: its effect and scope. *International Journal of Science Education,* **21**(8), 883–902.

Shayer, M. and Adey, P. ed. (2002) *Learning intelligence: cognitive acceleration across the curriculum from 5 to 15 years.* Maidenhead: Open University Press.

Shayer, M. and Gamble, R. (2001) *Bridging from CASE to core science.* Hatfield: Association for Science Education.

Wadsworth, B. J. (1971) *Piaget's theory of cognitive and affective development.* 5th edn. White Plains New York: Longman.

Website

CASE (details of more publications and trainers): http://www.kcl.ac.uk/depsta/education/case.html

Chapter	27	Creativity in teaching and learning science

'Do you consider yourself to be creative in any part of your life?' 'Do you think that you are creative in science?' When asked these questions teachers cited a range of constraints that seemed to impinge on their ability to be creative in the classroom. This chapter explores the meaning and value of creativity in science education and examines what teachers feel constrains creativity in teaching and learning. It discusses the conditions and resources for supporting creativity, the role of information and communication technology (ICT) and language in fostering it and how signs of creative thinking can be recognised.

Rosemary Feasey

What is creativity?

There are many definitions of creativity. One of the most useful has been developed by the National Committee for Creativity and Culture in Education in the report *All our futures: creativity and culture in education* (NACCCE, 1999). This seminal report suggests that creativity is:

> *Imaginative activity fashioned so as to produce outcomes that are both original and of value.* (NACCCE, 1999, p. 29)

This definition is expanded in terms of characteristics of creativity as follows:

> *First, they [the characteristics of creativity] always involve thinking or behaving **imaginatively**. Second, overall this imaginative activity is **purposeful**: that is, it is directed to achieving an objective. Third, these processes must generate something **original**. Fourth, the outcome must be of **value** in relation to the objective.* (QCA Creativity in the National Curriculum, see websites)

This definition provides a useful starting point and it is easy to apply the statements to school science. Creativity should be a partnership between pupils and teachers.

Constraints on creativity

Teachers were asked the question, *'What do you think are the constraints for teaching and learning creatively in the classroom?'* The majority of responses focused on:

- increase in paperwork linked to school inspection;
- the high level of planning required;
- feeling exhausted and unable to find the time and energy to be creative;
- the amount of content required in terms of curriculum coverage;
- not enough time to allow pupils the opportunity to be creative in the classroom;
- the concern that, if they taught creatively, it would jeopardise school results in national tests and school positions in performance tables.

The survey was of a hundred primary teachers, but the above responses indicate a level of stress that has pervaded much of the teaching profession for a number of years, and they are equally typical of secondary science teachers. However, we cannot, as a profession, allow these responses to excuse lack of creativity in teaching and learning. Everyone has the right to be creative: teachers have the right to work creatively, and they also have the responsibility to encourage and develop the creative potential of pupils. In an ideal world creativity would not be singled out for special treatment. To do so:

> uncovers a basic misconception about the nature of creativity. Creativity is not an add-on to the curriculum but an integral part of thinking and planning for teaching and learning episodes. Creativity requires that teachers are open to different possibilities and also to appreciate that developing creativity is not an option to be disregarded but that as professionals we have a duty to be creative and develop creativity in children. (Feasey, 2005, p. 35)

Nevertheless, it is important to debate the nature of creativity and how to develop creative approaches to teaching and learning.

Pupils' views of creativity

Whilst teachers might understand the nature of creativity what about the pupils? How can they become partners in developing their creative potential in science? One way is to ask them what they think is special about a creative person. Box 27.1 shows just some of the responses of a class of pupils who were asked exactly that question.

What do the responses in Box 27.1 tell us? Well, certainly that these pupils are able to think about the concept of creativity and offer profound and intuitive contributions to the debate. Their ideas include many of those that researchers and writers in the area of creativity mention, and at times with more eloquence and a sense of excitement about creativity. They are important contributions and help to provide some basis for thinking about creativity in science. The idea that creativity in science should encourage free thinking is important since

> **Box 27.1**
>
> **Pupils' ideas on characteristics of a creative person**
>
> A creative person:
> - *is a free thinker;*
> - *is daring;*
> - *thinks of lots of ideas not just one;*
> - *is always thinking of new things;*
> - *reaches new heights;*
> - *is encouraging and joyful;*
> - *lets the imagination run wild.*
>
> (Feasey, 2005, pp. 9–10)

it recognises that pupils should be engaged in thinking that is not bound by the existing knowledge and expectations of the teacher. Allowing them to collaborate and discuss their ideas encourages pupils to share ideas and spark ideas off each other, supporting a free flow of many ideas. You may be surprised to know that these profound responses were from a mixed class of 8–11 year-olds. These are the children who bring their ideas to our secondary classrooms.

The idea of being daring, a risk taker, is an important one, mentioned by writers such as Sternberg (1999) and the NACCCE report (1999). Risk is often associated with situations that are potentially harmful in science, such as using a Bunsen burner or chemicals. In the context of creativity, risk relates to a person being able to take a risk with ideas, with solutions to problems. These ideas might be different from those of their peers; they might sound ridiculous at first hearing, or be 'off the wall'. In a learning environment that supports and celebrates creativity in science, pupils will feel able to risk sharing ideas and ways of working with teachers and peers. To develop creativity in science pupils need to be encouraged to move out of their comfort zone and think the unusual. This might also require the teacher to do the same. A good example of this is the use of 'concept cartoons' (Keogh and Naylor, 1997), an important tool for eliciting pupils' ideas in science. The cartoons are in themselves a creative teaching approach, but used carefully they can encourage pupils to think and work creatively, particularly where the teacher encourages them to:

- share their thinking;
- consider alternative ideas;
- explore ways of challenging and testing the ideas.

'Always thinking of new things' is another important aspect of creativity. In this context *'new things'* are relative to the pupils and their peers, and just because the teacher already knows a solution to a problem it should not invalidate pupils thinking of the same idea, since it may be the first time that a pupil has come up with that idea. It is also important that the teacher allows pupils to work through ideas, problems and solutions. Too often teachers give pupils the answer in science, either because of perceived time constraints or because they worry about frustrating learners. It is important to remove the barriers to risk taking and failing. Where teachers iron out problems and make choices for pupils (e.g. resources, solutions), this denies them opportunities to:

- tackle problems;
- consider and try out alternatives;

- take risks with their ideas and strategies;
- work as a team;
- persevere when things do not work.

The suggestion that in the process of being creative a person is able to '*reach new heights*' is exactly what we as teachers strive to do, helping a child to shift his or her personal parameters for how they think and work scientifically.

Finally, the enthusiasm and energy of a creative person is acknowledged by pupils' suggestions that a creative person is '*encouraging and joyful*' and is able to let their '*imagination run wild*'. This underlines how important it is for the teacher to be enthusiastic and be willing to take a risk in his or her approaches to science.

What might creative science look like in the classroom?

Creativity in science is less likely to flourish where schools have a rigid approach to science based on a scheme of work that merely reiterates the bare bones of the National Curriculum or examination specification and that lacks the basic tenets of creativity. Of particular interest are the links between school science and everyday contexts that are local and personal to the pupils and school. Science needs to be freed from the constraints of being taught in a 'curriculum' vacuum. Links can be made across different aspects of science and with other areas of the curriculum and pupils' experience.

A science display cabinet in a public area of the school, with frequently changed displays of interesting and awesome objects, can inspire creativity. It may be combined with a competition, for example to identify this week's mystery object or to write a poem about displayed items. Similarly, a dedicated notice board in the science corridor can host fascinating newspaper articles and intriguing photographs, again with provoking questions. Management of the display could be delegated to a science club or to a rota of different classes. The aim of these displays is not to teach to a formal curriculum but to offer pupils opportunities to be fascinated, awed and inspired by something and encouraged to explore and engage in a free flow of ideas and suggestions that are not bound by right or wrong. Creativity in science also requires carefully structured lessons where the teacher offers pupils a rich and wide range of experiences that capitalise on their enthusiasm and on their different learning styles and interests.

Resources for creative teaching and learning

In planning for creativity, teachers should consider the kind of resources needed to support creative teaching and learning in science. While it is important to resource the department with commercially supplied scientific materials, imaginative use of everyday objects can complement these (see Chapter 21, Box 21.3). Many topics lend themselves to improvised models, such as a tennis ball in a sock to simulate peristalsis, or a length of string pulled out of the teacher's shirt to show the length of the gut. A more elaborate but imaginatively prepared resource on this theme is a knitted alimentary canal (Healey, 1987; Lock, 1990) or a can of 'dog food' for the teacher to eat (a recipe of jelly and *Mars* bar set in a cleaned and re-sealed dog-food can). Creative impromptu use of the school environment can make an impact. For example, taking a class outside on a bright sunny day to stand under a big tree is a more awesome introduction to photosynthesis than picking a leaf off a potted geranium in the lab!

Some items can be purchased with the intention of supporting creativity, such as touchable bubbles (bubbles that do not burst when they are touched or land on objects) that challenge pupils' ideas about common substances. This material does the unexpected and therefore challenges expectations, provides a stimulus for pupils' questions, offers opportunities for problem-solving and participation in 'mind investigations'. Teachers use touchable bubbles in the context of talk about polymers and also get pupils to work out what they would add to ordinary bubble mixtures to make them touchable. Pupils can investigate whether the touchable bubbles behave the same way in the same conditions, or whether the mixture is changed by adding water.

The role of language

Pupils' creativity is often expressed in the language of their questions. It is important that teachers should not undermine this by ignoring or dismissing as 'unscientific' the more bizarre or currently irrelevant questions (see Chapter 21). However, planning for creative teaching and learning of science must take account of the fact that different kinds of language are crucial, relating to:

- science – concepts, skills and processes;
- mathematics – metres, graphs, percentages;
- comparison – similarities and differences;
- awe and wonder, beauty, grace, horror, the unexpected and disgusting.

Ways to encourage pupils to learn and enjoy language in science include scientific word puzzles, matching words, word bingos, riddles, SPLAT games, charades and human graphs. Further discussion of the language of science, as well as creative approaches to developing language in science, can be found in Wellington and Osborne (2001).

In order for pupils to share their ideas, solve problems, take risks and think the unthinkable, they need language to express themselves. That much is obvious. What is less obvious is the potential of pupils to be creative in communicating their science with humour and eloquence. Boxes 27.2 and 27.3 gives examples of poems, from pupils at different

Box 27.2

The journey of the seed
By Lizzie, aged 11

I watch the seed fly silently
Across the flower scattered meadow
And as the seed hovers close to me
I see how it is carefully designed
And aerodynamic, suited to fly
It is whisked away by the gentle breeze.

Then other seeds come floating by
And each have the same qualities
As the other seed, now far away
On the soft, rich soil of the farmer's field.

(from Feasey, 2001)

Box 27.3

The journey of a water molecule
By Clare, an A-level student

Whenever you see the rain, known as H_2O,
Do you ever begin to think where it has to go?
We land on soil and sink down deep, until we find a root,
Then into a selectively permeable membrane we must shoot.
Once inside the root hair, a decision must be made:
By which method will I reach the final palisade?
Do I take the apoplast path, or even the symplast way?
Or shall I go the vascular route, I really cannot say.

Now I know which way I'll go, it's the apoplast way for me,
Along cell walls, in tiny spaces, 50% is free!
By mass flow I will travel, to areas of low concentration.
I'm just doing my tiny bit in the process of transpiration.

So on I go across the cortex, passing many things,
The odd cellulose and transcellular strings,
Through the endodermis, to my next port of call,
The xylem vessel, up the stem, which can be very tall,
The boring bit yet to come when I reach another cell wall.

On I go forever up, by root pressure and transpiration,
It's not far to go now to my destination.
Again, round I go, past many cells shaped not unlike cases
Luckily in front of me are substomatal spaces.
I'm going to evaporate soon, I'm certain that I will
But unfortunately in front of me is an overweight mesophyll.
So here I stay until my turn, I always have to wait,
Until the cells decide that I must evaporate.

(from Lock, 1997)

ends of the secondary age range, in which the pupils confidently and creatively combine scientific vocabulary and ideas with descriptive language.

Many generations of teachers have set homework tasks for pupils to write about the journey of a cheese sandwich through the digestive system or the adventures of a water molecule through the water cycle, so these may appear 'old hat'. However, such tasks are novel for each cohort of pupils and encourage creative writing and more focused thought on the science behind it. In a creative science department in Yorkshire some pupils designed travel brochures extolling the benefits of various planets of the solar system as holiday destinations, others wrote cartoon-strip stories about particles for an audience of younger children, and others wrote imaginatively about journeying through a plant cell (see QCA website).

Encouraging creative use of language in science is not just about poetry and story telling, but about providing pupils with the tools to explore ideas, tackle problems, take risks with ideas and ways of working and collaborating – all those elements that are important to the development of creative potential in science.

This means that teachers should model the use of language not only in relation to scientific terminology, but also to describe and to explore the emotions and awe and wonder of science. It is a challenge to introduce the WOW! factor in science. Objects viewed microscopically (perhaps using a digital microscope), spectacular chemical reactions (with due regard to risk assessment, see Chapter 14) and demonstrations of electrostatics, still provoke awe even in 'cool' pupils assuming disaffection. Pupils need to develop descriptive language in order to be able to talk about their observations and emotions and share their curiosity and wonder.

The National Curriculum for England states that pupils must be taught 'about the ways in which scientists work today and how they worked in the past, including the role of ... creative thought in the development of scientific ideas' (Programme of Study for Key Stage 3, Sc1, 1c, DfEE, 1999). Scientists across the centuries have been fascinated by nature, awed by its complexity and indeed its simplicity, its patterns and effects. This is a model for pupils learning science today, often forgotten in pursuing the prescriptive, concept-based, aspects of the National Curriculum.

Use of ICT to develop creativity

Planned uses of ICT have several important functions in developing pupils' creative potential in science, since ICT can:

● engage and motivate;
● collect and handle data that pupils would not normally be able to do, for example, collecting data during the night;
● offer collaborative ways of working;
● offer opportunities for devising new uses of ICT;
● provide problem-solving opportunities;
● offer contexts that stretch the imagination;
● encourage creative ways of communicating science.

Creative use of ICT is enabled by the use of computer data-loggers in science. Pupils can be challenged to ask more demanding questions, propose more challenging hypotheses and carry out more extensive recording than if they were restricted to manual measurements in a short lesson slot (see also Chapter 13).

Recognising creativity

So how do we know when pupils are thinking and behaving creatively? The QCA (see websites) suggests that we will see pupils:

● questioning and challenging;
● making connections and seeing relationships;
● envisaging what might be;
● exploring ideas, keeping options open;
● reflecting critically on ideas, actions and outcomes.

Promoting creativity

The ultimate in creativity in science would be for teachers not to have to think of it as a discrete feature of provision, but for it to be second nature in terms of teaching and learning. In the future, teachers will need to become risk-takers in their own thinking and practice and be prepared to try out new ideas and approaches. Importantly, schools must celebrate creativity and raise its profile in science by:

- involving pupils in discussion about what creativity is and in developing their own creative potential in science;
- inviting visitors into school who have links to science, from industry, universities, clinics, environment agencies;
- linking science with arts projects from music to sculpture, poets to drama;
- reconsidering resources to ensure teachers and pupils are stimulated by the resources and equipment available to them;
- developing pupils' higher-order skills linked with risk-taking and problem-solving;
- displaying science around the school;
- involving pupils, staff, parents/carers and visitors in science days, science weeks and fairs, clubs and award schemes (e.g. CREST);
- celebrating pupils' achievements and creativity in science at every opportunity.

In all of this, an imperative for science will be to allow children time to think, to let ideas gestate and to explore and experience their world, so that they can be surprised, awed, shocked, angry and humbled, experiencing in science emotions ranging from humour and beauty to sadness and happiness.

We must remember that, in order to develop creativity, children need to be given time to stand, stare, reflect, think and to be surprised and awed by their world. Sometimes we don't need to do anything with that experience in science, the experience in itself will be enough to feed the creative mind, because sometimes:

> *Rainbows are just to look at, not really to understand.*
> (http://www.juliantrubin.com/kidsquotes.html)

Acknowledgement

Valerie Wood-Robinson contributed to this chapter, especially examples of creativity from secondary school science departments.

References

DfEE (1999) *Science: The National Curriculum for England*. London: Department for Education and Skills. Available on: www.nc.uk.net

Feasey, R. ed. (2001) *Science is like a tub of ice cream – cool and fun! A collection of 100 science poems by primary and secondary school children*. Hatfield: Association for Science Education.

Feasey, R. (2005) *Creative science – achieving the WOW factor with 5–11 year-olds*. London: David Fulton.

Healey, J. (1987) Knit yourself a gut! *Journal of Biological Education*, **21**(2), 85–86.

Keogh, B. and Naylor, S. (1997) *Starting points for science*. Sandbach, Cheshire: Millgate House.

Lock, R. *et al.* (1990) A knitted model gut – extending the possibilities. *Journal of Biological Education*, **24**(2), 74–75.

Lock, R. (1997) Post-16 biology – some model approaches? *School Science Review*, **79**(286), 33–38.

NAACCE (National Advisory Committee on Creative and Cultural Education) (1999) *All our futures: creativity, culture and education*. London: DfEE.

Sternberg, J. ed. (1999) *Handbook of creativity*. Cambridge: Cambridge University Press.

Wellington, J. and Osborne, J. (2001) *Language and literacy in science*. Buckingham: Open University Press.

Websites

QCA Creativity in the National Curriculum: www.ncaction.org.uk/creativity
www.ncaction.org.uk/search/item.htm?id=185 (planets brochure)
www.ncaction.org.uk/search/item.htm?id=222 (particles stories)
www.ncaction.org.uk/search/item.htm?id=184 (journey in plant cell)

Index